Children and Interparental Violence

Children and Interparental Violence

The Impact of Exposure

B. B. Robbie Rossman, Ph.D.
Department of Psychology
University of Denver

Honore M. Hughes, Ph.D.
Department of Psychology
Saint Louis University

Mindy S. Rosenberg, Ph.D.
Private Practice, Sausalito, CA

USA	Publishing Office:	BRUNNER/MAZEL *A member of the Taylor & Francis Group* 325 Chestnut Street Philadelphia, PA 19106 Tel: (215) 625-8900 Fax: (215) 625-2940
	Distribution Center:	BRUNNER/MAZEL *A member of the Taylor & Francis Group* 47 Runway Road, Suite G Levittown, PA 19057-4700 Tel: (215) 269-0400 Fax: (215) 269-0363
UK		BRUNNER/MAZEL *A member of the Taylor & Francis Group* 11 New Fetter Lane London, EC4P 4EE, Tel: 171 583 0490 Fax: 171 583 0581

CHILDREN AND INTERPARENTAL VIOLENCE: The Impact of Exposure

1 2 3 4 5 6 7 8 9 0

Printed by Edwards Brothers, Ann Arbor, MI, 1999.
Cover Design by Nancy Abbott.
Edited by: Renee Hirsh and Jean Anderson

A CIP catalog record for this book is available from the British Library.
∞ The paper in this publication meets the requirements of the ANSI Standard Z39.48
1984 (Permanence of Paper)

Library of Congress Cataloging-in-Publication Data

Rossman, B. B. Robbie.
    Children and interparental violence: the impact of exposure /
B. B. Robbie Rossman, Honore M. Hughes, Mindy S. Rosenberg.
      p.   cm.
    Includes bibliographical references and index.
    ISBN 0-87630-958-9 (pbk. : alk. paper)
violence--Prevention. I. Hughes, Honore M. II. Rosenberg, Mindy Susan.
III. Title.
HQ784.V55R675   1999   99-44331
362.82'92--dc21   CIP

ISBN: 0-87630-958-9 (case)

We wish to dedicate this volume and express our gratitude to our families, friends, colleagues, and mentors who have provided support for our professional endeavors and lives across the years. We also wish to express gratitude to all of the families, personnel and administrators from community violence agencies, and educational institutions who have so generously given of their time and energy to help us learn about the struggles of children growing up in parentally violent families. This has been and continues to be a collaboration of caring.

Contents

Preface

The purpose of this book is to provide the reader with a systematic review of definitional issues and recent research concerning children growing up in parentally violent families, as well as discuss the existing conceptual models that account for effects of exposure, strategies for intervention, and implications for policy. The authors do this in the following chapters by presenting information regarding the ties among empirical data, conceptual/theoretical frameworks, and applications. Chapter 1 includes definitional and introductory information that sets the stage for the rest of the book. Chapter 2 provides a discussion of the general empirical findings to date and concludes with information regarding the heterogeneity of psychological effects seen among children exposed to parental violence. This prepares the reader for Chapter 3, in which individual differences in children and their responses to exposure are considered. Different combinations of individual factors are discussed as they relate to risk or resilience for exposed children.

Given these sets of findings, Chapter 4 presents conceptual models that provide explanations for the forms of impact observed, including information from social learning, cognitive behavioral, trauma, family systems, and relational theories. In Chapter 5, the authors expand the context of impact reviewed to include the influence of demographic factors such as socioeconomic status or ethnic group. Other types of family violence are also discussed, as is physical violence within nontraditional forms of the family, such as families with gay or lesbian parents. Chapter 6 reviews treatment and prevention programs that have been implemented for children exposed to parental violence, evaluates the efficacy of such programs that have been conducted, and makes recommendations for improving these approaches. Information related to children of battered women and the court system is discussed in Chapter 7 and includes such issues as child custody and the litigation of exposed children who commit violent crimes. The authors conclude the book in Chapter 8 with a summary of current needs within the field. Recommendations for future research, prevention and intervention programs, and policy related to research and clinical work are presented.

The authors have included many case examples to illustrate different points and help the families and children come alive. Some case examples are amalgamations of several families or children. In all cases the specific details and identity of individuals have been purposely disguised and changed so that they may remain anonymous.

CHAPTER

Exposure to Interparental Violence

What does it mean to say that children are "exposed" to interparental violence? Exposure is a broad term, and exposure to interparental violence is more easily defined anecdotally than scientifically. In everyday life children and youth may be exposed to physically aggressive behaviors between their parents or caregivers in a number of ways. For example, they may be exposed through being physically present in the room where the aggression is taking place, thereby receiving through all of their senses information about this conflict: the sight of pushing and hitting; the sound of yelling or crying; the smell of blood or gunpowder; the feel of being shoved against a wall when trying to intervene; and the taste of fear. Other forms of exposure may involve fewer of their senses, such as hearing terrified screams or someone being pushed against a wall or door, or seeing the resulting injuries such as a mother's black eye or damage to property such as a hole in the wall, or sensing the tension or dread in the spousal relationship.

For many years it was assumed that children were not affected by these occurrences. This assumption now has been challenged by almost 20 years of research suggesting that children are not oblivious to interparental violence. Some initial issues have to do with how this research came about, how frequently children experience these events, and how exposure is defined and related to emotional abuse within the context of a battering parental relationship.

☐ History of Research of Children Exposed to Interparental Violence

Violence toward women and children within families has been noted for centuries in the records of different civilizations (Dobash & Dobash, 1979). However, interest in and research on family violence is, in large part, quite recent, being spurred by concerns about child abuse (Helfer & Kempe, 1968). Further impetus came from examining violence in the entire family in the 1975 and 1985 National Family Violence Surveys (Straus & Gelles, 1990). Findings from these surveys suggested that a substantial portion, about one-third, of U.S. couples experience one or more physical assaults on a partner during a marriage. This and other research was aided by the development of the Conflict Tactics Scales (CTS; Straus, 1979, 1990), which provided a standard tool for researchers to assess partner violence. (Other scales have also been developed [e.g., Domestic Conflict Inventory, Margolin, Burman, John, & O'Brien, 1990; O'Leary–Porter Scale, Porter, & O'Leary, 1980]). The CTS hs recently been revised (Straus, Hamby, Boney-McCoy, & Sugarman, 1996) and expanded to include an updated parent-to-child aggression version (Straus, Hamby, Finkelhor, Moore, & Runyan, 1998) used in the 1995 Gallup Survey (Gallup Organization, 1995). Additional momentum for family violence research was provided by the First National Conference for Family Violence Researchers held in 1981 at the University of New Hampshire, which have continued every 3 years thereafter.

Initially concerns were mainly about abused wives (e.g., Pizzey, 1974). Soon it became clear that children were also at risk and were more likely to be physically abused in wife abusive homes (Carlson, 1984). Recent data from the 1985 National Family Violence Survey showed that the probability of child abuse by a violent husband increased from 5% with one marital violence event to over 90% with 50 or more marital violence acts (Ross, 1996). Marital violence was viewed as problematic, in part, because of its apparent exacerbation of child abuse.

Early studies by Rosenbaum and O'Leary (1981), Hughes and Barad (1983), and Hershorn and Rosenbaum (1985) raised yet another possibility, namely, that children's problem behaviors also might be enhanced by just witnessing the abuse of their mother. This and other work (e.g., Elbow, 1982) helped to raise the red flag that has generated 20 years of research of children exposed to interparental violence. The purpose of much of the work in the 1980s was to further document initial findings and to extend investigations to other domains of child functioning. Major facilitators and disseminators of this research have included the multiple books edited by Ammerman and Hersen (e.g., Ammerman & Hersen, 1999) and the seminal work by Jaffe, Wolfe, and Wilson, Children of Battered Women (1990), which has served as the "textbook" in this area for the last decade. In the current volume we hope to continue this tradition, highlighting the research of the 1990s.

☐ Incidence and Prevalence

An initial question must be about incidence: "How many children are exposed to interparental violence?" Incidence refers to the number of incidents of exposure during 1 year, whereas prevalence refers to the extent of the problem as a whole. Initial incidence estimates suggest that between 2.3 and 10 million children witness parental violence each year in the United States (Carlson, 1984; Straus, 1991). In addition, national surveys by Straus and Gelles and their colleagues have indicated that approximately one in six couples report some incident of physical violence in a year, and one-third of married women report at least one incident of physical violence during their marriage (Straus & Gelles, 1986), a figure that is thought to be an underestimate (Straus, 1993). Thus, a conservative incidence estimate is that 15% of children are exposed to aggression between their parents. It is not possible to make a prevalence estimate. However, if

33% of women experience some marital violence during their lives, it is reasonable to believe that lifetime prevalence rates for children would be high.

Estimates provided by these national surveys have strengths and weaknesses. These national community surveys have the advantage of querying the frequency of the specific conflict tactics of interest that have occurred between partners during the prior year through use of the CTS (Straus, 1979). For example, physically aggressive conflict tactics are clearly defined as those that involve pushing or shoving or more severe forms of interpersonal aggression such as beating up. A further advantage is that the surveys are by phone such that some segments of the population (e.g., higher socioeconomic status [SES] families) are represented. These families might not be as likely to come to the attention of domestic violence agencies or child protective services and thus be underrepresented. However, phone surveys also have the disadvantage of missing other segments of the population, such as those who would not agree to participate by phone or do not have telephones. In addition, these national surveys have the disadvantage of being based on the report of each of the spouses about themselves and their partners, rather than on reports made by a third party and investigated by a fourth. On the other hand, socially less acceptable behaviors such as intrafamilial violence are thought less likely to be reported (e.g., Bird, Gould, & Staghezza, 1992), meaning that even these subjective reports are likely to be underestimates of incidence. Nonetheless, these phone surveys are a critical source of information about violence between intimate partners in the United States. And phone survey results do not differ greatly from those done using private, in-person interviews. The National Alcohol Survey showed that 21% of the over 1,500 couples interviewed had experienced one act of spousal violence during the past year (Schafer, Caetano, & Clark, 1998).

National child abuse statistics also provide information about incidence of exposure. For example, as will be discussed, this exposure is thought to be psychologically abusive and therefore would be partially reflected in the National Center on Child Abuse and Neglect (NCAAN) survey under the emotional abuse category. In the 1994 NCAAN survey for the 48 reporting states there were an estimated 2.9 million children reported as victims of alleged child abuse and neglect. Approximately one million of these were substantiated/indicated and about 5% of these, or 47,097, fell into the emotional maltreatment category (NCAAN, 1996). However, a disadvantage of these survey data is that the proportion of cases in which maltreatment was linked to spouse abuse is not known. Nor do we know, more generally, the number of situations in which reports of other types of abuse were taking place in the context of parental violence or where parental violence occurred without child abuse. However, a possible advantage of these figures is that they are typically not based on self-report.

Two other types of survey data are particularly relevant for children's welfare. For example, medical record bases suggest that nearly 50% of abusive husbands batter their pregnant wives, resulting in four times the risk of low birth weight infants and a higher than expected level of birth defects (Chiles, 1988; U.S. Senate Hearings, 1990). In addition, Fantuzzo, Boruch, Beriana, Atkins, and Marcus (1997) surveyed police reports of domestic violence calls from five major U.S. cities. This database was gathered as part of the Spouse Assault Replication Program of the National Institute of Justice. Cases were included if there was verification of misdemeanor or felony physical assault of a female victim in a spouselike relationship and if the man had no outstanding arrest warrants at the time of the assault. Within this group of over 2,000 cases, several results were striking. These households were more than twice as likely to have children as census data would predict. Furthermore, these households had a significantly higher proportion of children younger than 5 years and of children living in poverty. This raises the question of whether younger children may be at even greater risk of exposure. This may be possible since the childrearing years for young families have been noted as particularly stressful. A survey of young couples showed that up to 40% reported the occurrence of some partner physical aggression (Magdol, Moffitt, Caspi, Newman, Fagan, & Silva, 1997).

Of course, there are both strengths and weakness in medical and police reports as well as community survey and abuse reports. All seem likely to underestimate true incidence (Bird et al., 1992). Whatever the actual numbers, they are large enough to constitute a serious physical and mental health problem for children in this country.

☐ Definitional Issues

Most researchers define children's exposure status based on the fact that the mother has been battered by her partner. Although many researchers have not asked the children specifically about what they have witnessed, women who have been beaten report that 90% of the time the children are either in the same room or the next room during the violence (e.g., Hughes, 1988; Rosenberg & Rossman, 1990). However, many parents do not realize that their children are aware of parental conflicts (O'Brien, John, Margolin, & Erel, 1994).

To investigate this more specifically, Rosenberg (1984, 1987a) used questionnaires and structured interviews with battered women and their children to determine the types and frequency of verbal and physical aggression witnessed by children in maritally violent and nonviolent families. She found that despite a parent's intention to shield children from the violence, nearly all such verbal and physical incidents were directly observed or heard or both by children of battered women in contrast to comparison group children. In addition, if children were exposed to verbal aggression in their families, they were significantly more likely to be exposed to physical aggression as well. Thus, the vast majority of the children are clearly aware of the physical violence as well as the verbal aggression that occurs. One study examining their awareness showed that children's and mothers' reports of the occurrence of physical aggression by mothers' partners were highly related ($r[99] = .54$, $p < .001$; Dominguez, 1995).

Researchers in this area have long been aware of controversy over whether spousal violence is "mutual combat" or one partner or the other engages in more physical violence (Feldman & Ridley, 1995). Some researchers indicate discrepancies between men and women in self-reported physical aggression with men obtaining significantly higher aggression scores (Rosenberg, 1984). However, when the self-reported physical aggression rates are similar for men and women, more often the woman is using physically aggressive tactics in self-defense, feeling in danger, and she is more often the victim of the most severe aggression of being beaten up and is more often physically injured and needing medical treatment (Carlos, Neidig, & O'Leary, 1994; Morse, 1995). Therefore, the current authors use the term spouse abuse or violence or interparental violence, but they acknowledge that woman battering remains the primary concern.

A further topic of current concern regarding definitions of violence has to do with how much interparental verbal and physical conflict make a difference for child adjustment and whether there are contexts in which conflict is not destructive. Jouriles, McDonald, and Norwood (1999) make the point that domestic violence is not as atypical as once believed. They cite studies of premarital partners (O'Leary, Barling, Arias,

Rosenbaum, Malone, & Tyree, 1989) and of young married couples (Magdol et al., 1997) suggesting that for around 40% some partner physical aggression has occurred. They speculate that perhaps this typically lower-level (e.g., pushing as opposed to being beaten up) and less frequent aggression is less destructive for children since that large a percentage (i.e., 40%) of children typically do not show clinically elevated levels of problem behaviors. These authors refer to this phenomenon as "ordinary" or "common" violence, which may occur during certain stages of a couple's relationship. Unfortunately, as they note, researchers have not generally discriminated between children exposed to "ordinary" versus more severe interparental physical aggression. There are some naturally occurring exceptions in studies where violent families from the community are included that show lower levels of aggression (e.g., Gordis, Margolin, & John, 1997; Rossman & Rosenberg, 1992). Interestingly, these lower levels of aggression still seem predictive of somewhat poorer adjustment for children. However, rates do not reach 40%, suggesting that factors such as if and how the parents resolve this more ordinary conflict may play a role (see Cummings & Davies, 1994). Clearly work remains to be done in the area of "ordinary" violence.

☐ Exposed Children as Psychologically Abused

Most researchers in this area acknowledge that a definition of emotional abuse or psychological maltreatment is difficult to establish, and much has been written toward that end (e.g., Garbarino, Guttman, & Seeley, 1986; Hart & Brassard, 1991; Hart, Germain, & Brassard, 1987; McGee & Wolfe, 1991; Vondra, Kola, & Radigan, 1992). In spite of these difficulties, Stuart Hart and Marla Brassard (1990) have constructed and empirically verified categories of adult behaviors that constitute emotional abuse. These have been studied, refined, and elaborated into the six behavioral categories put forth in the Practice Principles for evaluating psychological maltreatment from the American Professional Society on the Abuse of Children (APSAC, 1995). These include spurning, terrorizing, denying emotional responsiveness, isolating, corrupting/exploiting, and mental health, medical, and educational neglect. While children of battered women may not originally have been considered to be psychologically maltreated, the connection between woman battering and the emotional abuse of the children has become clearer (Rosenberg, 1987b; Rossman & Rosenberg, 1997). The primary example is that all exposed children experience terrorizing, which is defined, in part, as threatening or perpetuating violence against a child or a child's loved ones or objects (APSAC, 1995).

However, the abuse of a mother by her partner may not only find expression in overt acts of violence. Any one or more of the psychologically maltreating behaviors typically take place when there is battering in the home. For example, spurning or the repeated devaluation of the child often occurs when the child is the topic of the spousal dispute. The child and mother may be continually blamed for various things, cursed at, or called stupid. In addition, batterers tend to want to isolate the child and family from outside contacts in order to feel more control and keep the battering secret contained within the family. This may also take the form of not allowing the child to participate in peer or educational activities such as such as speech or language therapy. The child is also corrupted or missocialized by seeing that aggression is the way to get needs met or gain control and often is exposed to alcohol and drug abuse. All categories of psychologically maltreating behaviors experienced contribute to a domestic ambiance, which children are bound to experience either as victims, observers, or both (Graham-Bermann, 1996).

Children also may experience outright hostility and aggression during marital conflict since the conflict can "spill over" to the parent–child relationship (Fincham, Grych, & Osborne, 1994). Family violence researchers found early on that the cooccurrence of different types of violence (e.g., spousal violence with physical abuse of children) is rather high, with estimates in the 40% to 60% range (Forrstrom-Cohen & Rosenbaum, 1985; Rosenbaum & O'Leary, 1981; Straus, Gelles, & Steinmetz, 1980). As further support, Ross (1996) provides additional evidence that it is not unusual for both spouse abuse and child physical abuse to occur in the same family. Using a retrospective reporting method, she found that as the frequency of spouse abuse rises, the probability of child physical abuse also increases dramatically. This relationship was stronger for husbands than wives. More recently, Appel and Holden (1998), having reviewed a large number of studies, concluded that the median cooccurrence rate is 40%. Thus, as previously noted, children in homes with interparental violence are at risk for abuse themselves.

Similarly, Cummings and Davies (1994) describe as "contagious" the negative emotional climate when there is marital conflict. This negative emotionality experienced by the parent(s) could result in further negativity directed toward the child, expressed as either overt hostility or withdrawal from the child. Thus, the atmosphere in the home is one of tension and coercion, such that children living in these households experience psychological abuse, including terrorizing and spurning.

As will be discussed in more detail later in this volume, many children exposed to parental violence display adaptational difficulties linked to this exposure. It is difficult, given the current research, to make statements tying amount of exposure with degree of adaptive difficulty, particularly as one looks at the heterogeneity of outcome across children. The literature does not allow us to formulate dose-response relationships. Although research suggests that trauma symptomatology and other measures of distress are related in a positive, possibly linear, fashion to amount and severity of exposure or the number of different types of parental violence witnessed, more research is needed to clarify that relationship (Mallah et al., 1996; Rossman & Rosenberg, 1992).

☐ Dynamics of Battering and Relationship to Emotional Abuse

One of the most common questions asked in relation to battered women is, "Why do they stay?" The dynamics of battering provide some answers to this question. The abuse of a woman by her partner may not only find expression in overt acts of violence but also in psychological abuse, isolating tactics, or threats to the woman that he will kill her if she leaves (Gondolf & Fisher, 1991).

Geffner and Pagelow (1990) also describe the circumstances of battered women as terrifying: "intense and continuous degradation or intimidation for the purpose of controlling the actions or behavior of the other person, or placing that other person in fear of serious bodily injury to self or another" (Geffner & Pagelow, 1990, p. 113). The women experience unpredictable episodes of verbal aggression and physical violence from the men with the result that they are living in a "reign of terror" (Gondolf &

Fisher, 1991, p. 275). Therefore, it is not surprising that the most commonly reported reasons for staying are related to fear, fear for their safety and for that of their children (Geffner & Pagelow, 1990), even though children's safety is a reason women report for ultimately leaving (Strube, 1988). The "battered woman syndrome" occurs as many abused women gradually become more confused and less confident, immobilized by their partner's verbal abuse and physical intimidation until they no longer believe that they have options other than to stay (Dutton & Painter, 1993; Walker, 1984). Within these dynamics it becomes clear that both battered mothers and their children need to be considered to be psychologically maltreated.

☐ Conclusion

This introduction closes with themes that will echo throughout this volume. The high incidence and prevalence of children's exposure to violence between caregivers is alarming. It makes clear the need for a developmental perspective in research and treatment. It is also critical to persist in clarifying and elaborating definitions and dimensions of exposure, and its intensity, severity, and context. Such elaboration highlights the importance of incorporating an ecological perspective as well, where attention is paid to multiple dimensions of family and societal context and multiple risk factors over more than one year of a child's life. Perhaps most importantly, we must continue to integrate across the literatures on domestic violence, child development, developmental psychopathology, child abuse, and trauma, collaborations that can inform both thinking and intervention.

☐ References

American Professional Society on the Abuse of Children (APSAC). (1995). *Practice guidelines: Psychosocial evaluation of suspected psychological maltreatment in children and adolescents*. Chicago, IL: Author.

Ammerman, R. T., & Hersen, M. (Eds.). (1999). *Case studies in family violence* (2nd ed.). New York: Plenum Press.

Appel, A. E., & Holden, G. W. (1998). The co-ocurrence of spouse and physical child abuse: A review and appraisal. *Journal of Family Psychology, 12*, 578–599.

Bird, H. R., Gould, M. S., & Staghezza, B. (1992). Aggregating data from multiple informants in child psychiatry epidemiological research. *Journal of the American Academy of Child and Adolescent Psychiatry, 31*, 78–85.

Carlos, A. L., Neidig, P. H., & O'Leary, K. D. (1994). Injuries of women and men in a treatment program for domestic violence. *Journal of Family Violence, 9*, 113–125.

Carlson, B. E. (1984). Children's observations of interparental violence. In A. R. Roberts (Ed.), *Battered women and their families* (pp. 147–167). New York: Springer.

Chiles, L. (1988). *Report of the National Commission to Prevent Infant Mortality, death before life: The tragedy of infant mortality* (16). Washington, DC.

Cummings, E. M., & Davies, P. (1994). *Children and marital conflict: The impact of family dispute and resolution*. New York: Guilford.

Dobash, R. E., & Dobash, R. (1979). *Violence against wives*. New York: Free Press.

Dominguez, M. L. (1995). *Children's perceptions of and reactions to marital conflict and violence*. Unpublished doctoral dissertation, University of Denver.

Dutton, D. G., & Painter, S. L. (1993). The battered woman syndrome: Effects of severity and intermittency of abuse. *American Journal of Orthopsychiatry, 63*, 614–622.

Elbow, M. (1982). Children of violent marriages: The forgotten victims. *Social Casework, 63*, 465–471.

Fantuzzo, J., Boruch, R., Beriana, A., Atkins, M., & Marcus, S. (1997). Domestic violence and children: Prevalence and risk in five major U.S. cities. *Journal of the American Academy of Child and Adolescent Psychiatry, 36*, 116–122.

Feldman, C. M., & Ridley, C. A. (1995). The etiology and treatment of domestic violence between adult partners. *Clinical Psychology: Science and Practice, 2*, 317–348.

Fincham, F. D., Grych, J. H., & Osborne, L. N. (1994). Does marital conflict cause child maladjustment? Directions and challenges for longitudinal research. *Journal of Family Psychology, 8*, 128–140.

Forrstrom-Cohen, B., & Rosenbaum, A. (1985). The effects of parental marital violence on young adults: An exploratory investigation. *Journal of Marriage and the Family, 47*, 467–472.

Gallup Organization. (1995). *Disciplining children in America: A Gallup Poll report*. Princeton, NJ: Author.

Garbarino, J., Guttman, E., & Seeley, J. W. (1986). *The psychologically abused child*. San Francisco: Jossey-Bass.

Geffner, R., & Pagelow, M. D. (1990). Victims of spouse abuse. In R. T. Ammerman & M. Hersen (Eds.), *Treatment of family violence* (pp. 113–135). New York: Wiley.

Gondolf, E. W., & Fisher, E. R. (1991). Wife battering. In R. T. Ammerman & M. Hersen (Eds.), *Case studies in family violence* (pp. 273–292). New York: Plenum.

Gordis, E. B., Margolin, G., & John, R. S. (1997). Marital aggression, observed parental hostility, and child behavior during triadic family interaction. *Journal of Family Psychology, 11*, 76–89.

Graham-Bermann, S. A. (1996). Family worries: Assessment of interpersonal anxiety in children from violent and nonviolent families. *Journal of Child Clinical Psychology, 25*, 280–287.

Hart, C. H., Germain, R., & Brassard, M. (1987). The challenge: To better understand and combat psychological maltreatment of children and youth. In M. Brassard, R. Germain, & S. Hart (Eds.), *Psychological maltreatment of children and youth* (pp. 3–24). New York: Pergamon.

Hart, S. N., & Brassard, M. R. (1990). Psychological maltreatment of children. In R. T. Ammerman & M. Hersen (Eds.), *Treatment of family violence: A sourcebook* (pp. 77–112). New York: Wiley.

Hart, S. N., & Brassard, M. R. (1991). Psychological maltreatment: Progress achieved. *Development and Psychopathology, 3*, 61–70.

Helfer, R., & Kempe, C. (Eds.). (1968). *The battered child*. Chicago: University of Chicago Press.

Hershorn, M., & Rosenbaum, A. (1985). Children of marital violence: A closer look at the unintended victims. *American Journal of Orthopsychiatry, 55*, 260–266.

Hughes, H. M. (1988). Psychological and behavioral correlates of family violence in child witnesses and victims. *American Journal of Orthopsychiatry, 58*, 77–90.

Hughes, H. M., & Barad, S. J. (1983). Psychological functioning of children in a battered women's shelter: A preliminary investigation. *American Journal of Orthopsychiatry, 53*, 525–531.

Jaffe, P. G., Wolfe, D. A., & Wilson, S. K. (1990). *Children of battered women*. Newbury Park, CA: Sage.

Jouriles, E. N., McDonald, R., & Norwood, W. D. (1999, February). *Documenting the prevalence of children's exposure to domestic violence*. Paper presented at the Asilomar Conference on Children and Intimate Violence, Pacific Grove, CA.

Magdol, L., Moffitt, T. E., Capsi, A., Newman, D. I., Fagan, J., & Silva, P. A. (1997). Gender differences in partner violence in a birth cohort of 21-year-olds: Bridging the gap between clinical and epidemiological approaches. *Journal of Consulting and Clinical Psychology, 65*, 68–78.

Mallah, K., Kimura, S., Sorensen, C., West, J., Diaz, L., Brooks, K., Backes, M., Acker, M., Frohlick, P., & Rossman, B. B. R. (1996, May). *What do child witnesses witness?* Abstract in the *Proceedings of the Developmental Psychobiology Research Group Ninth Biennial Retreat*, Estes Park, CO.

Margolin, G., Burman, B., John, R. S., & O'Brien, M. (1990). *Domestic conflict inventory*. Unpublished manuscript, University of Southern California, Los Angeles. Developmental Psychological Research Group, Denver.

McGee, R. A., & Wolfe, D. A. (1991). Psychological maltreatment: Towards an operational definition. *Development and Psychopathology, 3,* 3–18.

Morse, B. J. (1995). Beyond the conflict tactics scale: Assessing gender differences in partner violence. *Violence and Victims, 10,* 251–272.

National Center on Child Abuse and Neglect of the U.S. Department of Health and Human Services (NCAAN). (1996). *Child maltreatment 1994: Reports from the states to the National Center on Child Abuse and Neglect.* Washington, DC: U.S. Government Printing Office.

O'Brien, M., John, R. S., Margolin, G., & Erel, O. (1994). Reliability and diagnostic efficacy of parents' reports regarding children's exposure to marital aggression. *Violence and Victims, 9,* 45–62.

O'Leary, K. D., Barling, J., Arias, I., Rosenbaum, A., Malone, J., & Tyree, A. (1989). Prevalence and stability of physical aggression between spouses: Longitudinal analysis. *Journal of Consulting and Clinical Psychology, 57,* 263–268.

Pizzey, E. (1974). *Scream quietly or the neighbors will hear.* London: Penguin.

Porter, B. K., & O'Leary, K. D. (1980). Marital discord and childhood behavior problems. *Journal of Consulting and Clinical Psychology, 57,* 263–268.

Rosenbaum, A., & O'Leary, K. D. (1981). Children: The unintended victims of marital violence. *American Journal of Orthopsychiatry, 51,* 692–699.

Rosenberg, M. S. (1984). *The impact of witnessing interparental violence on children's behavior, perceived competence, and social problem solving abilities.* Unpublished doctoral dissertation, University of Virginia, Charlottesville.

Rosenberg, M. S. (1987a). Children of battered women: The effects of witnessing violence on their social problem solving abilities. *Behavior Therapist, 4,* 85-89.

Rosenberg, M. S. (1987b). New directions for research on the psychological maltreatment of children. *American Psychologist, 42,* 166–171.

Rosenberg, M. S., & Rossman, B. B. R. (1990). The child witness to marital violence. In R. T. Ammerman & M. Hersen (Eds.), *Treatment of family violence* (pp. 183–210). New York: Wiley.

Ross, S. M. (1996). Risk of physical abuse to children of spouse abusing parents. *Child Abuse & Neglect, 20,* 589–598.

Rossman, B. B. R., & Rosenberg, M. S. (1992). Family stress and functioning in children: The moderating effects of children's beliefs about their control over parental conflict. *Journal of Child Psychology and Psychiatry, 33,* 699–715.

Rossman, B. B. R., & Rosenberg, M. S. (1997). Psychological maltreatment: A needs analysis and application for children in violent families. In R. Geffner, S. B. Sorenson, & P. K. Lundberg-Love (Eds.), *Violence and sexual abuse at home: Current issues in spousal battering and child maltreatment* (pp. 245–262). Binghamton, NY: Haworth.

Schafer, J., Caetano, R., & Clark, C. (1998). Rates of intimate partner violence in the United States. *American Journal of Public Health, 88,* 1701–1704.

Straus, M. A. (1979). Measuring intrafamily conflict and violence: The Conflict Tactics (CT) Scale. *Journal of Marriage and the Family, 41,* 75–88.

Straus, M. A. (1990). The Conflict Tactics Scale and its critics: An evaluation and new data on validity and reliability. In M. A. Straus & R. J. Gelles (Eds.), *Physical violence in American families: Risk factors and adaptations to violence in 8,145 families* (pp. 49–73). New Brunswick, NJ: Transaction Publishers.

Straus, M. A. (1991). *Children as witnesses to marital violence: A risk factor for life long problems among a nationally representative sample of American men and women.* Paper presented at the Ross Roundtable on "Children and Violence," Washington, DC.

Straus, M. A. (1993). Identifying offenders in criminal justice research on domestic assault. *American Behavioral Scientist, 36,* 587–600.

Straus, M. A., & Gelles, R. J. (1986). Societal change and change in family violence from 1975 to 1985 as revealed by two national samples. *Journal of Marriage and the Family, 48,* 465–479.

Straus, M. A., & Gelles, R. (1990). How violent are American families? Estimates from the national family violence resurvey and other studies. In M. A. Straus & R. J. Gelles (Eds.), *Physical violence in American families: Risk factors and adaptations to violence in 8,145 families* (pp. 95–112). New Brunswick, NJ: Transaction Publishers.

Straus, M., Gelles, R., & Steinmetz, S. (1980). *Behind closed doors: Violence in the American family*. New York: Anchor.

Straus, M. A., Hamby, S. L., Boney-McCoy, S., & Sugarman, D. B. (1996). The Revised Conflict Tactics Scales (CTS2): Development and preliminary data. *Journal of Family Issues, 17*, 283–316.

Straus, M. A., Hamby, S. L., Finkelhor, D., Moore, D. W., & Runyan, D. (1998). Identification of child maltreatment with the parent-child Conflict Tactics Scales: Development and psychometric data for a national sample of American parents. *Child Abuse and Neglect, 22*, 249–270.

Strube, M. J. (1988). The decision to leave an abusive relationship. In G. T. Hotaling, D. Finkelhor, J. T. Kirkpatrick, & M. A. Straus (Eds.), *Coping with family violence: Research and policy perspectives* (pp. 93–106). Newbury Park, CA: Sage.

U.S. Senate, Committee on the Judiciary, Hearings on Women and Violence. (1990). *Ten Facts About Violence Against Women*, at 78, Aug. 29 & Dec. 11.

Vondra, J. I., Kola, A. B., & Radigan, B. R. (1992). Psychological maltreatment of children. In R. T. Ammerman & M. Hersen (Eds.), *Assessment of family violence: A clinical and legal sourcebook* (pp. 253–290). New York: Wiley.

Walker, L. E. (1984). *The battered woman syndrome*. New York: Springer.

Impact of Exposure
to Interparental Abuse

Diane was married to Darryl for 12 years, and they had two children, Sheila and Warren, ages 11 and 6. Throughout the course of the marriage, Darryl had physically assaulted Diane approximately once a month, usually without warning. Sheila and Warren sometimes were present during the violent conflict and sometimes were in bed if the fight were at night. They always knew when their mother had been beaten because she had bruises on her face and body. Diane hardly ever went to the emergency room, except for the last time, due to the intensity of the beating and the severity of the injuries. Later that same day, after Diane was released from the emergency room, Diane filed for a temporary restraining order and a divorce. When Sheila and Warren were brought by Diane to the clinic, it had been approximately a year since they had seen their father. However, both were experiencing problems: Sheila was having academic difficulties in school as well as problems making and keeping friends; Warren was alternating between crying and saying he hated himself and being destructive to his toys and aggressive with the family pets.

****

Tiffany brought her daughter, age 4, to the clinic at least partially because she was required to do so by the day care staff as a condition of her daughter remaining at that center. Shaneise had been aggressive toward other children and disobedient with shelter staff and day care workers. Tiffany admitted that she also had problems managing Shaneise's behavior and getting Shaneise to do what she wanted. In addition, Shaneise had been recently acting aggressively toward her little brother, Rashad, who was 18 months old. The children had not seen their father for approximately 6 months, since their mother had decided to get off drugs and kicked her boyfriend (and father of the children) of 5 years out of the house. Tiffany had been drug-free for 6 months, going to support group meetings regularly while living in transitional housing.

How do we know what kind of impact being exposed to interparental violence could have on the children's adjustment and development, and what types of treatment might be appropriate for these family members? Research in the past two decades has helped us to understand the influences of growing up in a family in which there is interparental violence, and it has provided us with some ideas about what to do if children have adjustment problems after being exposed to this type of abuse.

In this chapter, some background and a brief overview of this area of research is provided first, with current knowledge regarding the impact of exposure to woman abuse subsequently discussed. By taking a historical perspective, one is able to note that there is a natural progression over time in the types of research questions asked by investigators and in the sophistication of methodologies utilized. The aim of initial research efforts often was to examine the clinical impressions of shelter workers and others that children of battered women were experiencing difficulties. However, more recently, many researchers' focus has been on obtaining more precise as well as more comprehensive descriptions and explanations of the children's adjustment and development. In addition, attempts have been made to investigate the potential processes involved in and mechanisms responsible for the impact seen. These findings and other recent advances in research investigations will be presented in this chapter (see also Chapter 3) along with some suggestions for improving future research. Implications for treatment will be briefly mentioned, with a more in-depth discussion of interventions in Chapter 6.

☐ Overview and Brief History

Initial Research

When one surveys this area over the past two decades, growth in both knowledge and sophistication of methods is apparent. It is clear that most of the early research was focused on descriptions of children's difficulties. Early research investigations regarding the adjustment of children of battered women were prompted by shelter workers and clinicians who wished to provide some type of intervention to alleviate distress for these often overlooked or forgotten victims of domestic violence (e.g., Carlson, 1984; Elbow, 1982; Hilberman & Munson, 1978; Hughes, 1982; Lystad, 1975; Pfouts, Shopler, & Henley, 1982).

Methodologically, early studies tended to employ interviews and informal observations, then moved to the use of standardized measures. Although case studies can provide in-depth information about several cases and are appropriate when research in an area is first initiated, more formal procedures and larger samples can increase the credibility and representativeness of the results obtained (e.g., Hughes & Barad, 1983; Jacobson, 1978; Porter & O'Leary, 1980; Westra & Martin, 1981).

Another advance occurred when researchers began using comparison groups (e.g., Hershorn & Rosenbaum, 1985; Hughes, 1988; Jaffe, Wolfe, Wilson, & Zak, 1986; Rosenbaum & O'Leary, 1981; Wolfe, Jaffe, Wilson, & Zak, 1985; Wolfe, Zak, Wilson, & Jaffe, 1986). Comparison groups are especially important in this area since they help guard against misinterpretation of results. Families staying in shelters for battered women are typically those with low income and few resources, who experience a number of different types of adversity additional to domestic violence. For example, behavior problems tend to be higher among working class than among middle income children. As such, several researchers found no differences between the children in shelters and the low-income comparison children on externalizing-type disorders; this was a result of high problem levels and risk among the comparison children as well as among the shelter youngsters (e.g., Christopoulos et al., 1987; Graham-Bermann, Levendosky, Porterfield, & Okun, in press).

In a pivotal summary and critique of the literature, Fantuzzo and Lindquist (1989) reviewed the state of the research from 1967 to 1987 and made recommendations regarding improvements in methodology. Of the 29 articles they found that dealt directly with children of battered women, 8 were "expository" papers, with no data included. In the remaining articles only about one-half included comparison groups. Children in those investigations were assessed regarding conduct and emotional problems, social functioning, intellectual/academic functioning, and physical development, with different researchers studying different combinations of variables. In general, Fantuzzo and Lindquist concluded that the researchers provided some evidence that the children of battered women experienced more difficulties and showed poorer adjustment in each of the areas of functioning.

The methodological critique of the area Fantuzzo and Lindquist provided was especially cogent, and their suggestions remain equally relevant today. In terms of definitions, they proposed that researchers specify the parameters of the violence to which the children were exposed and develop better measures of these criteria. Regarding design, they recommended that researchers employ comparison groups in order to investigate a number of family and individual child factors that also might influence the children's adjustment (e.g., ethnicity and sociocultural considerations, parenting style and skill, parental mental health, parental substance abuse and employment status, and children's gender, age, intellectual functioning, and experience with physical abuse). They also advocated collecting information from families additional to those in shelters for battered women. Finally, they suggested that investigators use multiple reporters and multimodal assessments of functioning, rather than rely on the single-source maternal report that characterized many investigations. For example, behavioral checklists, direct behavioral observations, child self-report, along with parent, counselor, and teacher reports could be employed to obtain information from a number of different perspectives.

Later Steps

Conceptual and Theoretical Development. Literature available since 1987 has provided substantial advances in knowledge, although increased sophistication in methodology has been slower. Researchers began to borrow concepts and information from other areas of literature related to children of battered women, such as emotional abuse, physical child abuse, marital conflict and discord, parenting and discipline, parent–child relationships and attachment, children of depressed parents, and traumatic stress. Theory and research findings from these areas were used to construct hypotheses regarding processes and mechanisms that contribute to the impact seen on the children from exposure to interparental abuse (see Chapter 4). Subsequently, research became less atheoretical and guided more by conceptual and theoretical writings as well as by empirical findings.

In another landmark article, Fincham (1994) concluded that there are well-documented findings that children of battered women are less well functioning than comparison children in a number of areas. Reinforcing the conclusions drawn by Fantuzzo and Lindquist (1989), Fincham recommended what he called "second generation" research. This means that researchers should focus more on the mediators and moderators of the impact of children's exposure (see Chapter 3), as well as on the mechanisms and processes involved.

Between 1987 and 1994, a number of researchers proposed several different, although related, theories regarding how exposure impacts children. A "family disruption" model having direct and indirect effects was proposed by Jaffe, Wolfe, and Wilson (1990), a "cognitive-contextual" prototype with proximal and distal effects was put forth by Grych and Fincham (1990), and an "emotional security" model based on parent–child attachment was suggested by Cummings and Davies (1994). Additional discussion regarding these and other models proposed is found in Chapters 4 and 6 of the current volume. In order to supply a context for the research findings to be discussed, a brief summary of models is provided here.

Direct mechanisms operate by having an impact on the child in a straightforward manner, without having an influence on another factor first. For example, direct mechanisms first mentioned by Grych and Fincham (1990) and Jaffe et al. (1990) include both (1) modeling of aggressiveness and (2) stress in the family, meaning that modeling and stress have an impact directly upon the child's adjustment. While examining the direct impact of modeling, researchers have focused on aggressiveness and other externalizing-type symptoms in the children. In addition, the direct impact of stress on children's functioning has lead to a concentration on internalizing-type problems and posttraumatic stress disorder (PTSD) symptoms among the children (and their mothers).

However, indirect mechanisms exert their impact by influencing another factor first, then influencing the child's adjustment. For example, family violence could have an effect on the way the parent functions, which then has an influence on the child's adjustment. Indirect mechanisms studied to date include characteristics of the parent–child relationship (e.g., quality of attachment or emotional availability, emotional negativity, parent–child aggression) and disciplinary practices (e.g., those that are exceedingly negative, harsh, inconsistent, ineffective). Researchers have also examined child characteristics that are relatively stable over time. For example, qualities such as temperament, self-esteem, cognitive abilities, coping skills, attributional style, age, and gender may contribute to children's reactions to exposure. Finally, attributes of the parental conflict must be considered; these include characteristics such as frequency, duration, or resolution.

Summary

It is clear in this brief chronological review that over the last 20 years researchers and clinicians have started asking different questions. While still trying to understand the impact of exposure, theoretical and conceptual models have been developed to guide inquiry. In addition, methodologies are becoming more sound and sophisticated. Mechanisms of direct and indirect impact have been proposed. The importance of a number of factors associated with these processes has been established. Thus, there is greater guidance as to which factors are most meaningful and crucial to include in investigations. Currently, researchers are attempting to examine these factors, taking into account the vast complexity of the factors and systems involved.

☐ Current Findings

Research findings indicate that, in general, witnessing interparental violence is a negative and often traumatic experience for children. To document this conclusion, results from investigations of exposed children's level of adjustment and development in a number of different areas are reviewed below. In this chapter, empirical results will be discussed more globally in terms of some of the associated child and family factors. In the next chapter, child factors are addressed in more detail, discussing their role as mediators or moderators of children's adjustment and development.

Exposed Children's Problems

A number of researchers have found that both behavioral and emotional problems are significantly higher in the children of battered women than in comparison youngsters (e.g., Christopoulos et al., 1987; Graham-Bermann et al., in press; Hershorn & Rosenbaum, 1985; Hughes, 1988; Hughes, Parkinson, & Vargo, 1989; Hughes, Vargo, Ito, & Skinner, 1991; McCloskey, Figueredo, & Koss, 1995; Rossman, Hughes, & Hanson, 1998; Sternberg, et al., 1993; Wolfe et al., 1986). Moreover, in the few studies conducted with children from non-shelter samples, these authors also found that violence against the mothers was associated with children's symptomatology (Fantuzzo et al., 1991; Graham-Bermann & Levendosky, 1998a; Spaccarelli, Sandler, & Roosa, 1994).

   Overall, there are consistent emotional and behavioral differences between children of battered women and nonexposed children in both internalizing (e.g., depressed, anxious) and externalizing (aggressive, disobedient) behaviors. In their review, Hughes and Graham-Bermann (1998) concluded that the evidence for a negative impact of witnessing spouse abuse on behavioral and emotional functioning of children is very strong. Similar conclusions were drawn by Kolbo, Blakely, and Engelman (1996) as well as Margolin (1998) and Kashani and Allan (1998) in recent reviews. However, the answer to how particular children might be affected is not a simple one, and it depends on how certain combinations of the factors interact, for example, age and gender. Researchers have also been investigating additional areas of adjustment within the last decade or so, including cognitive functioning and school performance, social interactions, and trauma-related symptoms. These will be covered in more depth in the next chapter on individual differences in children's reactions to exposure.

Severity of Exposed Children's Problems

It is possible to evaluate how serious the consequences for exposed children are by examining how many youngsters have severe difficulties; this is particularly important for purposes of intervention. "Severe" problems are defined as those that are substantially greater than those seen in a normative group. Severe problems are at a level high enough that the children are considered to be in need of clinical treatment.

A number of researchers and clinicians have investigated the percentages of children in shelter samples who have behavior problem checklist scores above the cutoffs that indicate the need for clinical services (e.g., the upper 2% to 10% of the standardization sample; Achenbach, 1991). The Child Behavior Checklist (CBCL) is the most commonly used and provides scores related to externalizing behaviors (e.g., aggressiveness, disobedience), internalizing behaviors (e.g., anxiety, depression), and social competence. Depending on the gender of the child, the type of violence experienced, and the T-score used as the cutoff, the percentages reported range from 25% to 75%. Rather consistently, on average, approximately 35% to 50% of the children fall above the clinical cut off (Christopoulos et al., 1987; Davis & Carlson, 1987; Graham-Bermann et al., in press; Hughes et al., 1991; Jouriles, Murphy, & O'Leary, 1989; Jouriles, Norwood, McDonald, Vincent, & Mahoney, 1996; Moore & Pepler, 1998; O'Keefe, 1995; Sternberg et al., 1993; Wolfe et al., 1986). By comparison in terms of base rates, approximately 25% of children in comparably low-income families have scores within the clinical range (Burns, Patterson, Nussbaum, & Parker, 1991). Thus, a substantial portion of these children are reported by their mothers as having serious problems and are in need of clinical treatment.

In addition, Jouriles et al. (1989) found that children of battered women were four times as likely to show high levels of psychopathology as were children living in nonviolent homes. McCloskey et al. (1995) also reported significant differences between the children of battered women and comparison youngsters in several types of child psychopathology, including diagnosable levels of attention deficit/hyperactivity disorder, separation anxiety, obsessive-compulsive disorder, and major depressive disorder.

Differences in problem severity have implications for intervention. Children having mild problems may need one approach to treatment, whereas the approximately 40% of youngsters with more severe difficulties may benefit from more intensive interventions. Appropriate types of interventions are addressed in Chapter 6.

Situational/Contextual Associated Factors

For the sake of discussion, the situational and contextual variables that can influence children's adjustment will be divided into two general categories: those factors more directly related to the children and those more directly related to the parents. Clearly it is difficult to totally separate these factors, and it should be kept in mind that they are related. As mentioned above, proposed factors that relate more closely to the youngsters include their past experience with all types of violence in their families, the perceived emotional climate in the family, maternal stresses or maternal mental health, and social support. Additional critical factors that have been considered are the emotional availability of the mother, parent–child aggression, and disciplinary strategies.

Type of violence experienced.   There are a number of different types of child maltreatment, including sexual abuse and physical neglect. However, more is known about exposure as related to physical and psychological violence toward women and children, so these will be the focus here. The co-occurrence of wife abuse and child abuse, long recognized by clinicians, is now coming to the attention of researchers and social agencies (e.g., Rossman & Rosenberg, 1998). As mentioned in Chapter 1, Appel and Holden's review (1998) concluded that the median co-occurrence rate is 40%.

The influence of this co-occurrence was examined in a study by Salzinger, Feldman, Hammer, and Rosario (1992) of physically abused children. They found that children's behavioral problems were mostly a function of violence in the child's immediate family, with violence against the child exerting the most powerful impact but with witnessing violence adding to that impact. Overlap in types of abuse was substantial, with path analysis indicating that child abuse is most likely to occur in households with spouse abuse, which co-occurs with severe discord and substance abuse. Jouriles, Barling, and O'Leary (1987) also found that children's problems were more associated with parent-to-child aggression than with spousal violence.

Similarly, McCloskey et al. (1995) reported a strong association among verbal, physical, and severe physical aggression toward both the women and the children. O'Keefe (1995) also reported that predictors of child abuse included greater frequency and severity of marital violence, less marital satisfaction on the mother's part, and poorer quality of the father–child relationship as perceived by the child.

Due to this overlap in types of family violence, a number of investigators have studied the adjustment of children who have been exposed to more than one type of family violence. Hughes and her colleagues have been investigating what they call the "double whammy": the hypothesis that although the effect of observing spouse abuse is negative, the impact is greater when children are also physically abused. This idea has been supported in several studies (Hughes, 1988; Hughes et al., 1989; Hughes et al., 1991). Other researchers examining children exposed to multiple types of family violence with similar patterns of results include Davis and Carlson (1987); McCloskey et al. (1995); O' Keefe (1995); Rossman, Heaton, Moss, Malik, Lintz, and Romero (1991); and Sternberg et al. (1993). Exposed abused boys (Cummings, Hennessy, Rabideau, & Cicchetti, 1994; Hennessy, Rabideau, Cicchetti, & Cummings, 1994) have also been found to be more reactive to interadult anger.

However, there is some research indicating that exposed abused children's aggressive behaviors, particularly when assessed by observers/mothers who see the children mostly in the violent home, may actually appear lower than those of similarly exposed but nonabused children (Rossman et al., 1991). This is not a consistent finding, but it could suggest that some exposed abused children opt to "keep their heads down" at home as a way of staying safe since the violence has extended beyond the marital system. And some of Sternberg et al.'s (1993) findings, wherein exposed children by some reports showed poorer adjustment than abused children, appear to fit this pattern. Mallah and Rossman (1998) also found that expectations a benign adult interaction videotape would end in aggression were greatest for exposed abused children. Grych's work (in press) provides one explanation. He found that children's appraisals of both the threat inherent in parental conflict and their pessimism about the outcome of parental conflict were greater for children who had experienced both spousal violence and higher levels of father-to-child aggression. Thus, no matter how doubly exposed children act out their distress or try to stay safe, in under- or overcontrolled behaviors or different delays, it is likely to be the case that they share frightening emotions and cognitions about what could happen. Thus, it would not be surprising if doubly exposed children were at greater risk.

Emotional Climate.   Emotional climate can be thought of as pertaining to the types of feelings that are primarily expressed in a family. For example, in one family there could be substantial amounts of yelling in expressing angry feelings, while in another family the parents could consistently give each other "the silent treatment."

Psychological abuse of women has recently come under more scrutiny as an important situational factor in its own right. For example, Jouriles and colleagues (1996) examined whether nonphysical forms of aggression might influence children's adjustment. They found that other forms of partner aggression, including verbal aggression, contributed unique variance after accounting for the impact of physical violence. The authors indicated that psychological aggression needs to be considered along with physical aggression as an important contributor to children's adjustment. They suggested that children exposed to interparental violence may be especially sensitive to the potential in their families for verbal aggression and other forms of psychological abuse to escalate into physical violence. Verbal aggressiveness and other forms of psychological aggression have been found to be more important than physical violence in predicting behavioral problems, especially for girls, in a number of other studies as well (e.g., Graham-Bermann & Levendosky, 1998a; Hughes & Luke, 1998; Moore & Pepler, 1998).

Emotional climate pertains to all members of the family; thus children's and mothers' symptoms cannot be viewed in isolation. (See also Emery and Laumann-Billings (1998) for a broader context, who reviewed other characteristics of violent families.) The abuser in the family has a major impact on the emotional climate. A batterer is often characterized by negative affectivity, lower impulse control and esteem, a heightened response to all stressors, and use of drugs and alcohol, which serves to disinhibit aggression. Holtzworth-Munroe and Stuart (1994) have described three categories of wife abusers: (1) those who are generally violent and antisocial and often abuse alcohol; (2) those who are violent only at home, are less severely violent, and show both suppressed anger and remorse (the majority of abusers); and (3) those who are only violent at home but are socially isolated and incompetent and characterized by dysphoric and schizoid/borderline symptoms. In addition, Gottman and colleagues (1995) found different patterns of physiological reactions for abusers similar to those in categories 1 and 2 above. The category 1 abusers showed a deceleration of heart rate in reacting to conflict, suggesting a sort of calming and ability to focus attention associated with their potentially violent responses. Those similar to the category 2 abusers showed heart rate acceleration with conflict, suggesting emotional upset and distress. Thus, women and children living in the types of situations described above would experience severe challenges to their psychological well-being.

Maternal Mental Health.   The symptoms with which a parent struggles are likely to influence her or his child in various ways. Developmentalists have noted a connection between maternal depression and children's problems, including problems with attachment (Carlson, Cicchetti, Barnett, & Braunwald, 1989). Battered mothers who were also depressed were more likely to have preschoolers with behavior problems and more ambivalent relationships with their mothers (Graham-Bermann & Levendosky, 1998a). One subgroup of exposed children experiencing difficulties described by Hughes and Luke (1998) were those characterized by having depressed and verbally aggressive mothers. Similarly, Hughes, Cole, and Ito (1988) found that maternal depression predicted between 45% and 51% of the variance in behavior problem scores. The amount of variance accounted for varied based both on the group (exposed versus exposed/abused) and on the particular behavior problem assessed. In addition, maternal self-blame, often related to maternal depression, was also related to girls' internalizing behavior problems (Brown & Kerig, 1995).

As discussed more in the next chapter, Hops (1995) put forth a gender intensification hypothesis wherein one effect of maternal depression was to accelerate a daughter's depression. This was reflected in Davies and Windle's study (1997) in which adolescent girls whose mothers had been depressed for longer than 1.5 years were more likely to be depressed and to show conduct and school problems. Maternal depression joined with family conflict, parenting impairment, low family intimacy, and other stressors to predict outcome for girls, especially the occurrence of delinquency and alcohol problems. However, results have been mixed regarding the impact of maternal psychopathology more generally (Margolin, 1998).

Other findings (using path analysis or structural equation modeling) related to the impact of maternal mental health on child functioning will be discussed in a subsequent section focusing on data analysis.

Maternal Stresses, Parenting, and Discipline. Other associated factors and indirect mechanisms include those related to maternal stresses, parenting stress, and discipline. Investigating potential variables associated with children's adjustment, Wolfe et al. (1985) assessed the impact of maternal stresses on child behavior problems. They found that maternal stress and family violence variables combined accounted for 19% of the variance associated with child behavior problems. Moore and Pepler (1998) also found that a mother's general health added modestly to the prediction of a child's emotional and behavioral difficulties.

Three general domains of study of the parenting relationship in violent families currently exist: those that attend to the attachment and emotional security children in spouse abusing families feel; those that examine the parenting stress and emotional availability of battered mothers to their children; and those that address parenting practices among battered women. Davies and Cummings (1994) succinctly reviewed the literature on parenting and attachment in conflictual families in presenting their emotional security hypothesis about how effects of marital conflict were passed on to children. They posit that it is the insecurity the child experiences connected with marital conflict that accounts for many of the negative effects of exposure. They identified almost the same three domains of study in their review: emotional negativity in parenting; actual child management practices; and, attachment security. The emotional negativity, which they saw as being rejecting of the child, ranged from outward parent-to-child hostility to parental withdrawal and neglect and was associated with various forms of maladaptation for children including passivity, low self-esteem and control, noncompliance, and low social competence. They saw insecure attachments as ways in which children deal with marital conflict and abuse and note that insecurely attached children are more vulnerable to fluctuating, unpredictable, and negative affective states.

In addition, they observe that in maritally conflictual families, parenting often does not reflect the desired close monitoring; authoritative, consistent discipline; and responsiveness that is most useful for children. As they and Grusec and Goodnow (1994) have noted, children in conflictual families are often fearful and anxious regarding parental interactions and this arousal state appears to interrupt the processing, acceptance, and internalization of parental disciplinary expectations and messages. It would not be surprising if children in conflictual families often felt confused, frightened, and insecure, not knowing how they felt nor being able to regulate their emotions well enough to produce the behaviors parents desire.

The review by Grych and Fincham (1990) also noted that the particular mechanism through which parental conflict has its effects, those noted as indirect effects, is not clear and likely is multidimensional. Children may model their parent's aggressive or withdrawal behaviors, the marital conflict and tension itself is undoubtedly upsetting, and disciplinary practices are likely to suffer when the parents are fighting. They also mention the high likelihood that a child's ability to understand or adaptively react to or process conflict events and whatever surrounds them in terms of child directives are likely to be disrupted by the child's arousal level. This would suggest that children would respond with more familiar and possibly developmentally earlier behaviors in the face of parental conflict.

Holden and his colleagues were some of the first to alert us to the amount of parenting stress battered mothers experience. Parenting stress is often measured with a scale wherein responses reflect endorsement of items expressing frustration about, for example, a child's slow learning rate, or lack of appreciation of maternal efforts, or parents feeling like they are trapped by parental responsibilities or that they cannot handle things very well. Holden and Ritchie (1991) noted that battered mothers reported greater parenting stress and inconsistency in discipline than nonbattered mothers. Further, maternal stress and ratings of paternal irritability were both predictors of children's behavior problems. Working with exposed 3- to 7-year-olds and both observations of and self-report from their mothers, Holden, Stein, Ritchie, Harris, and Jouriles (1998) found that maternal lack of control and aggression toward her partner were the best predictors of children's behavior problems. In a study of 5-year-old exposed children Ritchie and Holden (1998) reported that for battered, but not for nonbattered, mothers parenting stress was higher and was correlated with verbally deriding the child, spanking, less physical affection, and less positive reinforcement of the child.

Findings by Levendosky and Graham-Bermann (1998) and Hughes, Luke, Cangiano, and Peterson (1998) also revealed that parenting domain stress was predictive of internalizing and externalizing behavior problems. The parenting stress scale that they used allowed them to separate sources of stress into a child stress domain for those associated with characteristics of the child versus a parent stress domain for those associated with characteristics of the parent or her environment. In addition, Levendosky and Graham-Bermann (1998) also noted prediction due to interactions between mothers' marital psychological maltreatment and parent or child domain stress. The authors interpreted this as indicating that children's internalizing behaviors were associated with maternal behaviors, but their externalizing behaviors were due to the family violence and not mothers' stress levels.

Several investigators have addressed the question of what parenting practices are like in maritally violent homes. Levendosky and Graham-Bermann (1998) used the Parent Style Survey to examine parenting qualities of warmth, control, child centeredness, and effectiveness. They found support for a mediational model that showed that martial violence was related to poorer parenting when there was also marital dissatisfaction and mothers were experiencing greater symptoms of depression and trauma. A second study by these authors (1999), using observations of parenting and children's behaviors, showed that depressed battered mothers were less likely to show authoritative parenting but were more likely to use permissive and neglectful parenting processes. In fact, permissive parenting, and not marital violence, was the best predictor of children's observed behavior difficulties. The observed difficulties related modestly with those reported on the CBCL. Similarly, Chew and Hughes (1996), using a qualitative methodology, found that battered women described their parenting as inconsistent, being strict when the man is around and rather lax when he is not present. However, Sullivan, Nguyen, Allen, Bybee, and Juras (1999) also studied the parenting practices of battered women. They were interested in disciplinary strategies related to corporal punishment and found that the women used a number of methods, including time-out and removing privileges, in addition to spanking.

Moreover, Holden et al. (1998) report a series of three studies examining the parenting behaviors and beliefs of battered and nonbattered poor women. They found that battered and nonbattered poor mothers were similar in many ways, including the fact that both groups of mothers reported using more aggressive responses with sons, not differing on average in their repudiation of spanking. However, battered mothers were less likely to set limits and were less proactive in their interactions with their children. They also reported being less emotionally available to their children, especially the Hispanic battered mothers. Following another group of battered mothers of 32 4- to 9-year-old children for 6 months after they left a shelter, the authors determined that parenting stress, mother-to-child aggression, children's internalizing and externalizing behavior problems, and children's responses in play were all improved at the 6-month follow-up.

Other parenting mechanisms that may influence exposed children are those tied to parents' differential practices toward sons and daughters. In a study of 3- to 4-year-old community children from families experiencing differing amounts of marital dissatisfaction, Kerig (in press) noted that, especially in dissatisfied families, girls' assertive behaviors were most likely to be negated and those girls were least likely to respond positively to this. Across all families, parents, especially fathers, were more likely to respond positively to boys' versus girls' assertive responses and negated responses, and to girls' versus boys' positive responses. Early on children may be learning that the parental response to their behavior may depend on their gender.

Gender may also be involved in how various parenting tasks are performed. Margolin (1998) noted that parents play many roles for children. They provide opportunities for learning and social relationships in and outside the family, they teach and discipline, and they provide emotional support as well as modeling of emotion regulation. A good relationship with one parent or a sibling or peer, or an outside activity for which the child gets positive attention, appears to be protective for children. However, the modeling of violence to solve conflicts, the rationalization of its use, and the devaluing of women that occurs in violent families serve to put children at risk (Wolfe, Wekerle, Reitzel, & Gough, 1995).

But what about parent–child relationships with a battering father figure? In following battered mothers over several years, Sullivan, Juras, Bybee, Nguyen, and Allen (1999) examined the active participation of the children with mothers' assailants. They found that the level of assailants' involvement with the children, as well as the status of the man (i.e., biological father versus stepfather/father figure versus nonfather figure) played a role in the children's adjustment. Stepfather/father figures were more verbally abusive than biological or nonfather figures and children were more fearful of them. In addition, youngsters whose biological father was the abuser showed the lowest sense of social competence. The authors attributed this finding to either the greater amounts of physical violence against the mother or to the man's status as the child's biological father. This study highlights an area badly in need of more research regarding relationships with both parents, especially the batterer.

Marital Conflict Factors.   Included in the situational/contextual variables that are more directly related to the parents and the marital conflict factors are the following: frequency of the physical aggression, its intensity and duration, the content of the conflict, its resolution, whether it is overt or covert, and the child's age at the onset of the violence. Several researchers have examined these factors specifically related to children's adjustment. Rossman and Rosenberg (1992) reported that as the level of conflict and family violence increased, the children's levels of perceived competence fell and the children's behavior problems rose. Interestingly, Jenkins and Smith (1991) found in a community sample that, even after controlling for adverse parenting practices such as lack of care of the child and discrepancies between parents in parenting, parental conflict was still predictive of children's externalizing problems.

Regarding duration, Rossman, Mallah, Dominguez, Kimura, and Boyer-Sneed (1994) found that duration played an important role in children's adjustment. Their results indicated that the number of years the children had experienced family violence was more consistently related to outcome than the level of violence during the past year. Hughes and Luke (1998) also found that duration may play an important role in the extent of children's distress levels. Based on a cluster analysis, in a small sample of children they found that youngsters for whom the interparental violence occurred over their entire lives indicated substantial levels of internalizing distress.

One factor that may come into play for predicting child adjustment at lower levels and frequencies of violence is how or whether the conflict is resolved. Cummings and Davies (1994) have demonstrated, for verbal parental conflict, that children are less distressed when they see or hear of the conflict being resolved. They think of these contexts as being potential learning situations for children regarding constructive rather than destructive conflict.

Heterogeneity in Impact and Longer-Term Adjustment

Heterogeneity in Adjustment.   Although the above information is very important to understanding the functioning and adjustment of exposed children, as well as understanding mechanisms of impact and factors associated with impact, all findings are based on looking not at individual children but at groups of youngsters. The vast majority of the above findings are based on group differences in average scores, which may obscure individual variations in adjustment. Recently, another approach to an understanding of the impact of exposure has been employed. As a case in point, Hughes and Luke (1998) focused on delineating factors associated with domestic violence that can influence child outcomes and demonstrated that not all children have the same reactions to witnessing the abuse of their mothers. The researchers hypothesized that Anglo children ages 6 to 12 years who were residing in a shelter for battered women would show a range in adjustment, varying from little to substantial distress. Cluster analysis was used to identify subgroups of the children, based on similarities and differences among their behavior problem, internal distress, and self-esteem scores, which resulted in the identification of five distinct patterns in adjustment. The two largest clusters contained children who were at most only slightly distressed, accounting for approximately 60% of the children. These children had mothers who were less depressed and less verbally aggressive toward their male partners.

The other three clusters included children who experienced behavior problems, internal distress, and low self-esteem. Families in these latter three groups differed from the first two clusters in higher mothers' depression and verbal aggressiveness levels as well as in longer duration of the abuse of the mother. Additional attention to the individual needs of both the women and children in these groups, beyond the standard shelter services, was suggested. Recommendations for differential interventions for both children and mothers based on different patterns of distress were made (Hughes & Luke, 1998).

This approach was employed again in a second, rather different sample of families (primarily African American), and similar results were obtained (Hughes et al., 1998). Once again, a five-cluster solution fit the data, with one clear cluster of children with fewer problems (32%), three clusters of children with evident difficulties (47%), and one cluster that might be doing okay, although that is questionable (20%). For the youngsters who were experiencing problems, several factors distinguished them. Interestingly, they were significantly more likely to be younger children. In addition, their mothers indicated on measures of parenting stress and parenting that they felt they were experiencing problems managing their children, setting limits, and gaining cooperation, as well as expressing anger and irritability at or in front of their children. Other emotional climate factors that played a role in poorer adjustment included high levels of psychological aggression toward the child from both the mother and the father and especially high levels of psychological aggression from the mothers' partners to the mothers.

Longitudinal Perspectives.   It represents great progress in the field and courage on the part of investigators and families that some longitudinal investigations of battered mothers and their children are beginning to be done. It takes a great deal of work and time to establish a trusting relationship with women who have been abused so that they are willing to stay in touch with a research project. Sullivan, Rumptz, Campbell, Eby, and Davidson (1996) have developed good procedures (e.g., weekly calls or visits and help finding resources) for establishing these relationships such that they were able to follow 94% of battered women over 2 years.

Other researchers using some of the same procedures have tried to follow battered mothers. In one of the first investigations of adjustment over time, Emery, Kraft, Joyce, and Shaw (1984) reported on a 4-month follow-up of children who had been residents in a shelter for battered women. They found that with a small sample of 16 children, a significant improvement was seen in internalizing behaviors, although the reports were still approximately one standard deviation about the standardization sample mean score. No change was seen in externalizing scores. When adjustment was examined in relation to whether the family had returned to the batterer, few differences were noted. Scores for all of the children declined slightly, although the children whose mothers did not return were slightly higher at time of shelter stay and remained so at 4-month follow-up.

When follow-up studies were conducted approximately 6 months after shelter stay, all saw improvements in children's problem behaviors after mothers had found nonviolent shelter. Giles-Sims (1985) noted that mother-to-child aggression had decreased during the 6 months following a shelter stay. Wolfe et al. (1986) did postexposure assessments of children of former residents of a battered women's shelter and found that these children did not have levels of problem behaviors above those of a community sample. In addition, Andres and Moore (1995) also noted improvement in children's behavior problems 6 months after mothers had established a nonviolent residence.

Similarly, Holden et al. (1998) reported that among the shelter women there was a significant drop in depression levels as well as in parenting stress over 6 months. They also found significant differences in behavior problems over 6 months, with 36% of the children in their shelter sample above the cut-off indicating clinically significant levels of problems initially ($T > 67$); 6 months later, only 9% of the children met that criterion for level of difficulties. In addition, battered women's aggressive and punitive behavior toward their children also decreased if they left the battering situation.

Using the same shelter population as Emery et al. (1984), Emery (1996) found that as time passed, distress in family members decreased: over a 12-month period, mothers' depression levels dropped, as did the children's internalizing and externalizing scores. Emery also emphasized that a crucial variable to consider was whether the women returned to the batterer. Leaving or returning to her partner was a major factor in adjustment after one year, with children's internalizing scores significantly improved if the woman left and worse if she returned. In addition, women's depression levels decreased if they had not returned but increased if the women returned to the batterer.

Another longitudinal study was recently conducted by Rossman (1998b). She and her colleagues followed for almost a year over 100 5- to14-year-old children from disadvantaged shelter and community families that were characterized by different levels of marital conflict and violence. Over 90% of the exposed children had been in violent homes since age 2 or before. Researchers assessed initial and ongoing levels of poverty, marital violence, family life stressors, and children's PTSD symptomatology. In general, trauma symptoms and behavior problems decreased across follow-up for all violence-exposed children. However, school performance ratings improved slightly for exposed children if they had received 6 to 12 treatment sessions in the community. Three factors were associated with greater declines in symptoms and problems and lesser declines in school performance: the absence of ongoing interparental violence; the fact that children attended 6 to 12 treatment sessions on an outclient basis at area mental health agencies; and being male, because boys showed a greater decline in PTSD symptoms.

Finally, Jouriles and colleagues (1998) were able to show even more improvement in children's conduct disorder problems at 8 months for children specifically identified as above clinical cutoff, following a 6-month home-visitation treatment program. In their program, therapists helped mothers and children with pragmatic needs, as well as targeted parenting skills and children's behaviors that sustained conduct disorder problems. These findings are hopeful, suggesting that children are assisted by getting away from the violent home, and that children selected for a particular problem whose families receive assistance directed toward that problem as well as other family needs do show improvement.

Summary and Implications for Intervention

It is clear that for most children, there is a negative impact of exposure. However, it is evident also that the effects are not consistent across children. Child factors play a significant role in the difference in impact seen and will be discussed in greater detail in the next chapter. Situational/contextual factors also are quite important to consider in understanding the impact, which leads to a rather complex picture with so many factors interacting with each other, and in different contexts. At the present time, researchers have moved beyond simple linear cause-and-effect relationships and are trying to investigate this complexity through several methods.

One method is to test the theoretical models for direct and indirect effects and mechanisms of impact using path analysis and structural equation modeling. Evidence to date on direct or indirect impact of interparental violence on children's outcomes is mixed, and results vary depending on which direct and indirect factors are included in the particular study. Another method used is cluster analysis, which examines individual differences among children instead of studying group results. Some evidence for family factors that are associated with better and poorer adjustment of the children has been obtained, with some of those variables identified.

Thus, important factors to consider are type of violence in the family (verbal aggressiveness between partners or also toward the child and physical aggression between partners or also toward the child). These also include the mothers' mental health and duration of the physical abuse. Impact of characteristics of the batterer, for example, his level of violence, and his status as parent (all studies carried out so far have been with heterosexual couples) also likely play an important role. Parenting stresses and skills of the adults in the relationship are important and are part of the puzzle regarding how children are functioning. Differences in severity of impact are seen with approximately 35% to 50% of children above clinical cutoff levels. Longitudinal studies are beginning to be conducted, with results suggesting that 4 months after establishment of violence-free environment is not enough time to see much change in problem behavior, but after 6 to 12 months, fewer difficulties are seen.

All of the foregoing findings imply that interventions need to be individualized. Interventions with children will need to vary according to how severe the difficulties are, what symptoms the children may be showing, and what areas of functioning are disrupted. In addition, intervention efforts directed to the mothers need to be individualized as well. Mothers' mental health will vary, as will their parenting skills. More on interventions will be covered in Chapter 6.

☐   Implications for Research

Recent Advances in Research

Methodologically, researchers have been able to make improvements, with many studies becoming more sophisticated, although a good many of the recommendations made by Fantuzzo and Lindquist (1989) still stand. A more general discussion and recommendations for methodology are found in Chapter 8 of this volume.

Samples.   In terms of samples, researchers have gathered in increasing numbers participants from the community as well as shelters who are exposed to interparental violence (e.g., Fantuzzo et al., 1991; Graham-Bermann & Levendosky, 1998a; Jouriles et al., 1987, 1989; McCloskey et al., 1995; O'Brien, Margolin, & John, 1995; Rossman, 1998b; Rossman & Rosenberg, 1992; Sternberg et al., 1993). Although in some studies (e.g., McCloskey et al., 1995), the community participants have not been found to be different from shelter participants in terms of demographics or amount of violence experienced, in others more violence has been found in the shelter families (e.g., Rosenberg & Rossman, 1990; Rossman & Rosenberg, 1990). In addition, adjustment of children exposed to interparental violence from shelter versus community settings has been specifically examined by only a few researchers. Rossman and Rosenberg (1992) found that children in the violent-shelter group received significantly higher externalizing scores than the violent-home group of youngsters. In addition, there was a trend toward the violent-shelter children to obtain lower perceived competence scores than the violent-home youngsters.

In addition, participants from non-Anglo backgrounds are being included in studies (e.g., Graham-Bermann & Levendosky, 1998a, 1998b; Holden et al., 1998; Jouriles et al., 1996; McCloskey et al., 1995; O'Brien et al., 1995; O'Keefe, 1994, 1995; Rossman & Ho, in press). Also, participants who are of higher income are included (Jouriles et al., 1989; Kerig, 1998; O'Brien et al., 1995; Rossman & Rosenberg, 1992).

Definitions of Violence.   In order to more precisely define "exposure," researchers now more often ask either the children or the mothers where the children were when the fighting was taking place (e.g., Rosenberg, 1987). In terms of definitions of violence and exposure to interparental abuse, the CTS are still used the most frequently to document the types and amount of violence experienced. Several other instruments have been utilized, including the O'Leary–Porter Scale (Porter & O'Leary, 1980). The CTS have recently been revised and expanded to include more items, which are related to negotiation, psychological abuse, and physical assault (Straus, Hamby, Boney-McCoy, & Sugarman, 1996). However, researchers still have to ask whether the children were present or within earshot to be exposed to the particular behavior.

Measures and Measurement Techniques.   In terms of scales assessing adjustment and development, the majority of researchers use the CBCL (Achenbach, 1991). Others employ reasonably well-standardized instruments such as a structured diagnostic interview conducted with both women and children (e.g., McCloskey et al., 1995). In addition, investigators use self-report instruments that are standardized for use with children or adults, such as those that measure anxiety or depression. A non-self-report method brought to this area is the use of behavioral observations. These have been utilized by several investigators (Copping, 1996; Graham-Bermann & Levendosky, 1998a; Moore & Pepler, 1998) and provide very valuable information. Another innovative technique has been developed by Holden and Ritchie (1991), who devised a computer-administered format where they can provide the women with "person-alized" vignettes related to parenting. A general recommendation to be made is that various other developmental domains need to be measured more innovatively and extensively.

Associated Variables.   More recently, a substantial number of child-related and situational/contextual factors have been included in studies. As will be evident in the next chapter, researchers have been investigating the impact of individual child variables such as age, gender, ethnicity, attributional and cognitive styles, plus coping abilities. The situational factors that investigators have been pursuing, as discussed above, include the children's past experience with violence (e.g., with physical and psychological violence directed against them), the perceived emotional climate of the family, maternal mental health, maternal stress, and parenting practices. Variables that are more directly related to the conflict between the parents, in terms of intensity and duration, have been investigated to a limited extent recently as well.

Data Analysis.   The most recent literature reflects the fact that investigators have begun to examine the information they obtain in more sophisticated ways, with researchers using path analysis and structural equation modeling, in particular, to understand processes and mechanisms involved in the impact of spouse abuse on children's adjustment (e.g., Graham-Bermann et al., in press; Hanson, 1996; Hanson & Hughes, 1998; McCloskey et al., 1995; Rossman, 1998a; Salzinger et al., 1992; Sullivan et al., 1999). Much is to be learned from their findings, although many research questions remain unanswered.

For example, McCloskey et al. (1995), using structural equation modeling, found that there were direct effects of family violence on child adjustment according to both mother and child report, although the relationship was stronger based on mother report (56% of variance explained versus 12%). Interestingly, mothers' mental health did not mediate the relationship between exposure to interparental violence and child functioning. This large sample (*n* = 365) consisted of approximately 50% Anglo families and 35% Mexican American, all low income, with children between the ages of 6 and 12 years. The sample of violent families was gathered from both shelters and the community. Maternal mental health was measured by the Brief Symptom Inventory, while the Child Assessment Schedule (child- and parent-report versions) was used for child adjustment.

Sullivan, Nguyen et al. (1999) also studied child adjustment and parenting practices of battered women, as they are both influenced by the violence perpetrated against the women. Using path analysis, they found that the abuse of the mother had a direct impact on the child's adjustment, while the abuse had an indirect impact on parenting stress and use of discipline. The authors described the indirect effect as what happened when the children's problems increased the mother's parenting stress and her need to use more discipline.

In contrast, Hanson and Hughes (1998) used LISREL—a type of structural equation modeling data analysis technique—to test latent variable path models and found, based on mothers' reports of child functioning, that child adjustment was mediated by maternal mental health. These 100 families were low income and were 80% Anglo, with children between the ages of 4 and 16 years. These authors found that family violence seems to have an impact on children through its effect on maternal emotional distress. The direct causal pathway from family violence to child mental health was not supported by the analyses, although correlations between family violence and child adjustment were significant. Mother mental health was measured by a composite variable made up of the Beck Depression Inventory and State and Trait anxiety.

Similarly, Graham-Bermann et al. (in press) reported that maternal mental health mediated the impact of domestic violence on child behavior problems. Thus, as with Hanson and Hughes (1998), they concluded that exposure to domestic violence exerts its impact in an indirect fashion. They measured maternal mental health with a composite variable made up of the average of a mean stress score and a mean depression score. In addition, taking a contextual approach with their structural equation modeling, they also reported that a conflictual social network negatively moderated mothers' mental health.

Also employing structural equation modeling, Rossman (1998a), with a large sample of Anglo and mixed ethnic families, found support for two pathways of impact, one for behavioral problems and the other for cognitive difficulties. For the former, traumatic responding (PTSD-type symptoms) mediated adjustment problems. Interparental violence was linked with traumatic responding, which was then linked with behavioral difficulties. For cognitive problems, this type of difficulty was the mediator between family adversity and school problems. Family adversity was linked with cognitive difficulties, which were linked with school performance. That there would be two different pathways makes sense given the different outcome variables and the assessment of different areas of children's functioning.

Overall, the findings indicate some support for a direct influence of the impact of interparental violence on children; more substantial support was found for an indirect influence, with maternal mental health, posttraumatic symptoms, and cognitive difficulties as variables involved in indirect influence. Although there are discrepancies seen in the results discussed above, differences in findings are likely due to differences in samples, in measures used, and in data analysis procedures. The findings from these investigations are still instructive, and these studies are examples of the types of research that need to be replicated.

Also regarding data analysis, more attention is currently being paid to situational/contextual and developmental factors as they influence functioning. For example, approaches that allow for a more individualized examination of factors have been employed. As previously mentioned, cluster analysis has recently been used to tentatively delineate a number of factors that influence children's adjustment (Hughes & Luke, 1998; Hughes et al., 1998). These types of techniques allow for alternatives to the simple cause–effect linear model of relationships between interparental violence and impact of the exposed child, as suggested by Margolin (1998).

Suggestions for Future Research

Clearly there are number of needs in this area of research, all of which follow a developmental progression in sophistication of methodology. It will be helpful to continue to obtain more representative samples of battered women, including women from higher-income families, from sources other than shelters for battered women, and women who are individually and culturally diverse. See Chapter 5 of this volume for a discussion of ethnic minority and lesbian battered women.

Regarding measurement, continued use of standardized instruments, including those normed on children of battered women and their mothers, is a recommendation. In addition, continued use and development of innovative techniques, such as the behavioral observations and computerized vignettes noted above, would be helpful. In terms of measuring impact of exposure, clearer definitions of outcome would make assessment easier, as would more precise definitions of the violence the women have experienced. This same recommendation holds for violence the children have experienced, especially related to the distinction between corporal punishment and "violence." Moreover, there is a clear need, especially as we wish to study women from diverse backgrounds, to use qualitative methodologies in order to be more certain that we are obtaining the views of the women and children themselves, in their own words. A combination of qualitative/narrative and quantitative/standardized methods can be used to help us be more certain the information we receive is accurate and that we remain open to new areas of study.

There is a enduring need to acknowledge the complexity of the models and mechanisms of action proposed, and it will be very helpful to continue the investigation of direct and indirect mechanisms of influence. Questions remain regarding whether the impact of interparental violence takes place directly or whether it is mediated indirectly through other factors, such as mothers' mental health or children's cognitive difficulties. Clearly there is a need to continue building and testing multifactor models for ways the impact on youngsters is exerted.

Related to the situational context, it would be helpful to include additional family members and supplementary variables in the analyses. Sibling aggression and psychological abuse of the mother are prime examples of important contextual factors to consider in more depth and detail (e.g., Graham-Bermann et al., in press; Moore & Pepler, 1998). Duration of abuse is also a question that needs to be considered more often, in addition to intensity, frequency, or severity.

One important question regarding emotional climate pertains to whether types of aggressiveness are on a continuum and whether there is a qualitative difference if physical aggression, rather than only psychological aggression, is present. A number of researchers feel that when conflict between parents reaches the physical point, the impact on children is different from that of nonphysical conflict. For example, Fincham, Grych, and Osborne (1994) proposed that there may be a threshold between "garden-variety" marital conflict and more severe (i.e., physically aggressive) forms. In addition, several other researchers have pointed out that the dynamics in violent families are different from those that are verbally conflictual, because when psychological abuse and coercion are backed up by physical force, the climate changes (Graham-Bermann et al., in press; Jouriles et al., 1996).

However, currently the contribution of each type of aggressiveness is not entirely clear. Margolin (1998) points out that there is an important distinction between the role of couple violence and couple conflict. What is known currently is that violent, as opposed to nonviolent, conflict has been shown to lead to more extensive long-term problems as well as more negative immediate reactions. She suggests that we need to discover from the children what dimensions of the couple conflict, either violent or nonviolent, are most threatening to them.

Recently Jouriles, McDonald, and Norwood (1999) brought up the issue of what they call "ordinary violence." They base their argument on prevalence figures, saying that the prevalence of minor violence, such as pushing or slapping, is quite high (approximately 40% of couples). This is similar to the distinction between corporal punishment and "violence" toward children. Jouriles et al. (1999) propose that ordinary violence may not have the type of impact that more severe violence has. Clearly work remains to be done in the area of "ordinary" violence. The question remains regarding a continuum of violence or a qualitative difference, given the fact that psychological aggressiveness seems to have an impact, and in some instances a separate effect, from physical violence. Thus, emotional climate is a very significant factor to consider, and this is an important question that remains to be addressed in more detail.

The area of parenting and issues when there is battering highlights an area badly in need of more research. While some custody and visitation policies are changing, it is not uncommon to find battered mothers and exposed children who are mandated to have continuing contact with her abusive partner through visitation or the need to make arrangements for it. Research is needed to determine what types of parenting practices are used during visitation by battering fathers and how these are associated with child well-being. Several states now provide some access to formal visitation centers wherein the battered mother and her partner never need to have contact surrounding the children's required visits, and the visits can be done at the center and monitored if there is reason for concern.

Although much more difficult to conduct, there is a need for more follow-up and longitudinal studies. Regarding longitudinal investigations, Fincham et al. (1994) provided suggestions for the researchers in this area regarding directions research needed to go. They suggest a number of ways to make longitudinal findings more informative, which include testing numerous, competing models; assessing for the possibility of causal chains; being careful of assumptions regarding linear relationships among variables; and investigating individual differences more closely by using homogeneous groups of children. Even though sophisticated data analytic methods can be helpful in understanding mechanisms of impact, only longitudinal research will be able to provide clear answers to causal questions.

We also need more research that is treatment relevant. Although the results from all of the above studies are salient for interventions, investigations need to be tailored more specifically to addressing questions regarding interventions, including effectiveness of various types of treatment. Answers to some of these questions will guide the planning of interventions that will assist in alleviating distress. More on this is covered in Chapter 6.

☐ Conclusion

Overall, it is apparent that there are both strengths and weaknesses in this area of research. On the positive side, additional information has been gathered in the last decade regarding the psychological functioning of children of battered women. We know much more now about the mechanisms of influence as well as factors that are associated with the impact of exposure to interparental violence. We are also more clear about the types of questions that remain to be answered, having the benefit of the guidance of a number of theories. Moreover, the methodologies employed by researchers have become more sound and more sophisticated than previously. We are beyond simplistic investigations, and researchers are examining children of battered women and their functioning based on individual patterns of adjustment as well as the influence of a host of child-related and situational/contextual factors.

On the less positive side, a substantial amount of work remains to be done. We still do not know the exact combination of indirect and direct mechanisms that cause the impact on children. Chances are the combinations of mechanisms will be different for individual families as will the related variables. Additional improvements in methodologies are vital for advancing knowledge in the field. However, there is reason for hope and optimism, with many researchers committed to the area and conducting investigations that improve incrementally in a number of ways over the years, moving the field forward, even if in small steps.

☐ References

Achenbach, T. M. (1991). *Manual for the Child Behavior Checklist/4-18 and 1991 Profile*. Burlington, VT: University of Vermont Department of Psychiatry.

Andres, J., & Moore, T. E. (1995, March). *The adjustment of child witnesses to spousal abuse: A follow-up study*. Poster session presented at the meeting of the Society for Research in Child Development, Indianapolis, IN.

Appel, A. E., & Holden, G. W. (1998). The co-occurrence of spouse and physical child abuse: A review and appraisal. *Journal of Family Psychology, 12,* 578–599.

Brown, C. A., & Kerig, P. K. (1995, August). *Parent's and children's coping with interparental conflict*. Paper presented at the meeting of the American Psychological Association, New York.

Burns, G. L., Patterson, D. R., Nussbaum, B. R., & Parker, C. M. (1991). Disruptive behaviors in an outpatient pediatric population: Additional standardization data on the Eyberg Child Behavior Inventory. *Psychological Assessment: A Journal of Consulting and Clinical Psychology, 3,* 202-207.

Carlson, B. E. (1984). Children's observations of interpersonal violence. In A. R. Roberts (Ed.), *Battered women and their families* (pp. 147–167). New York: Springer.

Carlson, V., Cicchetti, D., Barnett, D., & Braunwald, K. G. (1989). Finding order in disorganization: Lessons from research on maltreated infants' attachments to their caregivers. In D. Cicchetti & V. Carlson (Eds.), *Child maltreatment: Theory and research on the causes and consequences of child abuse and neglect,* (pp. 494–528). Cambridge: Cambridge University Press.

Chew, C., & Hughes, H. M. (1996, June). *Parenting of battered women: A preliminary investigation.* Paper presented at the second Conference on Children Exposed to Family Violence, Austin, TX.

Christopoulos, C., Cohn, D. A., Shaw, D. S., Joyce, S., Sullivan-Hanson, J., Kraft, S. P., & Emery, R. E. (1987). Children of abused women: I. Adjustment at time of shelter residence. *Journal of Marriage and the Family, 49,* 611–619.

Copping, V. E. (1996). Beyond over- and under-control: Behavioral observations of shelter children. *Journal of Family Violence, 11,* 41–57.

Cummings, E. M., & Davies, P. (1994). *Children and marital conflict: The impact of family dispute and resolution.* New York: Guilford.

Cummings, E. M., Hennessy, K. D., Rabideau, G. J., & Cicchetti, D. (1994). Responses of physically abused boys to interadult anger involving their mothers. *Development and Psychopathology, 6,* 31–41.

Davies, P. T., & Cummings, E. M. (1994). Marital conflict and child adjustment: An emotional security hypothesis. *Psychological Bulletin, 116,* 387–441.

Davies, P. T., & Windle, M. (1997). Gender-specific pathways between maternal depressive symptoms, family discord, and adolescent adjustment. *Developmental Psychology, 33,* 657–668.

Davis, L., & Carlson, B. E. (1987). Observation of spouse abuse: What happens to the children? *Journal of Interpersonal Violence, 2,* 278–291.

Elbow, M. (1982). Children of violent marriages: The forgotten victims. *Social Casework, 63,* 465–471.

Emery, R. (1996, June). *A longitudinal study of battered women and their children: One year following shelter residence.* Paper presented at the National Conference on Children Exposed to Family Violence, Austin, TX.

Emery, R. E., Kraft, S. P., Joyce, S., & Shaw, D. (1984). *Children of abused women: Adjustment at four months following shelter residence.* Paper presented at the annual meeting of the American Psychological Association, Toronto.

Emery, R. E., & Laumann-Billings, L. (1998). An overview of the nature, causes, and consequences of abusive family relationships: Toward differentiating maltreatment and violence. *American Psychologist, 53,* 121–135.

Fantuzzo, J. W., De Paola, L. M., Lambert, L., Martino, T., Anderson, G., & Sutton, S. (1991). Effects of interpersonal violence on the psychological adjustment and competencies of young children. *Journal of Consulting and Clinical Psychology, 59,* 258–265.

Fantuzzo, J. W., & Lindquist, C. U. (1989). The effects of observing conjugal violence on children: A review and analysis of research methodology. *Journal of Family Violence, 4,* 77–94.

Fincham, F. D. (1994). Understanding the association between marital conflict and child adjustment: An overview. *Journal of Family Psychology, 8,* 123–127.

Fincham, F. D., Grych, J. H., & Osborne, L. N. (1994). Does marital conflict cause child maladjustment? Directions and challenges for longitudinal research. *Journal of Family Psychology, 8,* 128–140.

Giles-Sims, J. (1985). A longitudinal study of battered children of battered wives. *Family Relations, 34,* 205–210.

Gottman, J. M., Jacobson, N. S., Rushe, R. H., Short, J. W., Babcock, J., La Taillade, J. J., & Waltz, J. (1995). The relationship between heart rate reactivity, emotionally aggressive behavior, and general violence in batterers. *Journal of Family Psychology, 9,* 227–248.

Graham-Bermann, S. A. (1996). Family worries: Assessment of interpersonal anxiety in children from violent and nonviolent families. *Journal of Clinical Child Psychology, 25,* 280–287.

Graham-Bermann, S. A., & Hughes, H. M. (1998). The impact of domestic violence and emotional abuse on children: The intersection of research, theory, and clinical intervention. *Journal of Emotional Abuse*, 1(2), 1–22.

Graham-Bermann, S. A., & Levendosky, A. A. (1998a). The social functioning of preschool-age children whose mothers are emotionally and physically abused. *Journal of Emotional Abuse*, 1(1), 59–84.

Graham-Bermann, S. A., & Levendosky, A. A. (1998b). Traumatic stress symptoms in children of battered women. *Journal of Interpersonal Violence*, 14, 111–128.

Graham-Bermann, S. A., Levendosky, A. A., Porterfield, K., & Okun, A. (in press). The impact of woman abuse on children: The role of social relationships and emotional context. *Journal of Clinical Child Psychology*.

Grusec, J. E., & Goodnow, J. J. (1994). Impact of parental discipline methods on the child's internalization of values: A reconceptualization of current points of view. *Developmental Psychology*, 30, 4–19.

Grych, J. H. (in press). Children's appraisals of interparental conflict: Situational and contextual influences. *Journal of Family Psychology*.

Grych, J. H., & Fincham, F. D. (1990). Marital conflict and children's adjustment: A cognitive-contextual framework. *Psychological Bulletin*, 108, 267–290.

Hanson, K. L. (1996). *A proposed causal model of adjustment problems in children exposed to family violence*. Unpublished doctoral dissertation, Saint Louis University.

Hanson, K. L., & Hughes, H. M. (1998, August). *Children of battered women and adjustment problems: A proposed causal model*. Paper presented at the annual meeting of the American Psychological Association, San Francisco.

Hennessy, K. D., Rabideau, G. J., Cicchetti, D., & Cummings, E. M. (1994). Responses of physically abused and nonabused children to different forms of adult anger. *Child Development*, 65, 815–828.

Hershorn, M., & Rosenbaum, A. (1985). Children of marital violence: A closer look at the unintended victims. *American Journal of Orthopsychiatry*, 55, 260–266.

Hilberman, E., & Munson, K. (1978). Sixty battered women. *Victimology*, 2, 100–112.

Holden, G. W., & Ritchie, K. L. (1991). Linking extreme marital discord, child rearing, and child behavior problems: Evidence from battered women. *Child Development*, 62, 311–327.

Holden, G. W., Stein, J. D., Ritchie, K. L., Harris, S. D., & Jouriles, E. N. (1998). The parenting behaviors and beliefs of battered women. In G. W. Holden, R. Geffner, & E. N. Jouriles (Eds.), *Children exposed to marital violence: Theory, research, and intervention* (pp. 289–334). Washington, DC: American Psychological Association.

Holtzworth-Munroe, A., & Stuart, G. L. (1994). Typologies of male batterers: Three subtypes and the differences among them. *Psychological Bulletin*, 116, 476–497.

Hops, H. (1995). Age- and gender-specific effects of parental depression: A commentary. *Developmental Psychology*, 31, 428–431.

Hughes, H. M. (1982). Brief interventions with children in a battered women's shelter: A model preventive program. *Family Relations*, 31, 495–502.

Hughes, H. M. (1988). Psychological and behavioral correlates of family violence in child witnesses and victims. *American Journal of Orthopsychiatry*, 58, 77–90.

Hughes, H. M. (1991, August). Research concerning children of battered women: Clinical and policy implications. In R. Geffner & M. Paludi (Cochairs), *State-of-the-art research in family violence: Practical implications*. Paper presented at the annual meeting of the American Psychological Association, San Francisco.

Hughes, H. M. (1995, March). *Relationships between affective functioning of mothers and children in shelters for battered women: Clinical implications*. Paper presented at the Biennial Meeting of the Society for Research in Child Development, Indianapolis.

Hughes, H. M. (1997). Research concerning children of battered women: Clinical implications. In R. Geffner, S. Sorenson, & P. Lundberg-Love (Eds.), *Violence and sexual abuse at home: Current issues in spousal battering and child maltreatment*. (pp. 225–244). New York: Haworth.

Hughes, H. M., & Barad, S. J. (1983). Psychological functioning of children in a battered women's shelter: A preliminary investigation. *American Journal of Orthopsychiatry, 53,* 525–531.

Hughes, H. M., Cole, F., & Ito, E. S. (1988, August). *Maternal functioning and family violence as predicators of child adjustment.* Paper presented at the annual meeting of the American Psychological Association, Atlanta.

Hughes, H. M., & Fantuzzo, J. W. (1994). Family violence: Child. In R. T. Ammerman, M. Hersen, & L. Sisson (Eds.), *Handbook of aggressive and destructive behavior in psychiatric patients* (pp. 491–508). New York: Plenum.

Hughes, H. M., & Graham-Bermann, S. A. (1998). Children of battered women: Impact of emotional abuse on adjustment and development. *Journal of Emotional Abuse, 1*(2), 23–50.

Hughes, H. M., & Luke, D. A. (1998). Heterogeneity in adjustment among children of battered women. In G. W. Holden, R. Geffner, & E. N. Jouriles (Eds.), *Children exposed to marital violence: Theory, research, and applied issues* (pp. 185–222). Washington, DC: American Psychological Association.

Hughes, H. M., Luke, D. A., Cangiano, C. & Peterson, M. (1998, October). *Clinical implications of heterogeneity in psychological functioning among children of battered women.* Paper presented at the Fourth National Conference on Children Exposed to Family Violence, San Diego.

Hughes, H. M., Parkinson, D. L., & Vargo, M. C. (1989). Witnessing spouse abuse and experiencing physical abuse: A "double whammy"? *Journal of Family Violence, 4,* 197–209.

Hughes, H. M., Vargo, M. C., Ito, E. S., & Skinner, S. K. (1991). Psychological adjustment of children of battered women: Influences of gender. *Family Violence Bulletin, 7,* 15–17.

Jacobson, D. (1978). The impact of marital separation/divorce on children: II. Interparent hostility and child adjustment. *Journal of Divorce, 2,* 3–19.

Jaffe, P. G., Wolfe, D. A., & Wilson, S. K. (1990). *Children of battered women.* Newbury Park, CA: Sage.

Jaffe, P., Wolfe, D., Wilson, S., & Zak, L. (1986). Family violence and child adjustment: A comparative analysis of girls' and boys' behavioral symptoms. *American Journal of Psychiatry, 143,* 74–77.

Jenkins, J. M., & Smith, M. A. (1991). Marital disharmony and children's behavioral problems: Aspects of a poor marriage that affect children adversely. *Journal of Child Psychology and Psychiatry, 32,* 793–810.

Jouriles, E. N., Barling, J., & O'Leary, K. D. (1987). Predicting child behavior problems in maritally violent families. *Journal of Abnormal Psychology, 15,* 165–173.

Jouriles, E. N., McDonald, R., & Norwood, W. D. (1999, February). *Documenting the prevalence of children's exposure to domestic violence.* Paper presented at the Asilomar Conference on Children and Intimate Violence, Pacific Grove, CA.

Jouriles, E. N., McDonald, R., Stephens, N., Norwood, W., Spiller, L. C., & Ware, H. S. (1998). Breaking the cycle of violence: Helping families departing from battered women's shelters. In G. W. Holden, R. Geffner, & E. N. Jouriles (Eds.), *Children exposed to marital violence: Theory, research, and applied issues* (pp. 337–370). Washington, DC: American Psychological Association.

Jouriles, E. N., Murphy, C. M., & O'Leary, K. D. (1989). Interspousal aggression, marital discord, and child problems. *Journal of Abnormal Child Psychology, 57,* 453–455.

Jouriles, E. N., Norwood, W. D., McDonald, R., Vincent, J. P., & Mahoney, A. (1996). Physical violence and other forms of marital aggression: Links with children's behavior problems. *Journal of Family Psychology, 10,* 223–234.

Kashani, J. H., & Allan, W. D. (1998). *The impact of family violence on children and adolescents.* Thousand Oaks, CA: Sage.

Kerig, P. K. (1998). Gender and appraisals as mediators of adjustment in children exposed to interparental violence. *Journal of Family Violence, 13,* 345–363.

Kerig, P. K. (in press). Gender issues in the effects of exposure to violence on children. In R. Geffner & P. Jaffe (Eds.), *Children exposed to family violence: Intervention, prevention and policy implications.* Binghamton, NY: Haworth.

Kolbo, J. R., Blakely, E. H., & Engelman, E. (1996). Children who witness domestic violence: A review of the empirical literature. *Journal of Interpersonal Violence, 11,* 282–293.

Levendosky, A. A., & Graham-Bermann, S. A. (1998). The moderating effects of parenting stress on children's adjustment in woman-abusing families. *Journal of Interpersonal Violence, 13,* 383–397.

Levendosky, A. A., & Graham-Bermann, S. A. (1999). Behavioral observations of parenting in battered women. *Journal of Family Psychology.* Manuscript submitted for publication.

Lystad, M. (1975). Violence at home: A review of the literature. *American Journal of Orthopsychiatry, 45,* 328–345.

Mallah, K., & Rossman, B. B. R. (1998). Social information processing for children exposed to family violence. *Journal of Child Clinical Psychology.* Manuscript submitted for publication.

Margolin, G. (1998). Effects of domestic violence on children. In P. K. Trickett & C. J. Schellenbach (Eds.), *Violence against children in the family and community* (pp. 57–102). Washington, DC: American Psychological Association.

McCloskey, L. A., Figueredo, A. J., & Koss, M. P. (1995). The effects of systemic family violence on children's mental health. *Child Development, 66,* 1239–1261.

Moore, T. E., & Pepler, D. J. (1998). Correlates of adjustment in children at risk. In G. W. Holden, R. Geffner, & E. N. Jouriles (Eds.), *Children exposed to marital violence: Theory, research, and intervention* (pp. 157–184). Washington, DC: American Psychological Association.

Moore, T., Pepler, D., Weinberg, B., Hammond, L., Waddell, J., & Weiser, L. (1990). Research on children from violent families. *Canada's Mental Health Journal, 38,* 19–23.

O'Brien, M., Margolin, G., & John, R. S. (1995). Relation among marital conflict, child coping, and child adjustment. *Journal of Clinical Child Psychology, 24,* 346–361.

O'Keefe, M. (1994). Racial/ethnic differences among battered women and their children. *Journal of Child and Family Studies, 3,* 283–305.

O'Keefe, M. (1995). Predictors of child abuse in maritally violent families. *Journal of Interpersonal Violence, 10,* 3–25.

Pfouts, J. H., Shopler, J. H., & Henley, H. C., Jr. (1982). Forgotten victims of family violence. *Social Work, 27,* 367–368.

Porter, B., & O'Leary, K. D. (1980). Marital discord and childhood behavior problems. *Journal of Abnormal Child Psychology, 8,* 287–295.

Ritchie, K. L., & Holden, G. W. (1998). Parenting stress in low income battered and community women: Effects on parenting behavior. *Early Education & Development, 9,* 97–112.

Rosenbaum, A. & O'Leary, K. D. (1981). Children: The unintended victims of marital violence. *American Journal of Orthopsychiatry, 51,* 692–699.

Rosenberg, M. S. (1987). Children of battered women: The effects of witnessing violence on their social problem-solving abilities. *The Behavior Therapist, 4,* 85–89.

Rosenberg, M. S., & Rossman, B. B. R. (1990). The child witness to marital violence. In R. T. Ammerman & M. Hersen (Eds.), *Treatment of family violence* (pp. 183–210). New York: Wiley.

Ross, S. M. (1996). Risk of physical abuse to children of spouse abusing parents. *Child Abuse & Neglect, 20,* 589–598.

Rossman, B. B. R. (1998a). Descartes' error and Post-Traumatic Stress Disorder: Cognition and emotion in children who are exposed to parental violence. In G. W. Holden, R. Geffner, & E. N. Jouriles (Eds.), *Children exposed to marital violence: Theory, research, and applied issues* (pp. 223–256). Washington, DC: American Psychological Association.

Rossman, B. B. R. (1998b, October). *Time heals all: How much and for whom?* Paper presented at the Fourth National Children Exposed to Family Violence Conference, San Diego.

Rossman, B. B. R., Bingham, R. D., & Emde, R. N. (1997). Symtomatology and adaptive functioning for children exposed to normative stressors, dog attack, and parental violence. *Journal of the American Academy of Child and Adolescent Psychiatry, 36,* 1–9.

Rossman, B. B. R., Heaton, M. K., Moss, T. A., Malik, N., Lintz, C., & Romero, J. (1991, August). *Functioning in abused and nonabused witnesses to family violence.* Paper presented at the annual meeting of the American Psychological Association, San Francisco.

Rossman, B. B. R., & Ho, J. (in press). Posttraumatic response and children exposed to parental violence. In R. Geffner, P. Jaffe, & M. Suderman (Eds.), *Children exposed to family violence: Intervention, prevention, and policy implications.* Binghamton, NY: Haworth.

Rossman, B. B. R., Hughes, H. M., & Hanson, K. L. (1998). Victimization of school-aged children. In B. B. R. Rossman & M. S. Rosenberg (Eds.), *Multiple victimization of children: Conceptual, developmental, research, and treatment issues.* (pp. 87–106). Binghamton, NY: Haworth.

Rossman, B. B. R., Mallah, K., Dominguez, M., Kimura, S., & Boyer-Sneed, B. (1994, August). *Cognitive and social information processing of children in violent families.* Paper presented at the annual meeting of the American Psychological Association, Los Angeles.

Rossman, B. B. R., & Rosenberg, M. S. (1992). Family stress and functioning in children: The moderating effects of children's beliefs about their control over parental conflict. *Journal of Child Psychology and Psychiatry, 33,* 699–715.

Rossman, B. B. R & Rosenberg, M. S. (Eds.). (1998). *Multiple victimization of children: Conceptual, developmental, research, and treatment issues.* Binghamton, NY: Haworth.

Salzinger, S., Feldman, R. S., Hammer, M., & Rosario, M. (1992). Constellations of family violence and their differential effects on children's behavioral disturbance. *Child and Family Behavioral Therapy, 14,* 23–41.

Spaccarelli, S., Sandler, I. W., & Roosa, M. (1994). History of spouse violence against mother: Correlated risks and unique effects in child mental health. *Journal of Family Violence, 9,* 79–98.

Sternberg, K. J., Lamb, M. E., Greenbaum, C., Cicchetti, D., Dawud, S., Cortes, R. M., Krispin, O., & Lorey, F. (1993). Effects of domestic violence on children's behavior problems and depression. *Developmental Psychology, 29,* 44–52.

Straus, M. A., Hamby, S. L., Boney-McCoy, S., & Sugarman, D. B. (1996). The Revised Conflict Tactics Scales (CTS2): Development and preliminary data. *Journal of Family Issues, 17,* 283–316.

Straus, M. A., Hamby, S. L., Finkelhor, D., Moore, D. W., & Runyan, D. (1998). Identification of child maltreatment with the parent-child Conflict Tactics Scales: Development and psychometric data for a national sample of American parents. *Child Abuse and Neglect, 22,* 249–270.

Sullivan, C., Juras, J., Bybee, D., Nguyen, H., & Allen, N. (1999). *How children's relationships to their mother's abuser affects their adjustment.* Manuscript submitted for publication.

Sullivan, C. M., Nguyen, H., Allen, N., Bybee, D., & Juras, J. (1999). *Beyond searching for deficits: Evidence that battered women are nurturing parents.* Unpublished manuscript.

Sullivan, C. M., Rumptz, M. H., Campbell, R., Eby, K. K., & Davidson, W. S. (1996). Retaining participants in longitudinal community research: A comprehensive protocol. *Journal of Applied Behavioral Science, 32,* 262–276.

Wekerle, C., & Wolfe, D. A. (1996). Child maltreatment. In E. J. Mash & R. A. Barkley (Eds.), *Child psychopathology* (pp. 492–540). New York: Guilford.

Westra, B. L., & Martin, H. P. (1981). Children of battered women. *Maternal and Child Nursing Journal, 10,* 41–51.

Widom, C. S. (1989). Does violence beget violence? A critical examination of the literature. *Psychological Bulletin, 106,* 3–28.

Wolfe, D. A., & Jaffe, P. (1991). Child abuse and family violence as determinants of child psychopathology. *Canadian Journal of Behavioural Science, 23,* 282–299.

Wolfe, D. A., Jaffe, P., Wilson, S., & Zak, L. (1985). Children of battered women: The relationship of child behavior to family violence and maternal stress. *Journal of Consulting and Clinical Psychology, 53,* 657–665.

Wolfe, D. A., Wekerle, C., Reitzel, D., & Gough, R. (1995). Strategies to address violence in the lives of high-risk youth. In E. Peled, P. G. Jaffe, & J. L. Edelson (Eds.), *Ending the cycle of violence: Community responses to children of battered women* (pp. 255–275). Thousand Oaks, CA: Sage.

Wolfe, D. A., Zak, L., Wilson, S., & Jaffe, P. G. (1986). Child witnesses to violence between parents: Critical issues in behavioral and social adjustment. *Journal of Abnormal Child Psychology, 14,* 95–104.

Individual Differences in Response to Exposure: Risk and Resilience

Selena, age 6, Josh, age 10, and Rebecca, age 14, are the children of Margie and Thomas, who have been married for 17 years. The first 5 years of their marriage were uneventful, with Thomas fulfilling his duties at the Army base and Margie going back to teaching kindergarten when Rebecca was 3 years old. Then it felt like tragedy struck the family when Thomas's unit was called up for Desert Storm. Thomas spent over a year in the Middle East before his unit was relieved and personnel sent home. After Thomas returned home he seemed edgy and irritable, always worried and never satisfied that things were going as they should. He continued his duties at the base but expressed stronger and stronger beliefs that Margie belonged at home and that they should raise more children. In time Margie became pregnant with Josh and promised to retire from teaching when he was born. She felt responding to Thomas's wishes could help him relax and save their marriage. Their relationship had stayed close sexually, but emotionally Thomas seemed to grow more and more distant. After Josh was born, Thomas seemed to come out of what Margie had termed his postwar stage and was happier and interacted more with her and the children. This did not last long. Soon he was irritable and moody again and began making more demands of her. Thinking that fulfilling his wish for one more child might bring him all the way out of this stage she agreed to become pregnant again and Selena was born. Unfortunately this did not help Thomas. He became more demanding, difficult to please, isolative, and ultimately physically abusive of Margie. He felt she was not listening to him, did not keep the house well, and was not spending enough time raising their children. Now, 8 years later, wife abuse is the family secret and the children are showing various problems. Selena is doing well in school but is very withdrawn and anxious. Josh is failing in school and will pick a fight with anyone. Rebecca is average in school but is very aggressive with peers and has few friends.

Why do these children have such different behavior profiles? Most studies, as noted in the previous chapter, have examined differences between groups of children experiencing different levels of exposure to parental conflict and violence. This is not surprising as an initial strategy for understanding exposure effects. However, within these groups that are globally similar with regard to exposure there are notable individual differences between children, even those within the same family. Thus part of the recent paradigm shift in research in this area has been to examine mechanisms and characteristics of individual children, their families, and their support networks that may relate to or may modify or both the more global exposure effects.

Individual differences between children have been regarded as constituting potential vulnerability or protective factors, factors that may increase or decrease, respectively, the risk inherent in exposure. Surely these vulnerability and protective factors combine in some way to produce the evidenced behavior of exposed children. There are several models for how these factors may combine. Some researchers have worked with straightforward accumulation models, meaning that they see effects as additive. Having two vulnerability factors places a child at greater risk for poor outcome than having one (Rutter, 1983). Other investigators have assumed that children can absorb a certain number of adverse factors without negative effects, but those beyond that number begin interacting with each other to create even greater risk (Sameroff & Seifer, 1983). An additional emerging issue in this area of research has been that the direction in which factors operate, whether for protection or vulnerability, may depend on the context in which they are experienced. For example, while perspective taking (i.e., being able to see a situation from another's position) is regarded as a positive ability for children in normal families, it appears to place a child in a parentally violent family at greater risk (Rossman, Rosenberg, Rawlins, & Malik, 1991; West, Fraser, Ho, & Rossman, 1998). Therefore, the question of vulnerability and protection is not a simple one, either in terms of how factors combine or in terms of what direction they push a child in a violent family; normal developmental research findings cannot always guide researchers of family violence.

Davies and Cummings (1995) have highlighted the fact that the role of individual differences in children's responses to marital conflict has been greatly understudied. In this chapter we will review existing research findings for the individual difference factors that have been studied with exposed children. It is important to keep in mind that sometimes these factors interact to create a different outcome than either factor alone. For example, age and gender may interact. There is much evidence that while exposed boys are at higher risk for acting out behaviors and aggression during the school years, exposed girls may display equally or greater aggression during adolescence (Rosenberg, 1984). In addition, the guidelines for the review have been to examine results for investigations of both marital verbal and physical conflict since children in violent families are exposed to both and to use the newest studies available unless older studies are the only ones examining a particular child factor.

☐ Age

In general the literature has pointed to the greater vulnerability of younger children to exposure to spousal conflict and violence (see reviews by Emery & Laumann-Billings, 1998; Grych & Fincham, 1990; Hughes & Graham-Bermann, 1998; Lehmann, 1997; Margolin, 1998; or Grych, in press, regarding children's appraisals of threat inherent in parental conflict). This is ironic in view of the fact that these children are also at greater risk of exposure. Fantuzzo, Boruch, Beriana, Atkins, and Marcus (1997) found that children through age 5 years are disproportionately exposed to wife abuse and wife abuse with substance abuse. Since preschool and younger children have fewer capacities developmentally to regulate feelings and cognitively process and evaluate environmental information, they are more dependent on cues from parents regarding the meaning of events. Thus, it is not surprising if they are more vulnerable to dysregulation of their affect and behavior with exposure. However, Holden and Ritchie (1991) found their youngest children (ages 2 to 5 years) had fewer problems than their older children. Perhaps younger children's problems are less noticeable to adult observers. An additional insight on younger children's problems is provided by a study by Erel, Margolin, and John (1998). They found the negative features of both younger and older siblings' interactions (age range 3.5 to 8.5 years) in community families were related to negative features of the mother–child relationship, but that negative dimensions of the marital relationship were linked only to older siblings' behaviors. They suggested that the impact of marital conflict on younger siblings may be through the mother–child and sibling relationships.

There is the suggestion that younger children are more likely to show internalizing types of problem behaviors (e.g., depression, social withdrawal, and somaticizing) in response to marital conflict (Jouriles et al., 1991; Rossman et al., 1991). These behaviors are not unlike some of the symptoms characterizing posttraumatic responses. But these are also the types of symptoms that are less likely to garner adult attention. For example, Achenbach, McConaughy, and Howell (1987) found that outside observers were more likely to show agreement about the occurrence of externalizing behaviors (aggression, hyperactivity) than internalizing behaviors. However, the greater occurrence of internalizing problems for younger children has not been confirmed in other studies (Fantuzzo et al., 1991) and one study found externalizing behaviors were elevated for younger girls (O'Keefe, 1994a). Epidemiological data on children's problems have led Hops (1995) to put forth a gender intensification hypothesis with regard to age. Boys' problems are noted as being most intense during childhood, while girls' problems appear to be more evident in adolescence. In the 2 to 5 year age range Cummings, Pellegrini, Notarius, and Cummings (1989) noted that exposed children's responses to adult verbal anger (i.e., preoccupation, concern, support seeking, and social responsiveness) increased with age, with the preoccupation of exposed boys being greater than that of nonexposed boys.

In reviewing studies of children exposed to marital verbal conflict, Davies and Cummings (1994) hypothesized that children's responses to adult verbal anger likely reflected the emotional insecurity they felt when exposed and that the form of their responses appeared to shift with age. Toddlers and infants as young as 6 months reacted to adult anger with attempts to comfort or distract. Preschoolers showed the concern mentioned above and were also more likely to try to mediate the dispute than older children, but also to show acting-out and noncompliant behaviors. El-Sheikh and Cheskes (1995) found that their 6- to 7-year-olds were more likely to endorse intervening in parental conflict through siding with one party or through use of authority tactics, whereas older children endorsed resolution through submission. By late childhood and adolescence children's reactions were more passive, showing dysphoria and depression. So the point here would be that children at all ages are responsive to parental conflict but the form of the response may change; some behavioral responses may be more noticeable to parents or observers than others (Achenbach et al., 1987).

It should be noted that not all studies find child age to make a difference. Jouriles, Norwood, McDonald, Vincent, and Mahoney (1996) found that age did not contribute to the prediction of behavior problems in a sample of children from a battered women's shelter. The pattern where some studies find of no age differences whereas others do also characterizes the child trauma literature more generally (Pynoos, Steinberg, & Goenjian, 1996). One speculation has been that at very high levels of distress and trauma factors such as age or gender no longer exert much influence on children's responses (Rossman, Bingham, & Emde, 1997). This might be called an "overwhelmedness" effect wherein children become more homogeneous in their responses to severe trauma, showing basic traumatic stress responses. Since younger children have fewer resources to use in dealing with such an event, another prediction would be that factors such as age and gender would be even less influential for them. This is a hypothesis awaiting further investigation. Another hypothesis noted above would be that as adults we simply do not as readily note age differences in responding for a certain group of children, since the form of their response is less obvious.

A third possibility, noted by Cummings, Davies, and Simpson (1994), is that effects due to factors such as age may not be noted when tested by looking at group differences (e.g., the average internalizing problems for 4- to 5-year-olds versus those for 9- to 10-year-olds). What is needed is for investigators to look for differences in patterns of relationships among variables for different age groups. This point will be reiterated in discussing gender differences. What their comment suggests is that age (or gender) acts as a moderator or mediator variable, thus affecting the relationships among other variables. Stated briefly, a moderator variable is a preexisting characteristic or circumstance that influences the direction of the relationship between exposure and outcome. For example, were social support a moderator, high versus low social support may be associated with greater differences in outcome at high stress than at low stress. A schematic representation of this type of effect is presented in Figure 3.1. This suggests that the children's ratings of their self-worth do not drop with increased family adversity if those children have higher levels of social support, but that for children with lower social support there is a negative relationship between their ratings of self-worth and levels of family adversity.

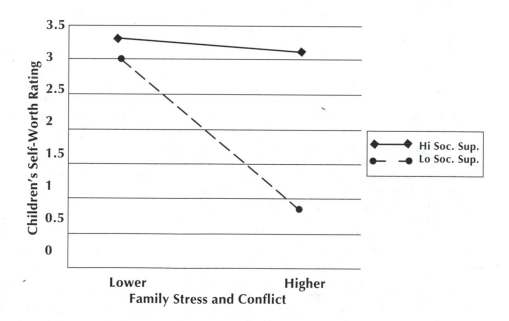

FIGURE 3.1. Schematic Drawing of a Moderator Effect of Social Support

A mediator variable, however, is like a catalyst in a reaction. You can have an event, but without the presence of the mediator you will not get a reaction so there will be no relationship between the event and the outcome. For example, a deaf child asleep upstairs will not be distressed by ongoing verbal conflict between his parents downstairs, because presumably his or her distress would need to be mediated by the process of hearing. The mediator comes between the event and the outcome and is most compellingly demonstrated with longitudinal data over at least three time points. However, mediation is sometimes descriptively examined in concurrent data sets where all variables are measured at the same time. Sometimes a variable can be thought of and found to act both as a moderator and a mediator. For example, a positive mother–child relationship could better prepare a child to face adversity before it happened, but it could also act to help the child use maternal support while the adversity was ongoing.

If age were a moderator (i.e., preexisting condition prior to the exposure) of the relationship between exposure and externalizing problems, that would mean that 4- to 5-year-olds might show fewer externalizing problems as exposure severity increased while older children would show more externalizing problems. This pattern of relationships might not be reflected in mean differences between arbitrarily defined age groupings. If age were a mediating variable between exposure severity and externalizing problems it could be the case that there was no relationship between externalizing problems and exposure for preschoolers but that the relationship was positive for older children. This could also result in weak age group differences, again depending on how age groups were defined. These different forms of influence that individual difference variables might have are complex and not required for understanding the research findings discussed. Their existence does, however, highlight the complexity of the task researchers, clinicians, teachers, and so on face in trying to understand what factors might be important for a helping a particular child.

☐ Gender

Gender does not show a consistent pattern of results as to whether boys or girls are at higher risk for poor outcome due to parental conflict or violence exposure (see Table 3.1 for a summary of studies; also see the review by Hughes & Graham-Bermann, 1998). In an early study, Jaffe, Wolfe, Wilson, and Zak (1986) noted that exposed girls had greater internalizing problems but exposed boys had greater internalizing and externalizing problems. In a later paper (Jaffe, Hurley, & Wolfe, 1990) it was noted that more boys than girls were above clinical cutoff on behavior problems. Working with exposed 8- to 11-year-old children in the community, O'Brien, Margolin, John, and Krueger (1991) found that boys showed more involvement in and more arousal from audiotaped adult verbal conflict. Reporting on children's responses to marital conflict, Grych and Fincham (1990) noted that school-age girls in community families with greater parent hostility and aggression also had higher conduct disorder scores than girls from less hostile but equally maritally satisfied families. In their review they note that it is more common to find school-age boys responding more aggressively to stronger marital conflict and girls responding with greater distress but that many of the studies showing boys to be at greater risk have been conducted with clinical samples. In a subsequent study of community families these researchers (Grych & Fincham, 1992) found that for 10- to 12-year-olds, as interparental conflict increased boys showed greater internalizing

TABLE 3.1. Age and Gender Studies

Study	Sample	Ages	Gender	Findings
Jaffe, Wolfe, Wilson, & Zak, 1986	Shelter	School-age	Both	Girls: ⇧intern. prob. Boys: ⇧intern. & extern. prob.
Jaffe, Hurley, & Wolfe, 1990	Shelter	School-age	Both	More boys ⇧clinic. cutoff on tot. prob.
Posada et al., 1998	Community	3–4 years	Both	Girls: insecurity of attachment related to exposure Boys: no relation
Ritchie & Miller, 1996	Shelter & Community	3–8 years	Both	Exposed children felt less securely attached; no gender diff.'s reported
O'Brien et al., 1991	Community	8–11 years	Both	Boys showed more involvement in and more arousal to audiotaped adult verbal conflict
Grych & Fincham, 1990	Community	School-age	Both	Greater interparental agg. related to higher conduct disorder scores for girls
Sternberg et al., 1993	Community	Young adolescents	Both	Exposed girls: ⇧intern. & extern. prob. over exposed boys; effect reversed for nonexposed
Rosenberg, 1984	Shelter	School-age & adolescents	Both	With exposure to more severe agg. adol. girls ⇧boys; effect reversed for school-age
Hughes & Graham-Bermann, 1998	Shelter	School-age	Both	Exposed girls more likely to be ⇧ clinic. cutoff for problems
Jouriles & Norwood, 1995	Shelter	School-age	Both	Exposed boys more likely to also be targets of parental aggression & had ⇧extern. prob.
Kerig, 1991	Community	3–4 years	Both	In maritally distressed families girls' assertive responses more likely to elicit negative parental responses than boys'
Jouriles et al., 1987	Community	School-age	Both	Parent-to-child rather than spousal agg. related to prob. for boys, but to anx. & withdrawal for girls

Table 3.1 continues on page 42.

TABLE 3.1. Continued

Study	Sample	Ages	Gender	Findings
Cummings & Hennessey, et al. 1994	Community	4–6 years	Boys	Exposed abused boys more responsive to adult verbal anger than exposed; sensitization
Hennessy et al., 1994	Community	6–11 years	Boys	Exposed abused boys more reactive to adult verbal & physical anger than exposed; sensitization
Davies & Windle, 1997	Community	10th & 11th grade	Girls	Exposed girls depress., conduct & school prob. related to maternal depress. of 1.5 yr. or longer
Brown & Kerig, 1995	Community	7–12 years	Both	In marital conflict homes girls' intern. prob.⇧with maternal self-blame (depress. link), but boys extern. prob.⇧with paternal self-blame; maternal distancing coping related to boys' anx., but maternal avoidance coping related to girls' extern. prob.
Hops, 1995	Community	Adolescent	Both	Maternal depress.⇧girls' depress. but not boys
Kerig, 1998b	Community	7–11 years	Both	Boys using approach coping and girls using avoidance coping with spousal conflict showed fewer prob.
Gordis et al., 1997	Community	9–13 years	Both	For boys exposed specifically to marital physical agg., anx. & distraction were observed responses during mild parental conflict whereas withdrawal was observed for boys not exposed to physical agg.; for all girls distraction was observed related to past exposure to verbal & physical agg.
Warren et al., 1996	Community	School-age	Both	As marital conflict increased boys with externalized coping had fewer extern. prob., but girls with more internalized coping had more intern. prob.

Table 3.1 continues on page 43.

TABLE 3.1. Continued

Study	Sample	Ages	Gender	Findings
Doumas et al., 1994	Community	School-age	Both	Marital violence & child abuse in 2 previous generations predicted boys' agg. but not girls
Cummings & Moore, 1995	Shelter	School-age & early adolescent	Both	Exposed girls ↑boys in intern. & extern. prob. & ↑parental verbal abuse
Andres & Moore, 1995	Shelter	School-age & early adolescent	Both	6-month follow-up of Cummings & Moore showed exposed girls ↑behav. prob. than boys
Kerig, 1997, 1998a, 1998b	Community	School-age	Both	Boys in more agg. families had less ↓egalitarian attitudes toward women; boys focused on threat aspects of marital conflict↓ had ↑extern. prob. if threat & severity were high, but ↑prob. if severity high but not threat; girls, focused on self-blame, had ↑intern. prob.
El Sheikh & Cheskes, 1995	Community	School-age	Both	Boys saw physical vs. verbal adult anger as more angry & had more agg. impulses during verbal
El Sheikh et al., 1996	Community	4–5 years	Both	Boys from families with unresolved marital conflict more upset by adult conflict, & more likely to predict conflict outcome & girls less likely to endorse interven.
Mallah & Rossman, 1999	Shelter & community	School-age	Both	More exposed boys more likely to predict agg. ending to adult conflict
El Sheikh & Reiter, 1996	Community	4–7 years	Both	Girls more distressed to adult physical agg. videotape & more likely to want to stop it than boys

behavior problems while girls evidenced greater externalizing problems. Working with early adolescents, Sternberg et al. (1993) found that parents reported girls in the exposed group to show greater internalizing and externalizing problems than the boys, whereas the direction of difference was reversed in the nonexposed group. Based on child report, it was the girls in the exposed abused group who reported greater externalizing problems than the boys in that group. Adolescent exposed girls' aggression increased relative to the boys when the violence was more severe, whereas for school-age children the effect was reversed (Rosenberg, 1984). In their review, Hughes and Graham-Bermann (1999) cite five studies that suggest that while both boys and girls exposed to parental violence show problems in development, girls tend to show more severe problems, being more likely to be above clinically significant cutoffs. Retrospective studies suggest that, in young adulthood, there are lingering effects of witnessing parental violence. College students who had witnessed parental violence were more anxious than their nonwitness peers, and exposed women were both more depressed and aggressive than nonexposed women (Forsstrom-Cohen & Rosenbaum, 1985); and Maker, Kemmelmeier, and Peterson (1998) found greater interpersonal violence in the relationships of exposed college women who had greater exposure.

In sum, both boys and girls show behavioral disruption associated with exposure. This appears to be more evident for boys during school age and, perhaps, for girls following school age. There may be different mechanisms influencing boys' and girls' reactions at different ages or the same mechanisms, which garner different reactions from boys and girls. Some of these hypotheses have to do with the unfolding of gender role socialization in our culture as it may be linked to the following: the development of emotional security; being the recipient of personal abuse; children's reactions to battered and depressed mothers and attitudes toward women more generally; selection of coping strategies; and children's perceptions of interparental conflict. Studies reviewed below exemplify these different hypotheses.

Gender and Emotional Security

Davies and Cummings (1994, 1998) noted, working from Attachment Theory (Bowlby, 1973), that boys and girls may respond to marital conflict and resultant feelings of emotional insecurity differently: boys may respond by feeling the threat in the situation, whereas girls may respond more relationally by blaming themselves for the parental conflict. This could become more evident as gender roles further develop during puberty, since the boys are socialized to value independence and girls to value family relationships, making girls more sensitive to the conflict as they grow older (Davies & Windle, 1997).

One way of thinking about emotional security is through examining attachment security. In one of the two studies of children's attachment status in relation to parental violence Posada, Waters, Liu, and Johnson (1998) found that verbal and physical aggression against mothers and parental disagreements about child rearing were both associated with lower attachment security scores for girls aged 3 to 4 years. This trend was also evidenced for the boys, meaning that the amount of marital physical aggression (i.e., pushing, throwing, slapping were the forms noted in this sample) was significantly and negatively associated with attachment security. However, neither Ritchie and Miller (1996) nor Huth-Bocks, Levendosky, and Semel (1999) found gender differences in attachment security of exposed preschoolers, although exposure severity was related to poorer outcome. An important question may be what maternal or parenting practices are useful for engendering emotional security for exposed boys and girls at different ages. One possibility, raised later by Cummings and Moore (1995), is that as children grow into adolescence, security may be engendered for boys more by maternal structuring of the household and for girls by mothers' ability to remain emotionally close and deal with their own distress levels. More work in the area of emotional security and attachment is needed, but these studies provide a solid beginning.

Gender and Personal Abuse

Another mechanism differentially affecting boys and girls may be the amount of aggression that is directed toward the child in addition to the marital aggression. Jouriles and Norwood (1995) found, working with school-age children, that in more violent families boys were more often the victims of parental physical aggression (pushing and shoving) and showed more externalizing behavior problems than girls, even after controlling for the boys' own aggression as a possible eliciting factor. An earlier study (Jouriles, Barling, & O'Leary, 1987) had suggested that it was parent-to-child aggression rather than spousal aggression that was associated with most problem indices for school-age boys, but only with anxiety/withdrawal symptoms for girls. However, for toddlers, Jouriles, Pfiffner, and O'Leary (1988) noted that conduct problems/disobedience were associated with marital dissatisfaction for boys (but only marginally with marital conflict) and girls. Cummings, Hennessey, Rabideau, and Cicchetti (1994) noted that physically abused 4- to 6-year-old boys, where two-thirds were also exposed as compared with same-age nonabused boys where two-thirds were exposed, were more reactive to interadult verbal anger, showing both greater aggression and more problem focused coping. This finding for boys fits with a cumulative sensitization model of aggression experienced in different parts of the family system. Again studying abused exposed and exposed boys, ages 6 to 11, Hennessy, Rabideau, Cicchetti, and Cummings (1994) found evidence of the sensitization and overarousal in abused exposed boys' responses to nonverbal, verbal, and physical anger on videotapes. The abused exposed boys showed greater fear of all forms of anger, but they indicated less fear if the videotape also showed anger resolution. The finding of greater arousal of exposed boys replicates the O'Brien et al. (1991) result cited earlier, which had been for nonabused community boys. No doubt personal physical abuse can change the nature of a child's reaction to interparental aggression. However, more work needs to be done to clarify the role of a child's gender when she or he is the target of parental physical aggression and also sees other family members abused.

Gender and Children's Reactions to Battered Mothers

A further group of factors that may interact with child gender in influencing children's responses to interparental aggression has to do with the state of their battered mother. Stress and depression provide severe challenges for many battered mothers. Adolescent girls appear especially sensitive to their mothers' depression. A history of maternal depression of 1.5 years or longer was related to exposed tenth and eleventh-grade girls' depression, conduct, and school problems (Davies & Windle, 1997). Hops (1995) also reported that mothers' depression appeared to accelerate depression for their daughters but not their sons.

Cummings and Moore (1995) examined yet another set of mechanisms based on children's responses to their battered mothers. Working with school-age and preteen shelter children, they found that girls showed higher internalizing and aggressive problems than boys and had higher external locus of control scores. The girls had received greater parental verbal aggression (especially paternal), and their problems were better predicted by maternal stress and distress levels. They speculated, as had Pianta, Egeland, and Sroufe (1990), that boys and girls are sensitive to different aspects of maternal stress. The girls may respond more to mothers' distress, and the boys more to their mothers' ability to provide structure and an organized home. Therefore, if the girls received both more verbal abuse and were more sensitive to their mothers' distress they might be at a greater disadvantage, on average, since some of the mothers did provide greater structure and a less conflictual mother–child relationship, which was important for boys. A follow-up study 6 months later (Andres & Moore, 1995) showed that the shelter girls were still evidencing greater problem behaviors than the boys.

Finally, Kerig (1997, 1998a, 1998b) has carried out a series of studies looking at mechanisms having to do with community school-age children's attitudes toward women, perceptions of parental conflict, and coping responses. She reported findings similar to those by Jaffe, Wolfe, and Wilson (1990): boys in more aggressive families had less egalitarian and more stereotyped attitudes toward women than exposed girls or nonexposed children and that violent households were less egalitarian. In addition, the aspects of a conflict to which boys and girls seemed to be attending were different. When both perceived severity and threat were high, boys' externalizing behaviors were lower than when perceived threat was lower. This represents a replication of Rosenberg's (1984) violence severity finding. Alternatively, girls' appraisals appeared to focus on self-blame, which exacerbated their internalizing behavior problems. However, girls who relied on avoidance coping strategies showed lower internalizing problems. Thus, it appeared useful for the boys to recognize the threat and "keep their heads down" and for the girls to avoid the parental conflict.

Putting the puzzle pieces in this section together is tenuous. Clinicians and researchers know that for every pattern of factors there will be a family. Drawing from the emotional security section and viewing the exposed children as experiencing emotional insecurity and the children as viewing their mothers in a one-down position provides one piece. Then, if mothers are depressed and distressed and girls are more relationally sensitive and also experience greater maternal and paternal verbal abuse, the girls may show avoidance and self-blame when younger, but they may also be moving toward a more adolescentlike agitated depression including aggressive behaviors. At more severe levels of violence, the boys may be vigilant for paternal threat and need greater home structure to calm themselves and sense, wrongly in many instances, that greater household organization and their own "invisibility" may help them avoid paternal aggression. Clearly more research is needed. It will be useful to consider this and other hypotheses below in the broader context of exposed children's coping.

Gender and Coping

Another mechanism that appears to interact with gender for exposed children is coping style. Kerig (1998b), working with 7- to 11-year-old children from community nonviolent and violent families, found that exposed boys were showing greater internalizing problems than exposed girls. However, if the boys adopted approach styles of coping with parental conflict and girls adopted avoidance styles, they showed lower levels of problem behaviors. She termed the boys *warriors* and the girls *worriers* to reflect at least temporarily more effective coping strategies. This fits with another finding (Warren,

Kerig, Brown, & Fedorowicz, 1996) showing that with community school-age children boys who adopted more externally oriented defense mechanisms showed fewer externalizing problem behaviors as parental conflict increased, while for girls internally oriented defense mechanisms exacerbated internalizing problems. The authors suggested that it was disadvantageous for the girls to take more responsibility as conflict increased, but it was advantageous for the boys to express their distress and blame others besides themselves. These results seem contradictory to the "keep your head down" finding discussed above for boys until one considers the levels of violence. As mentioned earlier, on average, the community samples do not show the severe levels of interparental violence found with shelter samples.

Another socialization effect also may be in evidence. Kerig (1991) found that 3- to 4-year-old girls in the more maritally dissatisfied community families were more likely than boys to elicit negative responses to their assertive behaviors and positive responses to their positive behaviors. This was especially true for fathers' responses. And, when children were behaving negatively, boys garnered more positive responses than girls. Interestingly, Brown and Kerig (1995), working with 7- to 12-year-olds, found that mothers' self-blame for marital conflict was related to greater internalizing problems for girls, which is possibly a slightly different statement of the mother–daughter depression effects noted earlier. However, fathers' self-blame was related to greater externalizing problems for boys and girls. In addition, mothers' coping by distancing was related to boys' greater anxiety levels, whereas mothers' use of avoidance for coping was related to girls' greater externalizing problems. The picture is far from clear as to which coping mechanisms may best serve children in violent families and how these relate to the nonaggressive coping strategies of either of their caretakers.

Gender and Perceptions of Interparental Conflict

El Sheikh and colleagues (El Sheikh & Cheskes, 1995; El Sheikh, Cummings & Reiter, 1996; El Sheikh & Reiter, 1996) have conducted a series of studies examining gender in relation to different properties of the spousal conflict. In a study (El-Sheikh & Cheskes, 1995) examining school-age community children's perceptions of verbal versus physical adult conflict they noted that all children were distressed by both forms of anger: boys saw physical conflict as more angry (i.e., greater perceived threat found key to boys' perceptions in Kerig's work discussed above), whereas girls did not (i.e., perhaps some avoidance of affect), and boys were more likely to report aggressive impulses during verbal rather than physical conflict ("keeping their heads down"), whereas girls were not. In a study (El-Sheikh et al., 1996) examining the role of 4- to 5-year-olds' history of seeing resolved versus unresolved marital conflict, children with histories of unresolved conflict were more distressed by conflict, more likely to predict a conflictual outcome, and girls were less likely to endorse intervention. Similar results came from a study of slightly older children (El-Sheikh & Reiter, 1996; higher SES community of 4- to 7-year-olds) where physical adult conflict was more distressing, but here the girls showed greater distress and were more likely to want to intervene. Mallah and Rossman (1999) also found school-age children, and especially boys, from shelter families to be more likely to expect aggressive endings to neutral adult interaction tapes than were children from nonviolent families. These studies fit the notion that boys see greater threat with physical parental aggression, but they raise the possibility that the girls are more distressed.

Gender Across Generations

It is difficult to know how the types of factors and dynamics are influential for boys and girls of different ages, let alone to know how they might be transmitted across generations. McNeal and Amato (1998) found that parents' reports of their marital violence 4 to 12 years earlier predicted more violence in their offsprings' current young adult relationships independent of earlier reports of marital nonviolent conflict, divorce, abusive behavior toward the offspring, offspring gender, and parental drug and alcohol use. Doumas, Margolin, and John (1994) reported that child abuse and marital violence in the grandparent and parent generations predicted aggression in the sons but not in the daughters. And, Simons and Johnson (1998) found that models using intergenerational antisocial behaviors and beliefs were more successful in predicting marital conflict and harsh parenting in the younger generation than were models predicting based on legitimization of specific roles (e.g., harsh parenting predicts harsh parenting). This provides more of a sociological perspective on family gender-based habits and family system violence that may contribute to the variability in gender findings. Given the Doumas et al. (1994) finding, it is clear that more research is needed to understand how boys and girls may be differentially impacted by mechanisms, such as antisocial beliefs, that may sustain interpersonal violence across generations.

While a number of studies have reported gender related to outcome for exposed children, some have not (Fantuzzo et al., 1991, with 3 to 6 year-olds; Graham-Bermann & Levendosky, 1998b, for PTSD symptoms with exposed school-age children; Holden, Stein, Ritchie, Harris, & Jouriles, 1998, for preschool and school-age children; Jenkins & Smith, 1991, for school-age children; Jouriles et al., 1996, for school-age children; King, Padpour, Naylor, Segal, & Jouriles, 1995, for adolescents). Gender findings may be related to age as well as to mechanisms of gender socialization, coping, experiencing personal verbal or physical abuse, and perceived threat that varies with conflict severity levels and gender. Thus, the role of gender as a protective or vulnerability factor remains confused. Work is needed that simultaneously examines multiple factors to help clarify the picture.

☐ Ethnicity

The influence of a child's cultural and religious heritage on their response to parental violence has not been well studied. Work in Rossman's lab has suggested that being of ethnic minority heritage tends to be related to poorer outcome for exposed children. However, in our work with disadvantaged shelter and community families, minority background is so closely linked with economic and educational disadvantage and high family stresses that it is really inappropriate to link poorer adjustment with minority background. However, there are a few studies that have been more specifically directed toward examining effects of ethnic heritage. In their reviews of the literature for exposed children Margolin (1998) and Hughes and Graham-Bermann (1998) noted that exposed Anglo boys tended to have greater externalizing behavior problems than either African American (O'Keefe, 1994b) or Hispanic exposed boys (McCloskey, Figueredo, & Koss, 1995). McCloskey et al. have reported that exposed Hispanic children appeared to have more problems in the areas of anxiety and phobic reactions than children of other backgrounds. Finally, Holden et al. (1998) reported that, while battered mothers reported being less emotionally available to their children than nonbattered mothers, Hispanic battered mothers reported being least available. Clearly much more research in this area is needed. Given that the exposed children who participate in much of the research that includes non-Anglo families are also exposed to other sources of adversity, it may be the case that ethnic heritage in and of itself is not a strong predictor of children's responses. However, we need to consider the possibility raised by the results of McCloskey et al. (1995) that some ethnic minority children may be acculturated to express their distress more quietly, which could make them less noticeable to service providers. Another possibility is that interparental verbal or physical aggression are perceived differently depending on cultural background. This would not be unexpected given the gender findings discussed above that boys saw physical conflict as more angry (El Sheikh & Cheskes, 1995). Some also argue that the family is so central to some cultures (e.g., Asian Indian, Hispanic) that high levels of family conflict may be tolerated before any action is taken. However, cultural background does not seem to have protected non-Asian-Indian or non-Hispanic women from remaining in severely abusive homes. It seems premature to do anything other than note the few findings that exist and hope researchers will accept the challenge to do systematic research, particularly to help us understand variations in child outcome within groups of families who share the same ethnic heritage.

☐ Temperament

Temperament is another factor deserving of more study. A fearful temperament could easily predispose exposed children to greater distress and possibly higher levels of posttraumatic symptoms, thus acting as a vulnerability factor. For school-age children, Dickerson and Rossman (1993) found a relationship between exposure and greater shy or fearful temperament. The problem inherent in this and other studies of temperament is that the investigator is unable to determine preexposure temperament except through retrospective report, which may have been influenced by intervening family conflict and stress. However, there is evidence that exposed children are more worried about their mothers, siblings, and father's violence (Graham-Bermann, 1996) than nonexposed children. These worries were predictive of the children's internalizing behavior problems. Thus, some of what may appear to be greater fearfulness of temperament could be associated with the child's hostile environment.

Nonetheless, here may be a general arousability or irritability temperamental predisposition that is captured in the term, "difficult temperament" and scales used to assess it. As an individual difference factor, this could lead a child to be more reactive or less able to calm given exposure to spousal aggression. Holden and Ritchie (1991) reported that mothers of exposed children rated them as having more difficult temperament than did mothers of nonexposed children. Davies and Cummings (1994) noted that children with difficult temperament were more reactive to negative than positive events. This is interesting in light of their subsequent finding that induced negative emotion, with sadness being worst, tended to exacerbate hostile interpersonal expectations, recall of negative information, and emotional dysregulation and distress. Emery, Fincham, and Cummings (1992) remind us that not all effects of marital conflict on children are unidirectional. It may be the case that a child's attributes contribute to how that child is parented, and temperament could play a role in this.

One physiological mechanism that may underlie the greater reactivity of some children to exposure is vagal tone, an index of the ability of the mammalian vagal system to regulate rapid changes in metabolic output such as heart rate and blood pressure in response to stress (Porges, 1995). Gottman and Katz (1989) found that children's higher vagal tone was associated with higher levels of positive play and suggested that high vagal tone may contribute to a child's greater ability to modulate internal physiological arousal and thus distress. It seems likely that children's brain and body physiological reactions will be central in understanding the reactions of exposed children and all children dealing with traumatic events. The progress that has been made even in the last decade and will be made in the near future in developmental cognitive neuropsychology and the psychobiology of stress is likely to advance the understanding of exposed children's reactions and our ability to assist them. Given the interactions that have already been noted between environmental events and circumstances and changes in the development of brain structure and function (e.g., see LeDoux, 1996; Perry, 1997), it will be interesting to see whether we continue to use and think of phenomena such as fearful or difficult temperament as more genetically determined descriptions. It is clear, for example, that the greater a child's exposure to marital violence, the more sensitized to it that child appears (O'Brien et al., 1991). However, there is evidence of statistically significant heritability in parent–child conflict, negativity, and verbal punitiveness for both mothers' and fathers' behaviors (Plomin, Reiss, Hetherington, & Howe, 1994). Thus, both environmental and genetic contributions to physical arousability and modulation may turn out to provide explanations for some individual differences in children's reactivity to violence exposure.

☐ Posttraumatic Symptomatology

One situation in which a fearful or arousal-prone disposition or temperament would clearly put a child at a disadvantage is when witnessing abuse of his or her mother. It has only been within the past decade that researchers and clinicians (e.g., Jaffe, Wolfe, & Wilson, 1990) have begun to more seriously consider the possibility that some children may be traumatized by witnessing repetitive verbal and physical abuse of their mother, in some cases accompanied by personal abuse. It has been within this same decade that PTSD symptom checklists and other assessment devices have become more readily available (Kerig, Fedorowicz, Warren, & Brown, 1997). Wolfe and Jaffe (1991) also note that traumatic responses are likely to be the immediate responses to exposure, followed by other mechanisms that prolong the effects of exposure such as conditioning and generalization of conditioned reactions. In particular, the power of traumatic intrusions, nightmares, and reexperiencing of aspects of a witnessed event make it likely that children may continue to be reexposed even in the absence of further wife abuse events. This feature of traumatic reactions makes it less surprising that at least some of the children exposed to domestic violence do not show great improvements in either their trauma symptoms or behavior problems 6 months to a year later, even when they and their mothers have left the violent household (Emery, 1996; Holden et al., 1998; Jouriles et al.,1998; Rossman, 1998).

Some studies have shown that exposed and exposed abused children show levels of total PTSD symptomatology higher than nonexposed children (Rossman, 1998) or as high as children who experienced a severe attack by a dog that required emergency medical attention (Rossman et al., 1997). Other studies have utilized the patterns of symptoms reported for children or self-reported to determine the proportion of children who would qualify for a PTSD diagnosis (see Table 3.2). Graham-Bermann and Levendosky (1998b) found that 13% of exposed children would qualify for such a diagnosis using criteria from the *Diagnostic and Statistic Manual of Mental Disorders* (*DSM-IV*, American Psychiatric Association, 1994). In subsequent studies, over half of exposed children met diagnostic criteria (Devoe & Graham-Bermann, 1997; Lehmann, 1997), rates higher than those for natural disasters. These higher rates for violence exposure may reflect the more traumatic nature of the event or the difficulty children would have in being buffered by parents from violence in which the parents were involved or both. Studies in Rossman's lab (e.g., Rossman, 1999; Rossman & Ho, in press) have tended to find that approximately one-quarter to one-third of the children meet diagnostic criteria, and factor analyses of children's self-reported symptoms have yielded a slightly different pattern of symptoms than those used in *DSM-IV*. The *DSM-IV* diagnostic clusters include a group of intrusion and reexperiencing symptoms, a group of numbing and avoidance symptoms, and a group of hyperarousal symptoms. Our analyses iden-

Table 3.2.   Examples of Levels of Children's PTSD Symptoms following Traumatic Events

Study	Event	Ages	% Who Would Meet PTSD Diagnostic Criteria
Natural Disaster			
Lonigan (1993)	Hurricane Hugo	9–19 years	5.5%
La Greca et al. (1996)	Hurricane Andrew	8–11 years	39.1%
Violence Exposure			
Pynoos et al. (1987)	School sniper attack	5–12 years	40.0%
Saigh (1991)	War	9–12 years	27.0%
Graham-Bermann & Levendosky (1998b)	Exposure to parental violence	7–12 years	13.0%
Devoe & Graham-Bermann (1997)	Exposure to parental violence	7–12 years	51.0%
Lehmann (1997)	Exposure to parental violence	School-age	56.0%
Rossman & Ho (in press)	Exposure to parental violence	School-age	24.0%

tified an intrusion group of symptoms, but the other two factors were characterized, respectively, by a combination of avoidance and arousal symptoms (agitated avoidance) and by a grouping of depressive and irritability symptoms. Pynoos et al. (1987) also noted a slightly different factor structure for children's symptoms, including a factor reflecting children's fears.

One of the critical features of PTSD reactions is the extent to which lingering posttraumatic difficulties with depression and social withdrawal, concentration, and attention or with hyperarousal or irritability could lead these children to be misdiagnosed as depresssed, Attention Deficit Hyperactivity Disordered (ADHD), or conduct disordered (Rossman, 1994). For example, Goenjian et al. (1995) found a diagnosis of depression to be comorbid with PTSD for 13% to 75% of children exposed to an earthquake, with higher comorbidity closer to the epicenter. The existence of an additional disorder for exposed children would place them at greater risk.

Another critical feature of these lingering symptoms is the extent to which, for a more traumatized child, they may interfere with ongoing functioning and the achievement of developmental tasks. Ongoing and notable levels of distress and attentional problems could leave exposed children less able to take in new information and learn in school or therapeutic settings. Rossman (in press) found that PTSD symptoms acted as mediators of poorer outcome for exposed children and that, for all but exposed abused children where the picture of relationships was more chaotic, PTSD symptoms were negatively related to good intake of new information that was positively related to school and social adjustment.

This type of effect of high levels of arousal on cognitive functioning has also been noted by Crick and Dodge (1994) who have called it preemptive processing, referring to the fact that the children appear to rely on old ideas about interpersonal interactions rather than objectively evaluate each new interpersonal situation. They have noted that boys from punitive backgrounds are less able to take in sufficient new information to recognize that a new peer interaction situation is actually benign. Instead they display what these authors have called a hostile aggressive bias wherein they expect the intention of other peers to be hostile and thus they behave aggressively in preparation for needing to protect themselves. In addition, exposed children also have a tendency to expect peer aggression (West, 1997). Exposed children, particularly younger boys, show this aggressive expectation regarding the outcome of neutral adult interactions, being more likely to anticipate aggression than nonexposed children (Mallah & Rossman, 1999). Interestingly, children's expectations of peer aggression in neutral situations were significantly related to their internalizing behavior problems and PTSD symptoms, while their expectations of adult interaction aggression were related to higher externalizing behaviors (West, Rossman, Ho, & Mallah, 1999). And expectation of adult and peer aggressive endings were related significantly to each other. Children who demonstrated both biases also had higher internalizing and aggressive behavior problems than children who demonstrated only one or none. Since both types of biases were associated with posttraumatic symptoms, it appears likely that lingering posttraumatic reactions can interfere with a child's ability to use new information, instead of relying on preexisting ideas.

One physiological basis for this phenomenon has been discussed by LeDoux (1996) based on his studies of fear conditioning. He has evidence that potentially dangerous stimulus information has two routes for processing in the brain: a fast track that does not evaluate the information carefully that goes from the thalamus to the amygdala; and a slower but more carefully evaluative track that goes through the cortex to the amygdala. The fast track would be useful for quick response to dangerous circumstances, but it could be in error. However, for a child with a history of danger at home, his or her response system might have stronger connections in the brain for the fast track, meaning that he or she would be more likely to respond immediately as though in danger. More time, effort, and possibly training would be needed for this child to be able to ignore the initial danger signals until the slower but more careful cortical track had evaluated the significance of the situation.

The true extent of exposed children's PTSD problems and whether children need different diagnostic criteria is still unclear. What is clear is that exposure to wife abuse is traumatizing for a notable proportion of children and that trauma theory and treatment need to be part of how we conceptualize the needs of exposed children. It appears that traumatic symptoms can interfere with children's development and adaptive behaviors in a variety of domains in addition to representing ongoing distress experienced by these children. At this point in our understanding, both clinical and research information suggests that a child's development of significant PTSD symptomatology provides a vulnerability factor, placing him or her at greater risk for maladjustment (Putnam, 1998).

☐ Children's Relationships and Social Support

The social psychology literature has informed us for many years that, in general, social support provides a protective factor for those experiencing stress due to a number of events such as spouse or parent loss or illness (e.g., see Figure 3.1). Therefore, the role of children's relationships and social support resources in buffering the effects of parental conflict and violence is of special interest. Studies of exposed children are only beginning to be done. Several investigators (Graham-Bermann & Levendosky, 1998a; Jaffe, Wolfe, & Wilson, 1990; Moore et al., 1990; Rawlins & Rossman, 1991; Rosenberg, 1984) have provided evidence that social relationships and problem solving strategies are problematic for exposed children. These children tend to show more aggression with peers, generally display more negative affect in social interactions, and tend to have more conflictual relationships with siblings. In violent households where mothers encouraged family cooperation, however, siblings did appear to serve as protective factors for each other (Rawlings & Rossman, 1991). However, McCloskey et al. (1995) found that neither mother nor child report of mother or associated sibling supportive behaviors (e.g., hugs, plays with) was associated with better outcome for exposed children. The typical violent home might not be one that would facilitate great sibling warmth, as Brody and Stoneman (1988) have noted that parental disagreement, family conflict, and lack of interparental affection are all associated with negative behaviors between siblings. As noted earlier (Erel et al., 1998), marital conflict and mother–child negativity appear to be linked to negative sibling interaction for older siblings, but its effects influence younger sibling interactions through negative features of the mother–child relationship. It appears unlikely that siblings can consistently buffer each other. The one study that has examined exposed children's relationships both within and outside the family has produced somewhat different and more hopeful results. Graham-Bermann, Levendosky, Porterfield, and Okun (in press) examined the quality of all of children's fairly frequent relationships. They reported that greater positive relationships were associated with lower behavior problems. The message here may be, as it was from the studies of Werner and Smith (1982, 1992), that one or more positive relationships can contribute to the resilience of children. It just may be that those relationships are less likely to occur within violent families, and children need to be assisted in finding them outside the family as well.

☐ Children's Control Beliefs and Coping Behaviors

The original finding from the social psychology literature (e.g., Rotter, 1966) was that beliefs that one had internal control, as opposed to being controlled by external forces, were associated with better adaptation. This was also demonstrated for children's school performance in some work by Connell (1988). It appeared that having an internal locus of control was a protective factor. In that regard it is interesting that Pepler and Moore (1989, 1993) found, working with conflictual families, that mothers' and fathers' more frequent use of verbal reasoning to cope with conflict was associated with a greater internal locus of control for boys. In the subsequent study they noted that girls from violent families who were showing the poorest adjustment (higher internalizing problems, more aggression with siblings, greater mother–daughter verbal conflict) also had higher external locus of control scores. Thus being able to observe and learn nonviolent tactics to manage conflict may be a contributor to a useful sense of internal control.

Recently, the effectiveness of a child's coping, as reported in the coping literature, has been tied to the control a child can exert over the aversive event in question. Compas, Banez, Malcarne, and Worsham (1991) found that when children and teens matched problem-focused coping (i.e., efforts to solve the problem) with events over which they felt they had control, they showed lower distress. Their use of emotion-focused coping was associated with higher levels of distress. This has also been a trend of the findings for exposed children. Margolin and colleagues have carried out several studies in the community where they noted that children's distress was higher if they involved themselves in the conflict and lower if they distanced (O'Brien, Margolin, & John, 1995), and that emotion-focused strategies were more useful for coping with uncontrollable stressors and problem-focused strategies were more useful for controllable ones (Laumakis, Margolin, & John (1998). Distancing would be more emotion focused than instrumental. Rossman and Rosenberg (1992) reported that children from more stressed and violent families who retained the belief that they could behave in ways so as to control their parents' fighting (e.g., keep them from fighting by always being good or praying a lot) showed much lower self-esteem than children who did not hold these beliefs (see Figure 3.2). However, children in low adversity families with stronger control beliefs had higher self-esteem.

Kerig, Fedorowicz, Brown, Patenaude, and Warren (1998) found a gender difference in coping. If girls felt they could act to control parental conflict they tended to endorse approach coping, whereas boys endorsed venting of emotion. Interestingly girls, but not boys, who endorsed self-calming strategies for coping also endorsed both approach and avoidance. For girls approach coping appears to place them at risk since for them approach was related to both depression and anxiety, whereas avoidance was related to lower behavior problems. For boys the opposite pattern was revealed: their depression was related to avoidance and their lower behavior problems to approach. Kerig et al. noted that the girls appear to act as the emotion caretakers for the family in their spontaneous desire to approach the problem but that this creates trouble for them. Another clue that suggests the girls may be oriented toward taking care of family rela-

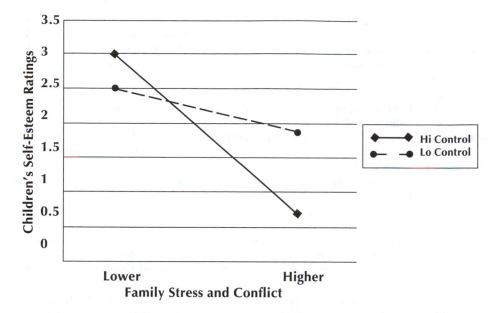

FIGURE 3.2.   Schematic Drawing of a Moderator Effect of Children's Beliefs in Control over Parental Conflict

tionships was noted in another study (Warren et al., 1996). In a community sample with varying levels of parental conflict, these researchers reported that girls tended to endorse internally oriented defense mechanisms, taking more responsibility for the conflict, which were associated with greater internalizing behavior problems as the conflict increased. The boys endorsed externally oriented defense mechanisms wherein they expressed their distress and did not blame themselves. These strategies were found associated with having lower externalizing problems in more conflictual families. In another community sample, Kerig (1998b) reported that self-calming coping strategies appeared useful for girls in higher conflict families in terms of being associated with lower anxiety. A final study (Kerig, 1997) reiterated the finding that for girls approach or venting coping strategies constituted vulnerability factors for internalizing problems, whereas avoidant strategies were more protective. For the boys in this study their sense that they were coping in an efficacious manner was a protective factor, but relationships with specific strategies did not act as moderators of adjustment. It is important to note that these coping behaviors may be working well for exposed school-age children. However, continuing to use an avoidant coping strategy as they develop to the exclusion of other strategies may not serve them well.

☐ Children's Understandings of Parental Conflict

A final "characteristic" that children take into their experience of a parental conflict event is their understanding of the meaning of that conflict. Several investigators, notably Grych and Fincham (1990) and Davies and Cummings (1994) have begun to explore children's perceptions of parental disputes and attributions and reactions children have associated with these perceptions. As noted, Davies and Cummings speculate that the negative effects of parental conflict result from the extent to which children's sense of emotional security is challenged. Thus, factors such as self-blame or the fact that the conflict remained unresolved could be predictive of more severe negative reactions. Their work has shown that unresolved conflicts proved more distressing for children. El-Sheikh et al. (1996) also noted that children with histories of witnessing resolved conflicts were less behaviorally distressed and predicted less likelihood of a conflictual ending to a tape showing a conflictional interaction where there was no resolution.

In light of these findings, it was interesting that Acker, Ho, Rossman, and Barnhart (1998) found that one of the main messages children got from their mothers' (battered and nonbattered) attempts to explain parental disputes to them had to do with how much negativity was conveyed about the status of the mother–child relationship. These authors also noted that mothers were more likely to convey positive information about the status of that relationship or to attend to the emotional needs of the child in their messages if the explaining took place in the context of an existing positive mother–child relationship.

Grych and Fincham (1990) have been more concerned with the how the properties of the conflict itself (e.g., whether the conflict was regarding the child, how severe it was, how frequent, whether it was resolved or not) related to children's attributions of responsibility and coping strategies. Following a Lazarus and Folkman (1984) stress and coping model they view children as processing parental conflict in two stages. First there is a primary processing stage where level of arousal may interfere with further processing, as may the child's developmental level, temperament, or threshold for attending or sensitivity to the environment. Next there is a stage of secondary processing where the child attempts to understand the conflict and determine how to cope. This stage involves the child's ideas about causation, which may vary with his or her perspective taking abilities and internal or external locus of control, about their ability to control the conflict, and about responsibility and blame. To investigate these ideas Grych and Fincham (1992) developed the Children's Perceptions of Interpersonal Conflict (CPIC) Scale. Working with community families who represented a range of parental conflict, they have noted (Grych & Fincham, 1992, 1993) that children are more distressed when arguments are about them and when they attribute blame to themselves. With 10- to 12-year-olds they found that perceptions of increased conflict were associated with greater internalizing problems for boys and greater externalizing problems for girls. Grych (in press), working with community and shelter families, found that children's appraisals of threat were greater for younger children and for those who had experienced interparental and father-to-child aggression violence. Higher intensity conflicts received more negative appraisals and stronger emotional reactions, especially from girls. Some of Hughes and Luke's (1998) most distressed children were also those who had witnessed the most prolonged violence. Jaffe, Hurley, & Wolfe (1990) note that exposed children feel most responsible for the violence and the safety of their mother and siblings when the violence has been more frequent and severe and observed across more partners.

Kerig (1998a, 1998b) also used the CPIC Scale in her work with violent and nonviolent community families where she noted gender differences described previously. Briefly restated, she found that as boys' appraisals of severity of the conflict increased, so did their behavior problems, except at very high threat levels when externalizing behaviors were lower. Girls tended to show greater internalizing forms of distress with high exposure. These findings are reminiscent of Rosenberg's (1984) finding of boys acting out less in more severely violent families, but not of Rosenberg's finding that the girls were more aggressive at high levels of exposure. It may be the case that Rosenberg's less severely violent families are similar in violence intensity to Kerig's more violent families, which would render this set of findings more compatible.

Reiterating the theme of greater severity being associated with greater child distress, El-Sheikh and Reiter (1996) found that all children aged 4 to 7 were more behaviorally distressed when viewing adults involved in physical conflict than verbal or covert conflict. El-Sheikh and Cheskes (1995) noted that school-age children were distressed by viewing both adult-to-adult and adult-to-child conflict and that this was more upsetting when the conflict involved physical rather than verbal anger. Lehmann (1997) underscored the toll taken by multiple forms of conflict in a family. In examining factors in the environments of children traumatized by exposure to parental violence, he reported that continuing parent–child conflict related negatively to children's recovery from posttraumatic reactions. This is consistent with findings reported earlier by Emery (1996) and Rossman (1998) regarding the deleterious effects of ongoing violence.

Finally, El-Sheikh, Buckhalt, and Parker (1999) examined children's understandings of parental conflict in situations involving substance abuse, an all too common occurrence. They had children view videotapes where both adult partners engaged in a discussion were described as having consumed a great deal of alcohol prior to the discussion, or just one or the other had consumed alcohol, or that alcohol was not involved. For children with domestic conflict and violence histories the presence of alcohol increased their distress noticeably.

Thus, research suggests that children are more distressed when they perceive the parental conflict to be more severe or more threatening, that they are more responsible for the conflict, and when they are less emotionally secure. This appears to be more likely for younger children. The picture as to what form their distress will take (i.e., more acting out, more laying low, greater internalizing problems, and anxiety) is unclear from the existing literature. Factors of the frequency and severity of exposure, age, and gender appear to be relevant. No doubt methodological differences across studies contribute to this lack of clarity. Shelter and community samples are both important but may differ in severity of parental conflict (e.g., Rossman & Rosenberg, 1992). In addition, studies coming from the family violence tradition have typically used the CTS to index conflict severity, whereas more developmentally oriented studies of children's understanding of parental violence in community families may use alternate instruments. Therefore, high and low conflict or violence may have different meanings in different studies. In addition, community volunteer families tend to be of higher SES than shelter families who would not be in a shelter if they had more resources. The simultaneous consideration of children's initial security levels, feelings about their control, exposure severity and duration, parental substance use and abuse, family SES, and residing at home or in a shelter would be useful to investigate since they all play a role.

☐   Conclusion

The research to date does not provide a clear list of protective and risk factors for children exposed to parental violence. The picture is more complex. For almost any of the factors examined there were positive results and negative or null results. Age and gender appear to interact in some findings, suggesting that school-age boys and adolescent girls are more at risk, but perhaps severely exposed younger children would be seen to be at greater risk if we followed them longitudinally over years, a study yet to be done.

Gender is complicated as a moderating factor in and of itself. These are perhaps the mechanisms through which gender makes a difference: the finding that there may be more parent-to-child aggression for boys, although boys' aggressive behaviors are more accepted, and that intergenerational aggression may effect boys more, pointing to a modeling mechanism for boys; the fact that girls are more influenced by maternal depression, supporting a gender intensification hypothesis; the fact that gender may influence which aspects of maternal distress children attend to, with boys responding adversely to less maternal structuring and girls responding to greater maternal distress; or the fact that boys and girls appear to attend to different aspects of adult conflict, with boys more likely to attend to the threat/danger aspects and sometimes appear to be better off if they try to act instrumentally and other times avoid, and with girls more attuned to relational and guilt aspects and be better off in the short term if they distance from the conflict. It seems risky for children to believe they can control parental behaviors that are beyond their influence and more productive for them to attend to reducing their emotional distress if they can. Some results are beginning to suggest that ethnicity and temperamental factors may influence both parental behavior and children's ability to regulate their distress or how they express it (see Chapter 6). In line with this, exposed children's PTSD symptoms would appear to place them at greater risk because reexperiencing may keep the conflict fresh, interfering with accurate social cognition and successful completion of developmental tasks due to overarousal and concentration problems and generally providing a heightened level of distress for children to manage. Children's distress appears heightened by self-blame, a more severe history of exposure, physical versus verbal conflict, and the involvement of parental alcohol use. Thus most moderating child factors studied appeared to be risk factors, at least in some circumstances.

Finally, one factor that may continue to show protective promise is a positive relationship with someone, whether it be the mother–child relationship or maternal structuring or a positive relationship outside the home. While there was some evidence to support this assumption, there were also examples of disconfirming evidence or null results. This leaves the picture unclear and more work is needed. However, what we know from this and other areas of research about the importance of a child's feelings of emotional security suggests that a relationship that can contribute to this security should be protective.

The message from this literature appears to be that we can intervene to help children through working with them around affect regulation, coping, valid perceptions of social situations in terms of danger and controllability, and establishing a trusting relationship with at least one person. We can also work with battered mothers to help them cope with the depression and distress they feel surrounding the battering, helping them to provide more access to a buffering relationship.

☐ References

Achenbach, T. M., McConaughy, S. H., & Howell, C. T. (1987). Child/adolescent behavioral and emotional problems: Implications of cross-informant correlations for situational specificity. *Psychological Bulletin, 101,* 213–232.

Acker, M., Ho, J., Rossman, B. B. R., & Barnhart, C. (1998). *Maternal communication about spousal conflict and violence: What do children understand?* Poster session presented at the Fourth International Conference on Children Exposed to Family Violence, San Diego.

American Psychiatric Association. (1994). *Diagnostic and statistical manual of mental disorders* (4th ed.). Washington, DC: Author.

Andres, J., & Moore, T. E. (1995, March). *The adjustment of child witnesses to spousal abuse: A follow-up study.* Poster session presented at the meeting of the Society for Research in Child Development, Indianapolis, IN.

Bowlby, J. (1973). *Attachment and loss: Vol. 2. Separation.* New York: Basic Books.

Brody, G. H., & Stoneman, Z. (1988). Sibling conflict: Contributions of the siblings themselves, the parent-sibling relationship and the broader family system. In F. Schachter & R. Stone (Eds.), *Practical concerns about siblings: Bridging the research practice gap.* New York: Haworth.

Brown, C. A., & Kerig, P. K. (1995, August). *Parent's and children's coping with interparental conflict.* Paper presented at the meeting of the American Psychological Association, New York.

Compas, B. E., Banez, G. A., Malcarne, V., & Worsham, N. (1991). Perceived control and coping with stress: A developmental perspective. *Journal of Social Issues, 47,* 23–34.

Connell, J. P. (1988). Context, self and action: A motivational analysis of self-system processes across the life-span. In D. Cicchetti (Ed.), *The self in transition: Infancy to childhood.* Chicago: University of Chicago Press.

Crick, N. R., & Dodge, K. A. (1994). A review and reformulation of social information–processing mechanisms in children's social adjustment. *Psychological Bulletin, 115,* 74–101.

Cummings, E. M., Davies, P. T., & Simpson, K. S. (1994). Marital conflict, gender, and children's appraisals and coping efficacy as mediators of child adjustment. *Journal of Family Psychology, 8,* 141–149.

Cummings, E. M., Hennessy, K. D., Rabideau, G. J., & Cicchetti, D. (1994). Responses of physically abused boys to interadult anger involving their mothers. *Development and Psychopathology, 6,* 31–41.

Cummings, J. G., & Moore, T. E. (1995). *The psychological adjustment of child witnesses to spousal abuse: Gender differences.* Paper presented at the meeting of the Society for Research in Child Development, Indianapolis, IN.

Cummings, J. S., Pellegrini, D. S., Notarius, C. E., & Cummings, E. M. (1989). Children's responses to angry adult behavior as a function of marital distress and history of interparent hostility. *Child Development, 60,* 1035–1043.

Davies, P. T., & Cummings, E. M. (1994). Marital conflict and child adjustment: An emotional security hypothesis. *Psychological Bulletin, 116,* 387-441.

Davies, P. T., & Cummings, E. M. (1995). Children's emotions as organizers of their reaction to interadult anger: A functionalist perspective. *Developmental Psychology, 31,* 677–684.

Davies, P. T., & Cummings, E. M. (1998). Exploring children's emotional security as a mediator of the link between marital relations and child adjustment. *Child Development, 69,* 124–139

Davies, P. T., & Windle, M. (1997). Gender-specific pathways between maternal depressive symptoms, family discord, and adolescent adjustment. *Developmental Psychology, 33,* 657–668.

Devoe, E., & Graham-Bermann, S. (1997). *Predictors of posttraumatic stress symptoms in battered women and their children.* Poster session presented at the Second International Conference on Children Exposed to Family Violence, London, Ontario, Canada.

Dickerson, L. K., & Rossman, B. B. R. (1993). *Child witness temperament and trauma: A preliminary investigation.* Poster session presented at the joint meeting of the Western Psychological Association and the Rocky Mountain Psychological Association, Phoenix, AZ.

Doumas, D., Margolin, G., & John, R. S. (1994). The intergenerational transmission of aggression across three generations. *Journal of Family Violence, 9,* 43–56.

El-Sheikh, M., Buckhalt, J., & Parker, K. (1999). *Do children expect more interadult and adult-child aggression when the adults are intoxicated versus sober?* Poster session presented at the meeting of the Society for Research in Child Development, Albuquerque, NM.

El-Sheikh, M., & Cheskes, J. (1995). Background verbal and physical anger: A comparison of children's responses to adult-adult and adult-child arguments. *Child Development, 66,* 446–458.

El-Sheikh, M., Cummings, E. M., & Reiter, S. (1996). Preschoolers' responses to ongoing interadult conflict: The role of prior exposure to resolved versus unresolved arguments. *Journal of Abnormal Child Psychology, 24,* 665–679.

El-Sheikh, M., & Reiter, S. (1996). Children's responding to live interadult conflict: The role of form of anger expression. *Journal of Abnormal Child Psychology, 24,* 401–415.

Emery, R. E. (1996, June). *A longitudinal study of battered women and their children: One year following shelter residence.* Paper presented at the First International Conference on Children Exposed to Family Violence, Austin, TX.

Emery, R. E., Fincham, F. D., & Cummings, E. M. (1992). Parenting in context: Systemic thinking about parental conflict and its influence on children. *Journal of Consulting and Clinical Psychology, 60,* 909–912.

Emery, R. E., & Laumann-Billings, L. (1998). An overview of the nature, causes, and consequences of abusive family relationships: Toward differentiating maltreatment and violence. *American Psychologist, 53,* 121–135.

Erel, O., Margolin, G., & John, R. S. (1998). Observed sibling interaction: Links with the marital and the mother-child relationship. *Developmental Psychology, 34,* 288–298.

Fantuzzo, J., Boruch, R., Beriana, A., Atkins, M., & Marcus, S. (1997). Domestic violence and children: Prevalence and risk in five major U.S. cities. *Journal of the American Academy of Child and Adolescent Psychiatry, 36,* 116–122.

Fantuzzo, J. W., DePaola, L. M., Lambert, L., Martino, T., Anderson, G., & Sutton, S. (1991). Effects of interparental violence on the psychological adjustment and competencies of young children. *Journal of Consulting and Clinical Psychology, 59,* 258–265.

Fincham, F. D. (1998). Child development and marital relations. *Child Development, 69,* 543–574.

Fonagy, P., Target, M., Steele, M., & Steele, H. (1997). The development of violence and crime as it relates to security of attachment. In J. D. Osofsky (Ed.), *Children in a violent society* (pp. 150–182). New York: Guilford.

Forsstrom-Cohen, B., & Rosenbaum, A. (1985). The effects of parental marital violence on young adults: An exploratory investigation. *Journal of Marriage and the Family, 47,* 467–472.

Goenjian, A. K., Pynoos, R. S., Steinberg, A. M., Najarian, L. M., Asarnow, J. R., Karayan, I., Ghurabi, M., & Fairbanks, L. A. (1995). Psychiatric comorbidity in children after the 1988 earthquate in Armenia. *Journal of the Academy of Child and Adolescent Psychiatry, 34,* 1174–1184.

Gordis, E. B., Margolin, G., & John, R. S. (1997). Marital aggression, observed parental hostility, and child behavior during triadic family interaction. *Journal of Family Psychology, 11,* 76–89.

Gottman, J. M., & Katz, L. F. (1989). Effects of marital discord on young children's peer interaction and health. *Developmental Psychology, 25,* 373–381.

Graham-Bermann, S. A. (1996). Family worries: Assessment of interpersonal anxiety in children from violent and nonviolent families. *Journal of Clinical Child Psychology, 25,* 280–287.

Graham-Bermann, S. A., & Levendosky, A. A. (1998a). The social functioning of preschool-age children whose mothers are emotionally and physically abused. *Journal of Emotional Abuse, 1,* 59–84.

Graham-Bermann, S. A., & Levendosky, A. A. (1998b). Traumatic stress symptoms in children of battered women. *Journal of Interpersonal Violence, 14,* 111–128.

Graham-Bermann, S. A., Levendosky, A. A., Porterfield, K., & Okun, A. (in press). The impact of woman abuse on children: The role of social relationships and emotional context. *Journal of Clinical Child Psychology.*

Grych, J. H. (in press). Children's appraisals of interparental conflict: Situational and contextual influences. *Journal of Family Psychology.*

Grych, J. H., & Fincham, F. D. (1990). Marital conflict and children's adjustment: A cognitive-contextual framework. *Psychological Bulletin, 108,* 267–290.

Grych, J. H., & Fincham, F. D. (1992). Assessing marital conflict from the child's perspective: The Children's Perception of Interparental Conflict Scale. *Child Development, 63,* 558–572.

Grych, J. H., & Fincham, F. D. (1993). Children's appraisals of marital conflict: Initial investigations of the cognitive-contextual framework. *Child Development, 64,* 215–230.

Hennessy, K. D., Rabideau, G. J., Cicchetti, D., & Cummings, E. M. (1994). Responses of physically abused and nonabused children to different forms of adult anger. *Child Development, 65,* 815–828.

Holden, G. W., & Ritchie, K. L. (1991). Linking extreme marital discord, child rearing, and child behavior problems: Evidence from battered women. *Child Development, 62,* 311–327.

Holden, G. W., Stein, J. D., Ritchie, K. L., Harris, S. D., & Jouriles, E. N. (1998). Parenting behaviors and beliefs of battered women. In G. W. Holden, R. Geffner, & E. N. Jouriles (Eds.), *Children exposed to marital violence: Theory, research, and applied issues* (pp. 289-336). Washington, DC: American Psychological Association.

Hops, H. (1995). Age- and gender-specific effects of parental depression: A commentary. *Developmental Psychology, 31,* 428–431.

Hughes, H. M., & Graham-Bermann, S. A. (1998). Children of battered women: Impact of emotional abuse on adjustment and development. *Journal of Emotional Abuse, 1*(2), 23–50.

Hughes, H. M., & Luke, D. A. (1998). Heterogeneity in adjustment among children of battered women. In G.W. Holden, R. Geffner, & E. N. Jouriles (Eds.), *Children exposed to marital violence: Theory, research, and applied issues* (pp. 185–222). Washington, DC: American Psychological Association.

Huth-Bocks, A. C., Levendosky, A. A., & Semel, M. A. (1999, April). *Attachment and cognitive development in preschoolers experiencing domestic violence.* Poster session presented at the meeting of the Society for Research on Child Development, Albuquerque, NM.

Jaffe, P. G., Hurley, D. J., & Wolfe, D. (1990). Children's observations of violence: I. Critical issues in child development and intervention planning. *Canadian Journal of Psychiatry, 35,* 466–469.

Jaffe, P. G., Wolfe, D. A., & Wilson, S. K. (1990). *Children of battered women.* Newbury Park, CA: Sage.

Jaffe, P., Wolfe, D., Wilson, S. K., & Zak, L. (1986). Family violence and child adjustment: A comparative analysis of girls' and boys' behavioral symptoms. *American Journal of Psychiatry, 143,* 74–77.

Jenkins, J. M., & Smith, M. A. (1991). Marital disharmony and children's behavioral problems: Aspects of a poor marriage that affect children adversely. *Journal of Child Psychology and Psychiatry, 32,* 793–810.

Jouriles, E. N., Barling, J., & O'Leary, K. D. (1987). Predicting child behavior problems in maritally violent families. *Journal of Abnormal Psychology, 15,* 165–173.

Jouriles, E. N., McDonald, R., Stephens, N., Norwood, W., Spiller, L. C., & Ware, H. S. (1998). Breaking the cycle of violence: Helping families departing from battered women's shelters. In G. W. Holden, R. Geffner, & E. N. Jouriles (Eds.), *Children exposed to marital violence: Theory, research, and applied issues* (pp. 337–370). Washington, DC: American Psychological Association.

Jouriles, E. N., Murphy, C. M., Farris, A. M., Smith, D. A., Richters, J. E., & Waters, E. (1991). Marital adjustment, parental disagreements about child rearing, and behavior problems in boys: Increasing the specificity of the marital assessment. *Child Development, 62,* 1424–1433.

Jouriles, E. N., & Norwood, W. D. (1995). Physical aggression toward boys and girls in families characterized by the battering of women. *Journal of Family Psychology, 9,* 69–78.

Jouriles, E. N., Norwood, W. D., McDonald, R., Vincent, J. P., & Mahoney, A. (1996). Physical violence and other forms of marital aggression: Links with children's behavior problems. *Journal of Family Psychology, 10,* 223–234.

Jouriles, E. N., Pfiffner, L. J., & O'Leary, K. D. (1988). Marital conflict, parenting, and toddler conduct problems. *Journal of Abnormal Child Psychology, 16,* 197–206.

Kerig, P. K. (1991). *Sequential analyses of parent-child interaction: Marital and gender effects.* Poster session presented at the meeting of the American Psychological Association, San Francisco.

Kerig, P. K. (1997). *Gender and children's coping efforts as moderators of the effects of interparental conflict on adjustment.* Paper presented at the meeting of the Society for Research in Child Development, Washington, DC.

Kerig, P. K. (1998a). Gender and appraisals as mediators of adjustment in children exposed to interparental violence. *Journal of Family Violence, 13,* 345–363.

Kerig, P. K. (1998b). Moderators and mediators of interparental conflict. *Journal of Abnormal Child Psychology, 26,* 199–212.

Kerig, P. K., Fedorowicz, A. E., Brown, C. A., Patenaude, R. L., & Warren, M. (1998). When warriors are worriers: Gender and children's coping with interparental violence. *Journal of Emotional Abuse, 1,* 89–114.

Kerig, P. K., Fedorowicz, A. E., Warren, M., & Brown, C. A. (1997). *Clinical issues in assessment and intervention with PTSD in children exposed to violence.* Paper presented at the Second International Conference on Children Exposed to Family Violence, London, Ontario, Canada.

King, C. A., Padpour, L., Naylor, M. W., Segal, H. G., & Jouriles, E. N. (1995). Parents' marital functioning and adolescent psychopathology. *Journal of Consulting and Clinical Psychology, 63,* 749–753.

La Greca, A., Silverman, W. K., Vernberg, E. M., & Prinstein, M. J. (1996). Symptoms of posttraumatic stress in children after Hurricane Andrew: A prospective study. *Journal of Consulting and Clinical Psychology, 64,* 712–723.

Laumakis, M. A., Margolin, G., & John, R. S. (1998). The emotional, cognitive, and coping responses of preadolescent children to different dimensions of marital conflict. In G. W. Holden, R. Geffner, & E. N. Jouriles (Eds.), *Children exposed to marital violence: Theory, research, and applied issues* (pp. 257–288). Washington, DC: American Psychological Association.

Lazarus, R. S., & Folkman, S. (1984), *Stress, appraisal, and coping.* New York: Springer.

LeDoux, J. E. (1996). *The emotional brain: The mysterious underpinnings of emotional life.* New York: Simon & Schuster.

Lehmann, P. (1997). The development of Posttraumatic Stress Disorder (PTSD) in a sample of child witnesses to mother assault. *Journal of Family Violence, 12,* 241–256.

Levendosky, A. A., & Graham-Bermann, S. A. (1998). The moderating effects of parenting stress on children's adjustment in woman-abusing families. *Journal of Interpersonal Violence, 13,* 383–397.

Levendosky, A. A., & Graham-Bermann, S. A. (1999). Behavioral observations of parenting in battered women. *Journal of Family Psychology.* Manuscript submitted for publication.

Lonigan, C. J. (1993, March). *Children's reactions to disaster: The role of negative affectivity.* Paper presented at the meeting of the Society for Research in Child Development, New Orleans.

Maker, A. H., Kemmelmeier, M., & Peterson C. (1998). Long-term psychological consequences in women of witnessing parental physical conflict and experiencing abuse in childhood. *Journal of Interpersonal Violence, 13,* 574–589.

Mallah, K., & Rossman, B. B. R. (1999). Social information processing for children exposed to family violence. *Journal of Child Clinical Psychology.* Manuscript submitted for publication.

Margolin, G. (1998). Effects of domestic violence on children. In P. K. Trickett & C. J. Schellenbach (Eds.), *Violence against children in the family and community* (pp. 57–102). Washington, DC: American Psychological Association.

McCloskey, L. A., Figueredo, A. J., & Koss, M. P. (1995). The effects of systemic family violence on children's mental health. *Child Development, 66,* 1239–1261.

McNeal, C., & Amato, P. R. (1998). Parents' marital violence: Long-term consequences for children. *Journal of Family Issues, 19,* 123–139.

Moore, T. E., Pepler, D., Weinberg, B., Hammond, L., Waddell, J., & Weiser, L. (1990). Research on children from violent families. *Canada's Mental Health Journal, 38,* 19–23.

O'Brien, M., Margolin, G., & John, R. S. (1995). The relationship among marital conflict, child coping, and child adjustment. *Journal of Clinical Child Psychology, 24,* 346–361.

O'Brien, M., Margolin, G., John, R. S., & Krueger, L. (1991). Mothers' and sons' cognitive and emotional reactions to simulated marital and family conflict. *Journal of Consulting and Clinical Psychology, 59,* 692–703.

O'Keefe, M. (1994a). Linking marital violence, mother-child/father-child aggression, and child behavior problems. *Journal of Family Violence, 9,* 63–78.

O'Keefe, M. (1994b). Racial/ethnic differences among battered women and their children. *Journal of Child and Family Studies, 3,* 283–305.

Pepler, D. J., & Moore, T. E. (1989, March). *Children exposed to family violence: Home environments and cognitive functioning.* Paper presented at the meeting of the Society for Research in Child Development, Kansas City, MO.

Pepler, D. J., & Moore, T. E. (1993, August). *Violence in adolescent relationships: Identifying risk factors and prevention methods.* Paper presented at the meeting of the American Psychological Association, Toronto, Ontario, Canada.

Perry, B. S. (1997). Incubated in terror: Neurodevelopmental factors in the "Cycle of Violence." In J. D. Osofsky (Ed.), *Children in a violent society* (pp. 124–149). New York: Guilford.

Pianta, R. C., Egeland, B., & Sroufe, L. A. (1990). Maternal stress and children's development: Prediction of school outcomes and identification of protective factors. In J. Rolf, A. S. Masten, D. Cicchetti, K. H. Nuechterlein, and S. Weintraub (Eds.), *Risk and protective factors in the development of psychopathology* (pp. 215–135). London: Cambridge University Press.

Plomin, R., Reiss, D., Hetherington, E. M., & Howe, G. (1994). Nature and nurture: Genetic contributions to measures of the family environment. *Developmental Psychology, 30,* 32–43.

Porges, S. W. (1995, March). *Stress: An evolutionary by-product of the neurogenic regulation of the autonomic nervous system. The poly-vagal theory of stress and distress.* Paper presented at the meeting of the Society for Research in Child Development, Indianapolis, IN.

Posada, G., Waters, E., Liu, X. D., & Johnson, S. (1998). *Marital discord and attachment security: Girls and boys.* Manuscript submitted for publication.

Putnam, F. W. (1998). Trauma models of the effects of childhood maltreatment. In B. B. R. Rossman & M. S. Rosenberg (Eds.), *Multiple victimization of children: Conceptual, developmental, research, and treatment issues.* Binghamton, NY: Haworth.

Pynoos, R. S., Frederick, C., Nader, K., Arroyo, W., Steinberg, A., Eth, S., Nunez, F., & Fairbanks, L. (1987). Life threat and posttraumatic stress in school-age children. *Archives of General Psychiatry, 44,* 1057–1063.

Pynoos, R. S., Steinberg, A. M., & Goenjian, A. (1996). Traumatic stress in childhood and adolescence: Recent developments and current controversies. In B. A. van der Kolk, A. C. McFarlane, & L. Weisaeth (Eds.), *Traumatic stress: The effects of overwhelming experience on mind, body, and society* (pp. 331–358). New York: Guilford.

Rawlins, C., & Rossman, B. B. R. (1991). *Siblingship as a protective factor for children in violent families.* Poster session presented at the meeting of the Society for Research in Child Development, Seattle, WA.

Ritchie, K. L., & Holden, G. W. (1998). Parenting stress in low income battered and community women: Effects on parenting behavior. *Early Education & Development, 9,* 97–112.

Ritchie, K. L., & Miller, G. (1996, June). *Familial conceptualizations and attachment in 3- to 8-year-old children of battered women.* Paper presented at the First International Conference on Children Exposed to Family Violence, Austin, TX.

Rosenberg, M. S. (1984). *The impact of witnessing interparental violence on children's behavior, perceived competence and social problem solving strategies.* Unpublished doctoral dissertation, University of Virginia, Charlottesville.

Rossman, B. B. R. (1994). Children in violent families: Current diagnostic and treatment considerations. *Family Violence and Sexual Assault Bulletin, 10,* 29–34.

Rossman, B. B. R. (1998, October). *Time heals all: how much and for whom?* Paper presented at the Fourth International Conference on Children Exposed to Family Violence, San Diego.

Rossman, B. B. R. (1999). *Frost Foundation Project final report,* unpublished manuscript, University of Denver.

Rossman, B. B. R. (in press). Risk factors, psychological maltreatment, and cognition/emotion linkages for children exposed to parental violence. *Journal of Aggression, Maltreatment & Trauma.*

Rossman, B. B. R., Bingham, R. D., & Emde, R. N. (1997). Symptomatology and adaptive functioning for children exposed to normative stressors, dog attack, and parental violence. *Journal of the American Academy of Child and Adolescent Psychiatry, 36,* 1–9.

Rossman, B. B. R., & Ho, J. (in press). Posttraumatic response and children exposed to parental violence. In R. Geffner, P. Jaffe & M. Sudermann (Eds.), *Children exposed to family violence: Intervention, prevention, and policy implications.* Binghamton, NY: Haworth.

Rossman, B. B. R., & Rosenberg, M. S. (1992). Family stress and functioning in children: The moderating effects of children's beliefs about their control over parental conflict. *Journal of Child Psychology and Psychiatry, 33,* 699–715.

Rossman, B. B. R., & Rosenberg, M. S. (1998). *Multiple victimization of children: Conceptual, developmental, research, and treatment issues.* Binghamton, NY: Haworth.

Rossman, B. B. R., Rosenberg, M. S., Rawlins, C., & Malik, N. (1991, June). *A needs perspective on risk and protective factors for children in violent families.* Poster session presented at the National Working Conference "New Directions in Child and Family Research: Shaping Head Start in the Nineties," Arlington, VA.

Rotter, J. B. (1966). Generalized expectancies for internal versus external control of reinforcement. *Psychological Monographs, 80*(1, Whole No. 609).

Rutter, M. (1983) Stress, coping, and development. In N. Garmezy & M. Rutter (Eds.), *Stress, coping, and development in children* (pp. 1–42). New York: McGraw-Hill.

Saigh, P. (1991). The development of posttraumatic stress disorder following four different types of traumatization. *Behavior Research and Therapy, 29,* 213–216.

Sameroff, A. J., & Seifer, R. (1983). Familial risk and child competence. *Child Development, 54,* 1254–1268.

Simons, R. L., & Johnson, C. (1998). An examination of competing explanations for the intergenerational transmission of domestic violence. In Y. Danieli (Ed.), *International handbook of multigenerational legacies of trauma* (pp. 553–570). New York: Plenum Press.

Sternberg, K. J., Lamb, M. E., Greenbaum, C., Cicchetti, D., Dawud, S., Cortes, R. M., Krispin, O., & Lorey, F. (1993). Effects of domestic violence on children's behavior problems and depression. *Developmental Psychology, 29,* 44–52.

Warren, M., Kerig, P., Brown, C., & Fedorowicz, A. (1996). *Defense mechanisms and adjustment in children exposed to interparental conflict.* Paper presented at the meeting of the American Psychological Association, Toronto, Ontario, Canada.

Werner, E. E., & Smith, R. S. (1982). *Vulnerable but invincible: A longitudinal study of resilient children and youth.* New York: Adams, Banister, Cox.

Werner, E. E., & Smith, R. S. (1992). *Overcoming the odds: High risk children from birth to adulthood.* Ithaca, NY: Cornell University Press.

West, J. C. (1997). *Exposure to interparental violence and children's social functioning.* Unpublished master's thesis, University of Denver.

West, J. C., Fraser, N. B., Ho, J., & Rossman B. B. R. (1998). *Cognitive moderators of parental violence exposure and trauma response.* Poster session presented at the Fourth National Head Start Research Conference, "Children and Families in an Era of Rapid Change: Creating a Shared Agenda for Researchers, Practitioners and Policy Makers," Washington, DC.

West, J. C., Rossman, B. B. R., Ho, J., & Mallah, K. (1999, April). *The relation of violence exposure to children's expectations of adult and peer aggression.* Poster session presented at the meeting of the Society for Research in Child Development, Albuquerque, NM.

Wolfe, D. A., & Jaffe, P. (1991). Child abuse and family violence as determinants of child psychopathology. *Canadian Journal of Behavioural Science, 23,* 282–299.

Wolfe, D. A., Wekerle, C., Reitzel, D., & Gough, R. (1995). Strategies to address violence in the lives of high-risk youth. In E. Peled, P. G. Jaffe, & J. L. Edelson (Eds.), *Ending the cycle of violence: Community responses to children of battered women* (pp. 255–275). Thousand Oaks, CA: Sage.

CHAPTER

Theoretical Explanations of Impact: Accounting for Change

Eddie was described in his mother Anna's journal as a fun-loving, sociable, and curious toddler. She documented his love of peek-a-boo and his mellow nature. He could take his naps almost anywhere and slid into sleep easily each night, not waking until morning. When Eddie was 3 his father, John, was laid off from his job due to corporate downsizing. John had a very good 8-year employment record and skills and began searching for a new job immediately and hopefully. Two years later the picture was quite different. John had been able to find only sporadic employment and had begun hanging out regularly at the neighborhood bar with other unemployed former coworkers. He would come home late, drunk and depressed. Anna felt shut out and abandoned, and her attempts to discuss this met with John's frustration and verbal anger. Over time the conflicts became louder and more physical until Anna's back was broken when she was shoved with great force into the edge of a kitchen counter. Eddie, approaching 6 years of age, was also quite different. He withdrew from people, became aggressive and inconsolable when his needs were not met, and he experienced regular nightmares in which he was being killed or killing someone.

What caused these changes? What theoretical tools do we have to help us understand? These issues are considered in the following discussion of impact and change.

All living involves change, and the task here is to account for change. With children exposed to family violence the change is usually referred to as the impact of exposure. In this context impact is usually thought of as negative. How can this change called impact be accounted for? Theories of coping are helpful here since they consider processes of change in stressful situations where harm is anticipated. Coping includes all the processes for managing, through cognitive, emotional, behavioral, or all of these activities, internal or external demands that are appraised as taxing or exceeding the resources of the person (Lazarus & Folkman, 1984). One may cope in an anticipatory manner by acting to prepare for a likely stressful event, and proactive coping includes actions taken well in advance of potentially stressful happenings to prevent or modify them even though their occurrence is uncertain (Aspinwall & Taylor, 1997). Thus theories of different kinds of coping consider change activities taken with regard to possible or actual negative events. They help us think about impact as a type of unconscious or conscious reaction of exposed children to try to manage the distress and possible danger associated with exposure. One can also consider changes people make in the absence of threat or negative consequences, but these are usually written about in the domains of self-actualization, curiosity, creativity, etc., rather than coping. Both changes made to avoid harm and in the absence of harm are integral to adaptation and growth.

☐ Impact as Coping

In the following discussion of theories used to account for the impact of children's exposure to parental violence, we assume that the changes or developmental trajectories needing explanation are those enacted to reduce distress or harm, which can be thought of in terms of a broad stress and coping framework. Coping behaviors can be positive or negative with regard to immediate or longer-term adaptation. For example, an exposed child who changes or develops cognitive schemas (e.g., interpersonal interactions are dangerous), emotional understandings or sequences (e.g., anger is uncontrollable), or behavioral repertoires (e.g., to escape is the safest strategy) which serve to minimize harm and maximize positive outcomes is coping. But this behavior may also be generalized beyond the violent home and used, say, to combat threats to self-esteem at school. The point is that much of the impact of witnessing parental violence, whether seen as positive or negative, can be understood within a global stress and coping framework that highlights processes of adaptation to adversity.

Within that framework, the coping activities used to manage the immediate threat of exposure may be seen to remain and become what we view as the signs of impact documented in the research literature (see Chapters 2 and 3). Signs of impact are the indicants of development or change elicited to manage threat to basic needs. It is important to note that these signs of impact are not necessarily the only coping mechanisms tried by exposed children. These are the ones that have stood the test of time (e.g., aggression, withdrawal, avoidance).

It is time to ask the question "From what prior state or from what nonexposed developmental trajectory has change occurred?" This is a critical question to ask when considering exposed children. Our premise has been, using the stress and coping framework, that there is change from normative developmental trajectories or from prestressor schemas, emotional reactions or behaviors or all three in order to manage the stressor and related affect. However, researchers working in the violence and trauma field rarely know what the preexposure state was. Inferences are drawn from comparisons of exposed and nonexposed children as to what the children might have been like without exposure. Inferences are also made from developmental theory about what should or is likely to be or have been. Therefore, in examining impact, researchers are left to find means that help them to infer initial or nonexposed state. Nonetheless, this is a useful approach. If we think we know how exposed children are currently behaving and how they might have been behaving plus the change processes involved, we are better prepared to consider those processes in interventions intended to move a child toward what "might have been." This is especially critical because many children may have been in violent homes since birth. In a recent longitudinal sample most shelter children who had been exposed to personal abuse or parental violence or both had experienced parental violence exposure for over 90% of their lives (Rossman, 1998a).

This raises another important point, namely, that change can be engendered by either adverse circumstances such as family violence or helpful circumstances such as education or therapy. The former we call adverse impact and the latter we call educational achievement or treatment outcome. This observation is critical because it opens more doors for considering accounts of change due to positive and negative circumstances; these are not often considered together. For example, catharsis (emotional release such as crying) has been studied as both a symptom of distress and a process that may underlie therapeutic change when combined with insight (L. S. Greenberg & Safran, 1987, 1989). Therefore, as we consider adverse change we can examine theoretical accounts additional to those commonly used for exposed children. And, using a stress and coping framework, we can see theories as differing in which threats to basic needs they highlight or which mechanisms or learning processes they emphasize or both. For example, a child may feel unsafe during a violent event. This provides the motivation to achieve a sense of safety. From observational learning he or she has noted that escape and hiding may achieve this goal. Therefore, the child chooses to hide in a dumpster on the school playground during a fight at recess. Learning is a fundamental mechanism for change, and meeting basic needs is a powerful motivator. Together these serve, in one form or another, as the basis for all theoretical accounts of the impact of exposure.

☐ Theoretical Accounts of Impact

Theoretical explanations of the impact on children will be viewed, as noted above, within the larger stress and coping perspective, as explanations of adaptation to an atypical rearing environment. What we view as maladaptative behaviors of exposed children have served them in some way in the violent home. This presents the functionalist view. We know less about how to apply structuralist thinking; although trauma theory implies changes in structure of neurotransmitter responses to adversity, systems and family systems theories focus on changes in family role and relationship structures. However, it is not the case that behaviors we see as functioning in a certain way or changes in structure are necessarily conscious choices of children. Their reactions to seeing a loved one assaulted are automatic, often resembling trauma reactions. Therefore, the theoretical explanations do not assume a child's conscious deliberation, although it may play a role.

Many theories have served to increase our understanding of the behavior of exposed children. The primary theoretical approaches used have been: behavioral and cognitive-behavioral theories that include cognitive processing and deficit models; trauma conceptualizations; family systems orientations; and relational theories that deal with the meaning of interpersonal violence for representations of self and other. Comments about the possible role of genetic factors are also made.

When we compare children witnessing parental violence with those not exposed, we find the following characteristics of child witnesses that theories discussed in Chapters 2 and 3 have sought to explain:

1. greater internalizing (i.e., depression, anxiety, or social withdrawal) behavior problems;

2. greater externalizing (e.g., hyperactivity, aggression) behavior problems;

3. more aggressive social problem solving strategies;

4. lower social competence;

5. lower self-esteem;

6. lower school performance and school achievement;

7. poorer informational intake capacities, lower levels of curiosity and distortion of neutral information;

8. poorer performance on intelligence tests;

9. greater PTSD symptomatology;

10. more frequent attributions of self-blame and guilt for the domestic violence;

11. less secure attachments with caregivers;

12. lower sense of personal control.

The comprehensiveness of this list is noteworthy, touching on most aspects of a child's life and development. In the most serious cases, these children appear to be dysregulated in many areas and to have experienced distorted developmental trajectories in most areas. It should be noted, however, that not all children experience all of these difficulties, some evidence very few, and that some of the problems appear enhanced if the child has also experienced personal sexual or physical abuse or neglect (see Rossman & Rosenberg, 1998).

Given the number of developmental domains that may be disrupted, it is difficult for any one theoretical approach to adequately account for all observed difficulties or for the varying patterns of problems and resilience that different children present. But different approaches provide insight into different areas. We turn now to these approaches and how they have tried to account for the behaviors of exposed versus nonexposed children. To aid integration across approaches, Table 4.1 highlights selected unique contributions of different conceptualizations.

Behavioral Theories

Behavioral and cognitive-behavioral approaches were some of the first used to explicate the apparent impact of parental violence exposure on children. This was because one of the most obviously different features of the behavior of many children seen in shelters was their out of control and often aggressive conduct. These behaviors were seen as due to modeling of a violent parent and to whatever reinforcement they receive for aggression in a home context where aggression appears valued and may serve as a means to gain control (Jaffe, Wolfe, & Wilson, 1990). These behaviors were then thought to inappropriately generalize to different targets and settings such as school, creating peer problems and poor achievement. There are other explanations for out of control behaviors that will be discussed below, but modeling of a male batterer remains a common explanation of children's, particularly boys', heightened aggression in violent families. Girls' possible modeling of female (or male) aggression is becoming of greater interest given findings that early teenage exposed girls showed greater externalizing problems than boys (Sternberg et al., 1993) and that adolescent exposed girls'

TABLE 4.1. Selected Contributions of Different Conceptual Approaches for Understanding Impact of Parental Violence Exposure for Children

	Conceptual Approaches					
Behavioral	Cog. Behavioral	Trauma	Family Systems	Relational	Genetic
Observational & instrumental learning of aggressive behaviors & their value & of protective & victim behaviors; absence of models of emotion & behavior regulation except through power & control	Learning of expectations & behavioral repertoires regarding the danger of interpersonal relationships; difficulty with intake of new information or modification of old scripts due to arousal & strength of the self-protective strategies	Prolonged activation of stress response system with associated fear conditioning, arousal & psychobiological changes; difficulty with deployment of attention and memory consolidation & thus new learning	The prolongation of roles and interpersonal interaction patterns including aggression through the functions that these systems serve in the family (& society); likely inflexibility of these patterns under stress	Initial innate motivation of child to maintain a sense of security within caretaker relationship & within a violent home the resulting working models or object representations that the child develops regarding the safety of self and other; the failure of integration of positive & negative self & other representations to assist with the development and stability of self-esteem, & emotion & behavior regulation; interruptions in the support of mastery attainment	Potential genetic underpinnings of & individual differences in arousability, fearfulness, aggression that may enhance effects of witnessing violence, stress, information distortion, & faulty relational and family systems

aggression increased relative to boys' when the violence in the home was more severe (Rosenberg, 1984).

Behavioral and cognitive behavioral approaches rely on two types of learning that have been the topic of study by learning theorists for some time: modeling, which is also called observational or incidental learning, and operant or instrumental conditioning, which is the learning through instruction that a reward may follow a behavior that is successfully carried out or punishment may follow failure. Observational learning has been studied by researchers such as Albert Bandura (1973). They have found that an action is more likely to be modeled if performed by an attractive (to the observer) person or a person who has more power or authority than the observer and if the behavior appears to yield outcomes that the observer would like. For example, a child observes a school bully regularly being given ice cream cups by other children from their lunches. This child begins shoving younger children into their lockers, picking fights at recess, and pushing other children down the stairs to the lunchroom. The study of operant conditioning (e.g., Tolman, 1932) has suggested that continuous reinforcement is useful in quickly establishing behaviors, that extinction of these behaviors appears to occur under conditions of no clear reward or punishment, and that behaviors that have been partially reinforced are particularly difficult to extinguish. For example, a child is instructed to put the dog's food and water on the back porch and receives praise and rewards for consistently doing this. Then a family of raccoons who love dog food moves into the neighborhood. The child is therefore instructed to keep the dog's food in the kitchen. The parents are surprised and angry when the previously conscientious child makes mistakes for a while, continuing to put the dog's food outside part of the time.

A third type of learning mechanism studied is classical conditioning, where a non-need-related (e.g., nonfood or nonshock) occurrence, such as the ringing of a bell, becomes linked with a behavior that is initially sustained by a need-related event (e.g., the reduction in painful anxiety). With repetition the non-need-related or conditioned stimulus comes to sustain the behavior in the absence of the need-related event. This mechanism is not as much a part of behavioral approaches that have been used with family violence. However, as we will see later, classical conditioning is used in trauma theory approaches to account for fearful and avoidant behaviors that are a part of the posttraumatic symptom picture. Conditioned fear responses may be impossible to extinguish (Le Doux, 1996). As an example of conditioned fear/avoidance imagine that when waiting at the front door for a hug from her father after work, a young girl instead encounters a very angry father who pushes her aside. She falls and cracks her head on the front steps. For several years the child refuses to use the front door.

While the modeling of aggression has been the major focus of behavioral accounts, other parental behaviors in a violent family could be learned through observation and contribute to children's problems. Parents in violent families, abused or abuser or both, have been variously characterized by research as having low self-esteem, experiencing depression and PTSD symptomatology, having a lower sense of personal control, making self- or other-blaming attributions for the violence, being socially withdrawn, and having impoverished social skills or networks or both (Brown & Kerig, 1995; Emery & Laumann-Billings, 1998; Graham-Bermann & Levendosky, 1998; Hamberger & Hastings, 1986; Holtzworth-Munroe & Stuart, 1994; Lynch & Graham-Bermann, in press). Because parents are both valued caretakers and in a position of authority over children, parental behaviors have a higher likelihood of being adopted. For example, imagine a battered mother who responds with helplessness and lack of confidence when required to make daily plans and decisions (e.g., what to put in school lunches, how to manage work, and get children home from school) and needs to be "rescued" by a neighbor. Her child may come to regard basic planning as beyond her or his capability in addition to feeling disappointed and angry that the mother can not do these things.

Cognitive behavioral theories have focused on modeling of schema and on how children process and gain meaning from the social information they receive in peer and family conflict situations. These conceptualizations have also been helpful in understanding the aggressive, social and personal competence problems of exposed children. Social Information Processing Theory (SIP, Crick & Dodge, 1994) and the Cognitive-Contextual Framework of Grych and Fincham (1990; 1993) examine the appraisals children make of parental conflict and how these may influence their emotional reactions, coping behaviors, attributions of responsibility, and informational processing capacities. For example, Crick and Dodge speculate about a mechanism they call preemptive processing, wherein heightened levels of emotion are thought to increase the likelihood that children will rely on existing family conflict scripts or schemas, possibly learned through observation or direct instruction, in understanding new situations. If an exposed child is highly socially anxious she or he may preemptively process a benign peer situation in a way that makes it seem threatening and produce an aggressive response. This erroneous expectation of an other's hostile intent has been termed a hostile aggressive bias (Crick & Dodge, 1994). Or Grych and Fincham (1993) and Cummings, Davies, and Simpson (1994) have found that parental fights about the child are more distressing and guilt inducing for children, and fights that are resolved in a reasonable way are less distressing. Thus, unresolved parental fights about the child's behavior may be preemptively processed using the child's existing "bad me" schema rather than listening for what seems accurate or inaccurate about the argument. And, Kerig, Fedorowicz, Brown, Patenaude, and Warren (1998) note, from research of school-age community children from conflictual families, that boys tend to make instrumental attributions of threat, which may lead them to enact protective, often aggressive behaviors (the "warriors") whereas girls tend to make more relational self-blaming attributions, which may result in greater distress and anxiety behaviors (the "worriers").

These appraisal-oriented cognitive-behavioral approaches are quite similar to the general Lazarus and Folkman (1984) stress and coping framework. A nice feature of these approaches is the avenue they open for probing children's understandings (i.e., what they have learned or imagined) of parental violence and interpersonal relationships at different ages. Such exploration has been carried out mainly with older school-age children (e.g., 10 to 12 years of age), since they are cognitively more able to respond to questions and verbally articulate different aspects of their understandings. However, were behaviors used to infer a child's understanding, as is the case in play therapy, younger children could be included in this theory-driven research.

Another type of cognitive behavioral approach, Cognitive Control Theory (CCT, Santostefano, 1985), has been used (Rossman, 1998b) to examine the difficulties some child witnesses experience with informational intake. This theory makes contributions such as those of SIP theory and the concept of preemptive processing to our understanding of why exposed children may not use new information well. However, CCT works from a base of Lewinian Field Theory and postulates that individuals use their information processing capacities unconsciously in a protective way to regulate emotional distress. Several features of information processing are examined in the theory, but the processing dimension that has been investigated with exposed children is called leveling/sharpening. This refers to the tendency either to take in new information and modify existing schemas very slowly or inaccurately or both (i.e., the leveling end of the dimension) or to process new information very quickly or accurately or both (the sharpening end); both are thought to occur in the service of distress regulation. Most adults operate somewhere in the middle, varying slightly depending on the emotion regulation needs of different situations, and children grow from greater leveling to this middle ground with development. Leveling provides protection from new and potentially distressing information by making its acquisition more gradual or familiar or both in fitting with existing schemas through distorting it so as to minimize the perception of threat. This would have the same functional effect as what is often referred to as denial. Sharpening, on the other hand, works to protect through preparedness, with a reduction in arousal resulting from the quick or careful or both search of the informational field so that plans can be made to deal with perceived threat. This process could account for the hypervigilant tendencies of some abused children (Rossman, Hughes, & Hanson, 1998).

Finally, a cognitive developmental approach using a Piagetian (1952) perspective is also useful. This approach is represented in the work of Fish-Murray, Koby, and van der Kolk (1987). They examined the accommodation skills of physically abused and nonabused school-age children. They did not specifically posit higher arousal as an interfering factor on the part of abused children, but later discussion by Murray and Son (1998) suggests that traumatic arousal may be part of the formulation. Accommodation skills are those where new information is taken in and existing schemas are changed to incorporate new information. In contrast, assimilation is where the information is changed or distorted to fit existing schemas. Piaget felt both processes were needed for the growth of intelligence. They found that abused children had weaker accommodation skills than similar nonabused children. Violence-exposed children would be at risk for delays in intellectual growth given this approach.

Probably the most complete account of the problems of exposed children comes through combining behavioral approaches. Working in a stress and coping framework, distortions in appraisals of meaning in a situation (e.g., overgeneralization) and associated heightened distress could be understood in terms of preemptive processing with its reduced use of new information associated with leveling or the overpreparedness that accompanies sharpening. The cognitive, emotional, and behavioral contents of schemas evidenced by exposed children are assumed to be learned by instrumental conditioning through experience with trying to avoid danger to self or others. The contents of coping repertoires, such as aggression or helplessness, could also be learned through modeling and the internalization of relationship dynamics. In sum, the complete explanatory package provided by behavioral approaches is highly useful. However, it does leave room for other conceptual approaches to contribute.

Trauma Explanations

Trauma "Theory" as such is only now evolving. It is, however, especially useful in highlighting the increased agitation and dysregulation of some exposed children as well as victims of other violence or adversity. Research over the past 15 years has provided the basis for integrating cognitive, emotional, behavioral, and psychobiological information about an individual's responses to terrifying events. Conceptually the main marker for trauma is the intense fear the person feels for his or her own psychological or physical safety or that of others or both and their feeling of helplessness to control the threat.

Instinctually many species, including humans, are programmed to respond to signs of danger with a fight or flight response, which is expressed in a number of bodily systems (Cox, 1978). This is a normal adaptive stress response process (Horowitz, 1986; Selye, 1956), which aids survival under conditions of threat to physical or psychological well-being, conditions labeled traumatic (*Diagnostic and Statistical Manual of Mental Disorders*, 1994, *DSM-IV*). However, when such stress is sustained over long periods of time by repetitive threat, there is prolonged dysregulation (van der Kolk, 1994). For example, some neurotransmitter systems increase output and others become depleted with chronic stress. Behaviorally there are more difficulties with attention and concentration, causing both greater irritability and a numbing of affect and behavior, and heightened arousal and startle responses. The brain/body system seems at some times to be on overload and at other times to be shut down. The typical return to modulated functioning that often occurs following acute stressors is not accomplished. When prolonged, this threat response may have negative physiological consequences and be generalized to circumstances beyond those of the initial threat. Ironically maladaptive consequences of this initially protective mechanism may emerge. For example, imagine a young boy is repeatedly raped in the bathroom at home. He may develop nightmares and other trauma symptoms in addition to manifesting bowel problems and avoiding bathrooms.

The learning process thought to account for these effects is classical conditioning, particularly aversive conditioning of fear/trauma to both dangerous and other stimuli, resulting in the PTSD avoidance behaviors elicited by reminders. The reminders have, through being associated with the initial threat, become conditioned to elicit similar emotional and behavioral responses to those naturally occurring with the original danger. Such avoidance could also gain instrumental value if rewarded by others; or, if it is punished, it could leave the individual paralyzed and unable to choose between aversive events (i.e., reexposure versus punishment). Classical conditioning currently serves as a major explanatory mechanism in trauma approaches.

Potential maladaptive consequences of prolonged threat and trauma responding are multiple and occur at different levels of functioning. Physiologically, a prolonged stress response, or chronic posttraumatic stress reaction, has been linked to changes in the functioning of the hypothalamic-pituitary-adrenal axis and neurotransmitters (Charney et al., 1994; van der Kolk, 1994, 1996). Changes have been found in the levels of several neurotransmitters that have implications for behavior and coincide with symptoms characteristic of PTSD. These include elevations in adrenalin and noradrenalin, glucocorticoids such as cortisol, endogeneous opiates, and dopamine, and a reduction in serotonin. Heightened adrenalin and noradrenalin creates increased heart rate and blood flow, preparing the body and muscles for quick action, fight or flight but also increased agitation, and, perhaps, increased intrusions, and decreased attention deployment capacities. In addition, with prolonged arousal, receptors for these neurotransmitters appear to decrease in number, perhaps to help the body reregulate arousal. Greater glucocorticoids help the body deal with injury through the reduction of inflammation, but they have been found also associated, at high levels, with the damage or death of cells in the hippocampus, one site of memory processes. High levels of endogeneous opiates reduce pain, but they are also linked to interference with memory consolidation processes. Excess dopamine in the frontal cortex stimulates thought processes, but it has been linked also to hallucinatory activity in schizophrenia (Berquier & Ashton, 1991) via the usefulness of dopamine antagonist drugs for that disorder. This same process could facilitate the intrusions and reliving experiences of PTSD patients, an interference to ongoing thought and reality testing. Finally, reduced serotonin levels are related to decreases in the body's ability to regulate emotional arousal, indexed by the usefulness of serotonin reuptake blockers such as fluoxatine (Prozac) for both depression and chronic PTSD.

It is not well known how prolonged neurotransmitter dysregulation affects children's brain/body functioning and development. Perry (1997) has speculated that the earlier the trauma, the more likely it is that early maturing brain systems (e.g., brainstem and limbic systems) may be affected, with cascading effects on the development of later systems (e.g., the cortex). These early systems control very basic activities such as heart rate and sleep/wake cycles. Thus, early severe exposure could have profound effects on a child's ability to develop basic regulatory functions. In addition, some of the dysregulation in neurotransmitter function, beginning to be documented in studies of abused children (e.g., Kaufman et al., 1997; Kaufman et al., in press), may also be seen in other aspects of physiological, immune, affective, and behavioral response. The hippocampus continues to develop to age 4, changing through use-dependent (environmentally sensitive) pruning of excessive branchings and myelination of neurons. For example, Perry (1997) studied the physiological responses of adolescents who had been incarcerated for violent stalking behaviors and those who had not as they contemplated danger and violence. Physiological responses of stalkers presented a pattern of calm, vigilant preparedness. Nonstalkers showed the typical increases in arousal and anxiety seen with impending danger. Perry has hypothesized that a critical effect of early chronic trauma may be structural and functional brain development that reflects brain usage during that time. Use-dependent brain architecture may result in a system that is highly responsive to managing trauma and traumatic arousal but less experienced in other aspects of function that are sculpted by nonviolent developmental experiences. At present speculation as to use-dependent brain development clearly needs further systematic empirical documentation.

While catharsis, the expressing of feelings and thoughts regarding negative situations, was once thought to account for positive change, research has shown this not to be the case (L. S. Greenberg & Safran, 1987, 1989). Increased understanding and reframing of the negative situation also needs to take place with catharsis for positive change to occur. This seems logical. Were catharsis enough, why would the emotional displays that accompany chronic posttraumatic reactions not help the victims more? Horowitz (1986) has suggested that the PTSD reliving of traumatic events can be useful for some victims as a reworking. These victims could be the assaulted adults studied by Foa, Riggs, and Gershuny (1995) who showed natural abatement of symptoms over several months. However, other change processes must also occur, since for some victims symptoms remained, particularly reliving experiences. The authors speculated that perhaps the longer-suffering victims were utilizing dissociative strategies to cope with intrusions rather than reworking, making their abatement less likely. Further discussion of PTSD treatment approaches is presented in Chapter 6.

The trauma process remains a complex puzzle. Perhaps some victims are more capable of providing or have social networks capable of providing the reframing, whereas others do not. Foa et al. (1995) noted that the initial symptom severity predicted prolonged symptomatology, and van der Kolk (1994, 1996) found severity and chronicity to be associated with greater preexposure psychiatric problems or life adversities or both. These would not bode well for an individual's ability to reframe. And these findings raise the question of how well exposed children, particularly younger children who have developmentally delayed capacities to reflect on their experience, could carry out needed reframing. For young children, pre- and during-exposure resiliency factors of buffering, temperament, and social support may be critical.

The basic point is that prolonged threat to survival may leave the individual in a dysregulated state, where perception, cognition, and emotional systems are functioning atypically, in part to compensate for dysregulation. This speculation and supportive research is based on the study of adult PTSD victims. It is not known what other changes might occur for children where brain development is still ongoing. However, there could be major consequences for ongoing cognitive and emotional behavior of traumatized children and perhaps for their developmental trajectories in these domains.

Trauma approaches suggest that the dysregulated behaviors of exposed children and difficulties with cognitive functioning as well as their fears may be, in part, accounted for by their natural reactions to trauma. These difficulties, which are assessed by *DSM-IV* as PTSD symptoms, are also assessed by behavioral symptom checklists such as the CBCL (Achenbach & Edelbrock, 1983) as externalizing behavior problems (e.g., aggressiveness, irritability, and arousal) or as internalizing behavior problems (e.g., somatic symptoms, anxiety, and social withdrawal). Trauma symptoms also could be linked to exposed children's poorer social competence. Briere (1992) has argued that, following initial and interim reactions to trauma, there may be a long-term phase where trauma reactions and behaviors solidify and become part of a person's character. Thus, some of the behavior problems noted for exposed children may have initially been part of their reaction to trauma. A severely traumatized child who presents as oppositional defiant or depressed may have gotten to that point differently than a nontraumatized child. This notion of multiple paths leading to a similar outcome illustrates the concept of equifinality as discussed by Cicchetti (1989). The companion concept of multifinality is also relevant for exposed children (e.g., siblings) who may have had similar antecedent exposure experiences but have ended up with different profiles of strengths and difficulties.

Returning to the issue and possibility that trauma symptoms may be misidentified as problem behaviors, research has shown substantial correlations between CBCL problem behavior internalizing and externalizing scales and PTSD symptom scores (Rossman, 1994). Thus, a trauma perspective on exposed children's behavior problems may have ramifications for the type of treatment needed (e.g., trauma versus conduct disorder interventions) for exposed children who, for example, present as oppositional/defiant, conduct disordered, depressed, or hyperactive. However, when traumalike symptoms persist it may be an indication that these behaviors have become the more fixed aspects of a child's behavior repertoire noted by Horowitz (1986), meaning that trauma-based intervention alone will not be sufficient. In sum, trauma explanations contribute in unique ways to understanding the problems noted for exposed children.

Family Systems Theories

Family systems approaches (see Aponte & VanDeusen, 1991) view the family as a unit and attempt to understand how the parental violence is serving a function for the unit. Its impact on exposed children needs to be understood in terms of the function of their family unit and their role in it. Further, family and larger social systems are viewed as networks of relationships among people. These relationships are typically characterized by the dimensions of boundary (i.e., the roles persons play in the network for certain tasks or functions), alignment (i.e., the joining with or opposition of one family member with others in carrying out some function), and power (i.e., the influence of a family member on the carrying out or outcome of an operation). A successfully functioning family is one where there is a good fit of the family's structural organization of relationships to the tasks or circumstances. Since most families face many tasks of child and adult development, daily organization and survival, interacting with the larger community around them, and so on, flexibility of members to move in and out of roles and alignments and power expectations is needed. Dysfunctional families, a term often applied to violent families, are often those where: boundaries are either too unspecified (i.e., *enmeshed* is a term used) or so predetermined that little social interchange is needed to carry out tasks (i.e., sometimes called *disengaged*); alignments are inflexible in various ways (i.e., *stable*, meaning the joining together of some family members against another in a consistent manner such that this exerts a dominant force on family interactions; *detouring*, meaning a stable coalition formed to reduce the stress between two family members by identifying another family member as the source of the distress and having relationship links with that person characterized by either attack or overconcern toward that person; and *triangulated*, meaning that two conflictual parties relate to a third in ways to seek that person's support for their position while the third party tends to move back and forth in terms of where they place their support) and power is distributed in ways that leave role designated persons without the power to carry out their tasks in the system (i.e., sometimes called *weak executive functioning*) or leave persons without the power to carry out developmental tasks (i.e., often called the *inhibition of developmental potential*).

Dysfunctional families are also characterized as underorganized, meaning that their relationship and functional structure is inconsistent, undifferentiated, and lacks flexibility. Learning processes of modeling, instrumental, and perhaps classical conditioning all serve as mechanisms through which dysfunctional and functional family structures evolve. Thus, learning deficits are relevant.

These families often have limited repertoires for organizing themselves to carry out functions or solve problems and may even be inconsistent in how these limited options are used. Limited systemic coping repertoires leave them at a disadvantage. Such repertoires often characterize families with limited social, financial, and educational resources. They are frequently impacted by adverse and disruptive social circumstances that have and continue to interfere with their learning of and more flexible use of different organizational structures in the family. Thus the system of relationships, roles, alignments, and power that characterize a family is used by family systems approaches to explain the difficulties of violent families and their children. Disadvantaged violent families tend to experience high levels of family and personal stressors, which would further deplete their resources to learn new organizational structures.

While parental violence is seen as caused by the whole family and larger social system, these approaches do not condone violence on the part of a perpetrator. They do seek to understand the role the violence plays in the functioning of the family and the family plays in its continuation. They also seek to understand what children and other family members are learning in the context of how this unit functions. Thus, the impact of wife abuse on the parenting abilities of mothers and their partners is of interest and is what Jaffe et al. (1990) have referred to in their model as the "indirect" effect of wife abuse on children. Interrupted parenting and atypical family boundaries, alignments, and power structures all provide a rich learning environment for exposed children. These family structural characteristics also imply that exposed children may be at a disadvantage in carrying out needed developmental tasks or may execute them in an atypical fashion, shaped by their family unit's structure and functioning.

Relational Approaches

Several developmental conceptualizations of human relationships have been used in thinking about the problems of exposed children such as attachment theory (Bowlby, 1988), a related emotional security hypothesis (Cummings & Davies, 1994; Davies & Cummings, 1994, 1995, 1998), and ego-analytic object relations theories (see review by J. R. Greenberg & Mitchell, 1983). Compared with the relationship conceptualizations of family systems approaches, relational approaches have focused more on dyadic relationships within the family, especially parent–child relationships due to their special evolutionary significance in keeping a young child safe.

While learning mechanisms per se are less the focus of relational approaches, observational and instrumental learning and classical conditioning all provide parts of the underlying support for the formation of attachment or emotional security bonds with caregivers. Even though the basic motivation for attachment and secure base behaviors is assumed to be instinctual initially, learning processes are needed to account for the form taken, secure or insecure, by the development of the attachment system and content of working models. Similarly, objects relations theory posits the child's internalizing of objects or part objects (Klein, 1949) is a result of observed or experienced interactions with others. Some believe that whole interactional sequences may be learned (Laing & Esterson, 1964).

Many relational approaches describe the expected course of development as unfolding through the child's establishment of a secure relationship with a parent. This experience sets the stage for development of a child's "working models" or internalization of object representations of self and others in relation to self. If the process is successful, others become viewed as safe or trustworthy, as in Erikson's (1950) first developmental stage of basic trust. If the process is not so successful, negative models may evolve wherein others are seen as dangerous or unpredictable or both in their caring and the self may be seen as bad or unworthy of care.

Object relations theorists have variable views, but most see normal development as proceeding through good enough mothering (Winnicott, 1965) such that positive and negative representations of self and other become integrated. Some (e.g., Klein or Mahler; see J. R. Greenberg and Mitchell, 1983, Chapters 5 and 9) suggest that an infant's initial good and bad partial representations of self or caregiver may fail to be integrated in adverse parenting circumstances where the needed balance of constancy of sensitive nurturing and limit setting may not have been available. There may be a need to retain a good representation independent of a bad representation to protect the positive part object from the presumed destructive power of the bad representation. For example, an abused child may need to keep separate the abusive part of a parent representation (or destructive anger of a self-representation) from more worthy or nurturing or safe features of an object representation in order to protect those features. The normal process of integration is thought critical for the development of a resilient and reality-based self-concept and internal regulatory processes that can modulate and remain fairly stable in the face of adversity. If an abused child needs to retain a split representation of caregiver such that benevolent features (real or wished for) can be retained, the child may also need to retain a split representation of self, where the "bad" self is congruent with and deserving of the abuse of a "good" caregiver.

The hostile aggressive bias of Crick and Dodge (1994), which is often seen as more cognitive behavioral, could also be seen as an aspect of a working model or negative object representation of other. In their work, the attributions children make of the safety/danger in social situations may dictate how the children respond. There is some evidence that abused and exposed children (Erickson, Egeland, & Pianta, 1989; Mallah & Rossman, 1999; West, Rossman, Ho, & Mallah, 1999) or those with punitive relationships with their mothers (Weiss, Dodge, Bates, & Pettit, 1992) expect others to be threatening and thus respond in more protective or aggressive ways. This could help explain the greater aggressive or social withdrawal or both behaviors of exposed children.

Cummings and Davies (1994) have offered an attachment-based emotional security hypothesis in trying to understand children's reactions to adult conflict. They suggest that children's reactions may be varied but can best be understood as children's attempts to establish or regain a sense of emotional security based on their attachments with caregivers. Thus, one could see defensive reactions to others that ranged from aggression to withdrawal to seeking reassurance as evolving from child witnesses' attempts to establish or reestablish some sense of emotional security.

The relational approaches seem well-suited to illuminate exposed children's difficulties in social situations and relationships, including their greater aggression, and reliance on aggressive social problem solving. Early caregiver relationships in parentally violent families are less likely to be able to focus consistently on the child's needs. Children may have learned that social interactions may not be safe, so they need to take precautions. In addition, the potential disruption of a caretaker attachment bond due to ongoing parental violence could change the success of other aspects of parenting and socialization. There is some evidence that young exposed children have developed less secure attachments with their mothers (Posada, Waters, Liu, & Johnson, 1998; Ritchie & Miller, 1996), but these findings need replication. To the extent that a battered mother is only sometimes experienced as available for the child and is not experienced as powerful, observational learning and modeling principles would suggest that developmental tasks or socialization roles valued by her would be less likely to be adopted by the child.

Relational theories, with their emphasis on the role of the caregiver in guiding the child through the completion of developmental tasks, highlight the need to consider mastery approaches for understanding children's development and the difficulties of exposed children. These mastery approaches could be discussed separately but also fit well within the relational arena, since a child's development of a sense of mastery seems inseparable from the provisions existing within her or his rearing environment. Mastery approaches provided by several theorists have attended to the importance of mastery or effectance motivation and behaviors for the development of the child. Piaget (1952) felt that through play the child was able to explore and discover her or his ability to act on the environment (assimilation) or be acted upon by the environment (accommodation). These processes supported the growth of intelligence for the child. Robert White (1959) also noted the importance of the development of a child's sense of effectance or capacity to bring about an outcome for the developing sense of self. Some of this sense of personal mastery comes from the accomplishment of developmental tasks through trial and error as well as instruction, caretaking provisions. In a violent family where much of the energy of family members, including children, becomes directed toward keeping an even keel to avoid further conflict and aggression, it is less likely that children's free exploration or even direct instruction may be accomplished in normative ways. Thus, it becomes less likely that exposed children would have the usual opportunities to develop an integrated sense of their own competence as well as its limitations. Harter (1998) and others have written about the likely disruption of a child's sense of self and competence in adverse rearing circumstances. Thus, exposed children's diminished provisions for accomplishing developmental tasks may form part of a cascading cycle of development where a realistic assessment of one's own mastery leaves the child feeling ineffective due to developmental lags and due to his or her inability to stop the family conflict.

Relational theories provide powerful explanatory tools that can be directed toward understanding the lowered self-esteem, difficulty with trust and interpersonal relationships, and emotion and behavior regulation difficulties of exposed and abused children. However, other approaches, including possible genetic contributions to exposed children's reactions to parental violence, introduce useful constructs.

Genetic Contributions

We have outlined ways in which current theoretical orientations have been used to account for child witness behavior. This was not meant to deny the possible role of genetics in some behaviors for some children. It simply seems improbable that genetic influences could account for problem behaviors in all child witnesses, because so many children, with likely different genetic heritage, are exposed.

However, there are legitimate ways in which genetic heritage may contribute to a child's reaction to exposure to parental violence. There is evidence that fearfulness, depression, hyperactivity or attention deficits or both, and aggression have genetic contributions (e.g., see Cicchetti & Cohen, 1995; Plomin, Reiss, Hetherington, & Howe, 1994; True et al., 1993). There is also evidence in the medical literature (e.g., sickle cell anemia) that environmental factors may contribute to gene expression. Therefore, a child's trauma reactions may be enhanced by a genetic tendency toward fearful temperament, his or her information processing difficulties exacerbated by a family history of Attention Deficit Disorder or Attention Deficit Hyperactivity Disorder (ADD/ADHD), and his or her aggressive behaviors strengthened by a genetic component. Similarly, genetic predisposition for disorders such as ADD/ADHD or depression may be enhanced by living in a stressful family environment where danger and unpredictability are common. For exposed children there is not sufficient evidence to evaluate the role of either genetic contributions to observed behaviors or environmental contributions to gene expression. Future research is clearly needed to help evaluate these possibilities.

☐ Conclusion

In sum, all of the theoretical approaches utilized in understanding the role of marital violence exposure in children's development are informative in different ways as we approach the task of preventing and treating children growing up in violent families. For the developing child the individual columns of theoretical contributions highlighted in Table 4.1 represent arbitrary separations. Different mechanisms likely act simultaneously, sequentially, and cyclically. If the lowered sense of self-worth and mastery, distrust of others, and weakness in self-modulatory capacities from relational theories are combined with the modeling and reward of interpersonal aggression and development of negative interpersonal schemas from cognitive/behavioral theories and with family systems dysfunctions and the heightened arousal, fear, and trauma responses appropriate to violent threat, the resulting picture of an exposed child's developmental environment is treacherous. Thus, all theoretical approaches contribute to form this picture, with learning and innate protective and relational processes providing the oil and canvas from which the picture is created. This conclusion highlights a main theme in this book, discussed in more detail in Chapter 6, that assessment and intervention for exposed children must be carried out using the tools and understandings provided by multiple theoretical approaches and with multiple targets in mind (e.g., psychobiological arousal, children's schemas and behavioral repertoires, the nature of dyadic interpersonal relationships, and the functioning of family and societal systems). For example, a traumatized child may be unable to benefit very quickly from a cognitive behavioral intervention for anger management until traumatic arousal is reduced or the family structure to which he or she much return each day is changed.

☐ References

Achenbach, T. M., & Edelbrock, C. S. (1983). *Manual for the Child Behavior Checklist and Revised Child Behavioral Profile.* Burlington, VT: University of Vermont.

American Psychiatric Association. (1994). *Diagnostic and statistical manual of mental disorders* (4th ed.). Washington, DC: Author.

Aponte, H. J., & VanDeusen, J. M. (1991). Structural family therapy. In A. S. Gurman & D. P. Kniskern (Eds.), *Handbook of family therapy* (Vol. 1, pp. 310–360). New York: Brunner/Mazel.

Aspinwall, L. G., & Taylor, S. E. (1997). A stitch in time: Self-regulation and proactive coping. *Psychological Bulletin, 121,* 417–436.

Bandura, A. (1973). *Aggression: A social learning analysis.* Englewood Cliffs, NJ: Prentice–Hall.

Berquier, A., & Ashton, R. (1991). A selective review of possible neurological etiologies of schizophrenia. *Clinical Psychology Review, 11,* 585–598.

Bowlby, J. (1988). *A secure base.* New York: Basic Books.

Briere, J. N. (1992). *Child abuse trauma: Theory and treatment of the lasting effects.* Newbury Park, CA: Sage.

Brown, C. A., & Kerig, P. K. (1995). *Parent's and children's coping with interparental conflict.* Paper presented at the meeting of the American Psychological Association, New York.

Charney, D. S., Southwick, S. M., Krystal, J. H., Deutch, A. Y., Murburg, M. M., & Davis, M. (1994). Neurobiological mechanisms of PTSD. In M. M. Murburg (Ed.), *Catecholamine function in PTSD: Emerging concepts* (pp. 131–158). Washington, DC: American Psychiatric Association.

Cicchetti, D. (1989). How research on child maltreatment has informed the study of child development: Perspectives from developmental psychopathology. In D. Cicchetti & V. Carlson (Eds.), *Child maltreatment: Theory and research on the causes and consequences of child abuse and neglect* (pp. 377–431). New York: Cambridge University Press.

Cicchetti, D., & Cohen, D. J. (1995). *Manual of developmental psychopathology.* New York: Wiley.

Cox, T. (1978). *Stress.* Baltimore, MD: University Park Press.

Crick, N. R., & Dodge, K. A. (1994). A review and reformulation of social information-processing mechanisms in children's social adjustment. *Psychological Bulletin, 115,* 74–101.

Cummings, E. M., & Davies, P. T. (1994). *Children and marital conflict: The impact of family dispute and resolution.* New York: Guilford Press.

Cummings, E. M., Davies, P. T., & Simpson, K. S. (1994). Marital conflict, gender, and children's appraisals and coping efficacy as mediators of child adjustment. *Journal of Family Psychology, 8,* 141–149.

Davies, P. T., & Cummings, E. M. (1994). Marital conflict and child adjustment: An emotional security hypothesis. *Psychological Bulletin, 116,* 387–411.

Davies, P. T., & Cummings, E. M. (1995). Children's emotions as organizers of their reactions to interadult anger: A functionalist perspective. *Developmental Psychology, 31,* 677–684.

Davies, P. T., & Cummings, E. M. (1998). Exploring children's emotional security as a mediator of the link between marital relations and child adjustment. *Child Development, 69,* 124–139.

Emery, R. E., & Laumann-Billings, L. (1998). An overview of the nature, causes, and consequences of abusive family relationships: Toward differentiating maltreatment and violence. *American Psychologist, 53,* 121–135.

Erickson, M. F., Egeland, B., & Pianta, R. (1989). The effects of maltreatment on the development of young children. In D. Cicchetti & V. Carlson (Eds.), *Child maltreatment: Theory and research on the causes and consequences of child abuse and neglect* (pp. 647–684). New York: Cambridge University Press.

Erikson, E. H. (1950). *Childhood and society.* New York: Norton.

Fish-Murray, C. C., Koby, E. V., & van der Kolk, B. A. (1987). Evolving ideas: The effect of abuse on children's thought. In B. A. van der Kolk (Ed.), *Psychological trauma* (pp. 89–100). Washington, DC: American Psychiatric Association.

Foa, E. B., Riggs, D. S., & Gershuny, B. S. (1995). Arousal, numbing, and intrusion: Symptom structure of PTSD following assault. American Journal of Psychiatry, 152, 116–120.

Graham-Bermann, S. A., & Levendosky, A. A. (1998). The social functioning of preschool-age children whose mothers are emotionally and physically abused. *Journal of Emotional Abuse, 1,* 59–84.

Greenberg, J. R., & Mitchell, S. A. (1983). *Object relations in psychoanalytic theory.* Cambridge, MA: Harvard University Press.

Greenberg, L. S., & Safran, J. D. (1987). *Emotion in psychotherapy: Affect, cognition, and the process of change.* New York: Guilford.

Greenberg, L. S., & Safran, J. D. (1989). Emotion in psychotherapy. *American Psychologist, 44,* 19–29.

Grych, J. H., & Fincham, F. D. (1990). Marital conflict and children's adjustment: A cognitive-contextual framework. *Psychological Bulletin, 108,* 267–290.

Grych, J. H., & Fincham, F. D. (1993). Children's appraisals of marital conflict: Initial investigations of the cognitive-contextual framework. *Child Development, 64,* 215–230.

Hamberger, L. K., & Hastings, J. (1986). Personality correlates of men who abuse their partners: A cross-validation study. *Journal of Family Violence, 3,* 121–130.

Harter, S. (1998). The effects of child abuse on the self-system. In B. B. R. Rossman & M. S. Rosenberg (Eds.), *Multiple victimization of children: Conceptual, developmental, research, and treatment issues* (pp. 147–188). Binghamton, NY: Haworth Press.

Holtzworth-Munroe, A., & Stuart, G. L. (1994). Typologies of male batterers: Three subtypes and the differences among them. *Psychological Bulletin, 116,* 476–497.

Horowitz, M. J. (1986). *Stress response syndromes* (2nd ed.) Northvale, NJ: Jason Aronson.

Jaffe, P. G., Wolfe, D. A., & Wilson, S. K. (1990). *Children of battered women.* Newbury Park, CA: Sage.

Kaufman, J., Birmaher, B., Dahl, N., Ryan, N., Perel, J., & Nelson, B. (1997, April). *Psychobiological sequelae of abuse.* Poster session presented at the meeting of the Society for Research in Child Development, Washington, DC.

Kaufman, J., Birmaher, B., Perel, J., Dahl, R., Moreci, P., Nelson, B., Wells, W., & Ryan, N. (in press). The corticotrophin releasing hormone challenge in depressed, abused, depressed non-abused and normal control children. *Biological Psychiatry.*

Kerig, P. A., Fedorowicz, A. E., Brown, C. A., Patenaude, R. L., & Warren, M. (1998). When warriors are worriers: Gender and children's coping with interparental violence. *Journal of Emotional Abuse, 1,* 89–114.

Klein, M. (1949). *The psycho-analysis of children.* London: Hogarth.

Laing, R. D., & Esterson, A. (1964). *Sanity, madness and the family.* London: Tavestock.

Lazarus, R. S., & Folkman, S. (1984). *Stress, appraisal, and coping.* New York: Springer.

Le Doux, J. E.(1996). *The emotional brain: The mysterious underpinnings of emotional life.* New York: Simon & Schuster.

Lynch, S., & Graham-Bermann, S. A. (in press). Self-esteem in mothers and children in woman abusing families. *Violence against Women*.

Mallah, K., & Rossman, B. B. R. (1999). Social information processing for children exposed to parental violence. *Journal of Child Clinical Psychology*. Manuscript submitted for publication.

Murray, C. C., & Son, L. (1998). The effect of multiple victimization on children's cognition: Variations in response. In B. B. R. Rossman & M. S. Rosenberg (Eds.), *Multiple victimization of children: conceptual, developmental, research, and treatment issues* (pp. 131–146). Binghamton, New York: Haworth.

Perry, B. D. (1997). Incubated in terror: Neurodevelopmental factors in the "Cycle of Violence." In J. D. Osofsky (Ed.), *Children in a violent society* (pp. 124–149). New York: Guilford.

Piaget, J. (1952). *The origins of intelligence in children*. New York: International Universities Press.

Plomin, R., Reiss, D., Hetherington, E. M., & Howe, G. (1994). Nature and nurture: Genetic contributions to measures of the family environment. *Developmental Psychology, 30*, 32–43.

Posada, G., Waters, E., Liu, X. D., & Johnson, S. (1998). Marital discord and attachment security: Girls and boys. Manuscript submitted for publication.

Ritchie, K. L., & Miller, G. (1996, June). *Familial conceptualizations and attachment in 3- to 8-year-old children of battered women*. Paper presented at the First International Conference on Children Exposed to Family Violence, Austin, TX.

Rosenberg, M. S. (1984). *The impact of witnessing interparental violence on children's behavior, perceived competence and social problem solving strategies*. Unpublished doctoral dissertation, University of Virginia, Charlottesville.

Rossman, B. B. R. (1994). Children in violent families: Current diagnostic and treatment considerations. *Family Violence and Sexual Assault Bulletin, 10*, 29–34.

Rossman, B. B. R. (1998a, October). *Time heals all: How much and for whom?* Paper presented at the Fourth International Conference on Children Exposed to Family Violence, San Diego.

Rossman, B. B. R. (1998b). Descartes' error and posttraumatic stress disorder: Cognition and emotion in children who are exposed to parental violence. In G. W. Holden, R. Geffner, & E. N. Jouriles (Eds.), *Children exposed to marital violence: Theory, research, and applied issues* (pp. 223–256). Washington, DC: American Psychological Association.

Rossman, B. B. R., Hughes, H. M., & Hanson, K. L. (1998). The victimization of school-age children. In B. B. R. Rossman & M. S. Rosenberg (Eds.), *Multiple victimization of children: Conceptual, developmental, research, and treatment issues*. Binghamton, New York: Haworth Press.

Rossman, B. B. R., & Rosenberg, M. S. (1998). *Multiple victimization of children: Conceptual, developmental, research and treatment issues*. Binghamton, New York: Haworth Press.

Santostefano, S. (1985). *Cognitive control therapy with children and adolescents*. New York: Pergamon Press.

Selye, H. (1956). *The stress of life*. New York: McGraw-Hill.

Sternberg, K. J., Lamb, M. E., Greenbaum, C., Cicchetti, D., Dawud, S., Cortes, R. M., Krispin, O., & Lorey, F. (1993). Effects of domestic violence on children's behavior problems and depression. *Developmental Psychology, 29*, 44–52.

Tolman, E. C. (1932). *Purposive behavior in animals and men*. New York: Appleton-Century-Crofts.

True, W. R., Rice, J., Eisen, S. A., Heath, A. C., Goldberg, J., Lyons, M. J., & Nowak, J. (1993). A twin study of genetic and environmental contributions to liability for posttraumatic stress symptoms. *Archives of General Psychiatry, 50*, 257–264.

van der Kolk, B. A. (1994). The body keeps score: Memory and the evolving psychobiology of posttraumatic stress. *Harvard Review of Psychiatry, 1*, 253–265.

van der Kolk, B. A. (1996). The body keeps score: Approaches to the psychobiology of posttraumatic stress disorder. In B. A. van der Kolk, A. C. McFarlane, & L. Weisaeth (Eds.), *Traumatic stress: The effects of overwhelming experience on mind, body, and society* (pp. 214–241). New York: Guilford.

Weiss, B., Dodge, K. A., Bates, J. E., & Pettit, G. S. (1992). Some consequences of early harsh discipline: Child aggression and a maladaptive social information processing style. *Child Development, 63,* 1321–1335.

West, J. C., Rossman, B. B. R., Ho, J., & Mallah, K. (1999, April). *The relation of violence exposure to children's expectations of adult and peer aggression.* Poster session presented at the meeting of the Society for Research in Child Development, Albuquerque, NM.

White, R. W. (1959). Motivation reconsidered: The concept of competence. *Psychological Review, 66,* 297–333.

Winnicott, D. W. (1965). *The maturational process and the facilitating environment.* New York: International Universities Press.

Exposure to Interparental Violence in Diverse Family Contexts: Impact on Children[1]

A Vietnamese woman, her 3-year-old son, and 5-year-old daughter entered a shelter that primarily served African American and Anglo families, with a staff consisting mostly of the latter as well. In a parenting group with an outside facilitator she discussed the difficulties the children were having, because the "food that was served for meals was very strange." In addition, she talked about the spankings she and the father gave the children, which were in accordance with their expected cultural practices, and the problems she had with the "no spanking" rule in the shelter. Other women in the shelter found her to be rather quiet and standoffish. Three days later she returned to her abuser, in spite of severe and frequent physical and psychological abuse.

****

A woman had called the shelter in order to obtain a safe residence and protection from her abuser. The shelter staff member had conducted a phone intake with the woman, and they were making plans for the woman to enter the shelter that evening with her two children. However, the woman then told the staff member that she was a lesbian and her abuser was another woman. At that point, the mother was then told by the shelter worker that she would not be able to receive services through the shelter, because her presence would make the other women "uncomfortable."

---

1. Chris Chew, Ph.D., contributed to this chapter. She is a former Saint Louis University student in the graduate program in clinical psychology and is now in a post-doctoral position at Geisinger Hospital, Danville, PA.

☐ General Issues for Diverse Types of Families

In this chapter, general issues for children who are not in families from the dominant culture within the mainstream are considered in terms of the impact of exposure to interparental violence. These youngsters include those who are members of ethnic minority groups or whose parents are gay men or lesbian women. This chapter is somewhat different from the previous ones, since much of what follows here is based on conjecture and on extrapolation from other samples of children. Even speculation is difficult, because in both areas of literature, children exposed to interparental violence and culturally or individually diverse youngsters, relatively little information is available. Models describing the impact of exposure for children, especially as it relates to their psychological adjustment, were presented in previous chapters. However, these models were not developed specifically for families from diverse backgrounds. In this chapter some empirically based and conceptually based arguments will be made that represent an educated guess regarding the impact of exposure on nonmainstream children. In addition, some literature will be presented that provides information regarding possibly unique ways children from various backgrounds might respond. This information will be based on material that both describes children in the individually and culturally diverse groups and their general adjustment and discusses typical ways they might respond to adversity and demonstrate distress.

Invisibility

In the past two decades few people conducting research in the area of family violence have paid attention to culturally and individually diverse types of families, rendering them in many ways "invisible." In general, these families have not been considered in terms of any services being designed with their special needs in mind. Some exceptions exist such as a shelter for Asian women in Boston or for Mexican American women in California (Valencia & Van Hoorn, 1999), although they are few and far between. In research, children from specific ethnic minority groups have, for the most part, been combined with Anglo families or with other types of ethnic minorities in samples, with the result that there is little evidence of cultural awareness seen in the literature. Moreover, any discussions related to children of lesbians or gay men have been singularly absent from the family violence literature. This neglect leaves these diverse children without a voice or advocates for their needs (e.g., Reinharz, 1994).

Currently, nontraditional families are in many places rapidly increasing in numbers. For example, it is predicted that non-White and Spanish-speaking youth under age 18 years will constitute 30% of the nation's child and adolescent population by 2005, and 38% by 2020 (Gibbs & Huang, 1989). In addition, it is estimated that there are between 1 and 5 million lesbian mothers in the United States (Falk, 1989; Gottman, 1990; Patterson, 1992), and there are an estimated 6 to 14 million children being raised by gay or lesbian parents. Clearly this invisibility needs to change, and in some places, is changing, though slowly.

Largest Ethnic Groups

At the time of the most recent census, Anglo families constituted approximately 70% of the population (U.S. Bureau of the Census, 1996). Making up the other 30% are a vast number of ethnic groups. Currently in the United States, the four largest ethnic groups are African American (approximately 12% to 15%), Latino (9%), Asian/Pacific (3%), and Native American (0.8% to 1%). The two fastest-growing groups are the Latino and Asian/Pacific. In terms of demographics, the percentages of families of color have been changing steadily over the last 30 years, largely due to immigration patterns. According to the 1995 census, between 1960 and 1990, 11.5 million persons immigrated to the United States (U.S. Bureau of the Census,1996). In 1990, the percentage of foreign-born Hispanic or Latino children was 33%, and for Asian children it was also 33%.

Within each of these groups there is great variety in customs and beliefs. The two largest Spanish-speaking subgroups are from Mexico (62%) and Puerto Rico (13%), while the largest percentage of Asians are of Chinese (22%), Filipino (21%), and Japanese (19%) descent (Aponte & Crouch, 1995). We must keep in mind that within each ethnic/cultural group is found enormous diversity, although we often place them together (e.g., all Mexican, Puerto Rican, or Cuban families as Latino) for ease of discussion. Nevertheless, within each broad group there are some general similarities. Where knowledge about different groups especially matters is in one's approach to intervention. The family's cultural heritage has important implications for conducting clinical work in a culturally sensitive, culturally competent manner (discussed more later and in Chapter 6).

Lesbian Women and Gay Men

Families headed by lesbians and gay men need to be included in the discussion of individual and cultural diversity. It is important to consider the impact on children of being reared in a nontraditional family, a family type that is frequently subject to oppression brought on by homophobia. Demographics indicate that 8% to 12% of parents are gay or lesbian, with an estimated 1.5 to 5 million lesbian mothers living with 6 to 14 million children (Parks, 1998). Most research in this area has focused on lesbian mothers.

Marginalized Groups and Stresses

These changing demographics have challenged researchers in many ways. As noted, these children have been "invisible" to family violence researchers, even though these youngsters live their lives with the experience of the oppression of their families by the dominant culture. Prilleltensky and Gonick (1994) define oppression as a "series of asymmetrical power relations between individuals, genders, classes, communities, nations, and states. These power relations lead to conditions of alienation, misery, inequality, and social injustice among human beings and to the conditions of exploitation, fragmentation, and marginalization" (p. 153). Thus, stressors for minority groups include migration, acculturation, poverty, oppression from racism, and language problems. Often these marginalized families are the ones who go unnoticed and underserved. Although there are parts of the United States where families of color may actually be in the majority (sections of California, Texas, Florida, or New York, for example), they are unlikely to have an equivalent amount of power in relation to the Anglo culture and are frequently subject to oppression.

As mentioned previously, the U.S. culture is becoming increasingly more ethnically and culturally diversified, a trend likely to continue into the next century (McRae, 1994). Social change creates many stressors, perhaps more likely to be noted in economically depressed, politically disadvantaged, or other socially disenfranchised sectors of the population. As a result, families from minority cultures have had to face multiple stressors (Yamamoto, Silva, Ferrari, & Nukarija, 1997). One of the biggest problems for ethnic minority families is poverty, and they are overrepresented in percentage of families below the poverty line. For example, of children and adolescents under the age of 18, 12% of Anglos, 40% of African Americans, 32% of Latinos, 17% of Asian/Pacific Islanders, and 40% of Native Americans live below the poverty line (Aponte & Crouch, 1995).

In a recent review examining the relationship between socioeconomic disadvantage and child development, McLoyd (1998) concluded that persistent poverty has detrimental effects on IQ scores, school achievement, and socioemotional functioning. She identified factors such as higher rates of perinatal complications, reduced access to resources, increased exposure to lead, and less home-based cognitive stimulation as partially accounting for the diminished cognitive functioning often seen in poor children. These factors, along with lower teacher expectancies, poorer academic-readiness skills, and possibly poorer educational opportunities, also appear to contribute to lower levels of school achievement among poor children. Moreover, a rise in the proportion of poor children who are from ethnic minority backgrounds has been noted, and McLoyd points out that both internalizing and externalizing problems become more prevalent the longer children have been living in poverty.

McLoyd contends that the link between socioeconomic disadvantage and children's socioemotional functioning may be at least partially mediated by harsh, inconsistent parenting and children's elevated exposure to acute and chronic stressors. Parental depressive symptoms and harsh, inconsistent parenting arise partly from the overwhelming number of negative life events and conditions that confront adults who are poor. According to McLoyd, poverty and economic stress contribute to these socioemotional problems in children partly by increasing parents' tendencies to discipline in a punitive and inconsistent fashion and to ignore children's dependency needs.[2] In addition, poor and low SES children themselves also experience more negative and undesirable life events and adverse conditions than nonpoor youngsters, and this overload then likely places demands on them that exceed their resources. In general, un-

---

2. However, results from Deater-Decker, Dodge, Bates, and Pettit (1996) indicate that one must be cautious in interpreting "harsh" parenting to include all corporal punishment, especially in ethnic minority families. Deater-Decker et al. found that in their study of physical discipline among African American and European American mothers and its links to children's externalizing behaviors, physical discipline was related to higher externalizing scores, but only for Anglo children. They pointed out that the meaning of physical discipline may differ depending on the family's cultural heritage. For example, among Anglos, the presence of harsh discipline may imply an out-of-control, parent-centered household for some families, whereas a lack of physical discipline among African American parents may indicate an abdication of the parenting role for others. Authoritarian parenting may not generalize across ethnic and cultural groups. Cultural meanings for children of forms of discipline must be considered.

desirable life events constitute a consistent predictor of socioemotional adjustment, and adversity that is chronic also takes its toll on children's mental health (McLoyd, 1998).

Professionals will likely need to respond to these associated problems that have traditionally plagued minority children and adolescents as well as other groups that have become socially disenfranchised. Problems such as family violence, substance abuse, PTSD, underemployment, and poverty are likely to continue to affect ethnic minorities. Although members of mainstream society face these problems, cultural and ethnic minority groups are at greater risk because they are overrepresented in socioeconomically disadvantaged groups that are likely to be experiencing stress, mental distress, and incidents of violence (Yamamoto et al., 1997).

Risk Factors

These stresses from oppression, poverty, and educational disadvantage can be risk factors for children's problems. Approximately two decades ago, Rutter (1979) in a now classic study identified six risk factors for child psychopathology, which included (1) marital conflict, (2) low social status, (3) overcrowding or large family size, (4), paternal criminality, (5) maternal psychiatric disorder, and (6) admission of child to foster care. However, these were established on mostly Anglo populations; therefore, they may or may not all apply for culturally/ethnically diverse families. It remains to be seen what role these factors will play in predicting children's difficulties in non-Anglo families. One of Rutter's main points was that the impact of stressors is likely to be cumulative. Nontraditional families with family violence are likely to experience a number of these stressors: marital distress/conflict; possibly overcrowding; and low social status (with a large percentage of families below the poverty line). Moreover, they very likely also have unique stressors, including racism and acculturation issues.

More recently, Emery and Laumann-Billings (1998) modified Brofenbrenner's ecological view of risk factors more specifically for situations of family violence. These included four levels that interact to produce an impact: (1) aspects of the individual, such as personality characteristics; (2) the immediate social context, especially the family, including family structure and size, acute stressors (such as loss of job or death in the family), characteristic styles of resolving conflicts or of parenting; (3) features of the community, which can include poverty, lack of social cohesion, social isolation, unemployment, inadequate housing, or other daily stressors, as well as community violence; and (4) factors in society, such as cultural beliefs and values, physical punishment, and violence in the media. The above risk factors might be helpful in terms of making "predictions" about the impact of interparental violence on children from diverse backgrounds.

Limitations of Current Literature

Knowledge in these areas is lacking because the literature that is available at present is sparse and methodologically limited. The research that has been conducted at the intersection of domestic violence and culturally diverse families suffers from the difficulties associated with both areas of literature. In domestic violence studies, some prevalence studies have been conducted. These have been primarily limited to incidence reports from public sources, survey-based research on family violence, and self-report surveys (Kanuha, 1997), each of which has its own source of bias and inaccuracy. Families outside the dominant culture have rarely been studied, and there are few descriptive or comparative investigations that assess the impact of domestic violence on women and children from diverse ethnic and cultural groups (Kanuha, 1997). Information that is available is discussed below.

☐ Ethnically, Individually, and Culturally Diverse Families

It is important to keep in mind when reading the following section that the information presented is meant to be informative. The following descriptions are intended to alert readers to the likelihood that families from different backgrounds possess particular beliefs or values. When working with families of color, it is important to ascertain their individual acculturation levels as well as how much they subscribe to a specific world view or how essential a particular value is to them.

African American Families

Like many other families of color, African Americans usually place great importance on family. The extended family provides support in many ways, including child rearing, financial assistance, or assistance to each other in times of crisis (Black, 1996). Religion and spirituality are valued sources of support, and many families are interested in preserving or reestablishing a focus on the music, arts, and food of Africa. A strong work ethic, emphasis on education, and an achievement orientation also characterize African American families. Frequently they use physical measures for discipline (M. K. Ho, 1992). Typically the gender roles are more egalitarian and flexible, with a less rigid division of family tasks (Hatchett, 1991). Also similar to other families of color, where there is a continuum of values from strongly ethnic to strongly Westernized, the African American families' values vary from strongly Afrocentric to strongly Anglo. Families generally fall into one of four categories of ethnic identity: Afrocentric, bicultural, Anglo, or marginal (Dana, 1993). Racism and discrimination are major social forces with which they must contend.

Latino Families

In Latino families, there is also a strong emphasis on extended family and family obligations. The emphasis is more on the group than on the individual, although this varies with acculturation level. The family guarantees protection and caretaking for as long as the person stays in the system. It also traditionally offers the individual a measure of control for aggression and violence (Garcia-Preto, 1996). Regarding gender roles, there is a sense of hierarchy, with the father being superior and head of the family; mothers are supposed to obey him (M. K. Ho, 1992). Spirituality and fatalism also are prominent values. At times their respect for authority may keep them from speaking up and asserting their rights. In terms of acculturation, many struggle with culture shock for years as well as with language differences. Again families vary along a continuum of embracing Hispanic or Anglo values or being bicultural. Hispanics also encounter racism, with darker-skinned Latinos experiencing more discrimination (Garcia-Preto, 1996).

Asian Families

Similar to the other families discussed so far, in Asian families the family unit is highly prized, and the group is emphasized over the individual. Traditionally, individuals' personal actions reflect not only on themselves, but also on their extended family (E. Lee, 1996). Obligations and shame are the mechanisms that traditionally were used to help reinforce societal expectations and proper behavior. If an individual behaves improperly, he or she will "lose face" and the family and community may withdraw support (M. K. Ho, 1992). Roles are clearly defined, based on age, gender, and social status. The husband assumes the role of leadership and authority and is the protector of the family, while the mother is dominated by his authority (E. Lee, 1996). The father's role is to discipline the children while the mother provides support.

　　Other Asian values include self-control (maintaining modesty, being humble and not intruding on another), inconspicuousness (being verbally passive at times), and the "middle position" (no one stands out from others). Also of importance are a sense of fatalism and stoicism as well as being highly sensitive to the opinions of peers and subordinating oneself to them (M. K. Ho, 1992). Asian families, too, can be found along a continuum of transition ranging from traditional values to Westernized values: traditional families, "cultural conflict" families, bicultural families, "American" families, and biracial families (E. Lee, 1996).

American Indian Families

In American Indian families, identity is tied not only to the family, but to the tribe as well (Sutton & Broken Nose, 1996). The extended family provides structure and obligations, and there is communal sharing of all possessions among the tribal members. Nevertheless, individuality and mutual respect are part of the value system. No one tries to control another. There is an emphasis on listening in communication, working together, getting along, and not being competitive. The spiritual relationship between man and nature is important as is harmony with nature and a sense that time is counted by natural phenomena (M. K. Ho, 1992). Fatalism, endurance, and patience are common themes. The acculturation continuum exists among American Indian families as well, with traditional, bicultural, acculturated, and "pantraditional" families (i.e., those who are struggling to redefine or reconfirm their lost culture; M. K. Ho, 1992).

☐ Interparental Conflict in Ethnically, Individually, and Culturally Diverse Families

As discussed by Kanuha (1997), there are a number of factors that affect the woman of color and her family differently than women of the dominant culture that will be briefly described in this section. For example, there are several reasons battered women of color do not currently utilize either mental health services or battered women's shelters as often as Anglo women. One reason is the impact of institutional racism. They may not have had their needs met from governmental agencies or service workers. In addition, women of color may be reluctant to bring attention to themselves for fear of contributing to the stigmatization of families of color as pathological (Kanuha, 1997). In addition, there is also the "superwoman" expectation, in which women of color are expected to be resilient in the face of all odds.

Another factor that contributes to lack of information and lack of help seeking is the racial/ethnic context of heterosexism and gendered role behaviors (Kanuha, 1997). Expectations regarding the role of women in different cultures contribute to women's oppression in a patriarchal society, and religious influences also contribute to the occurrence of domestic violence (Ferrer, 1998; C. K. Ho, 1996). Hetereosexism is most evident in battering between lesbian couples. As Kanuha points out, even in same-sex relationships between women, "one partner's implicit sanction to dominate or control her partner is an objective and logical extension of the patriarchal definition of relationships" (p. 438). All of these points need to be kept in mind in order to understand the struggles of nonmajority families.

Following from the above, one major issue when it comes to assessment and intervention for all diverse groups is that the clinical work must be conducted in a culturally competent, culturally sensitive fashion. Shelter programs that take the family members' ethnic/cultural background into account will be more helpful. Shelter workers and other service providers must be aware of the special needs of the children from diverse cultures and implement the services to them and their mothers in a culturally competent, sensitive manner (Hughes & Marshall, 1995). Children from groups different from the shelter workers need special attention paid to them so that their individual developmental and mental health needs are not overlooked.

Negative Impact on Children

As we discussed previously, we know from research with mainstream families that, for the most part, the impact on children of exposure to wife abuse is negative. However, the extent of the difficulties and their severity vary based on a number of factors that have been delineated in the previous chapters. Generally the impact is apparent in the following areas: behavioral and trauma-related, emotional, cognitive/school, and social (social skills and attachment) functioning. Based on research with children in shelters for battered women, overall the proportion of children with moderate to severe problems is approximately 40%. Other children seem to be more mildly affected, depending on what types of behaviors one is measuring and who provides the report.

Moreover, several factors have been identified that seem to be associated with greater or lesser difficulties (Hughes & Luke, 1998; Hughes, Luke, Cangiano, & Peterson,

1998). For example, the duration of the physical violence the children witness and the severity of the psychological abuse to which the children are exposed make a difference. If the length of abuse is the children's entire life or the psychological abuse is more frequent and more severe or both, this contributes to greater emotional and behavioral difficulties for the children. Furthermore, for African American children, the level of the mother's parenting stress, especially whether the mother experiences her child as difficult to care for, plus whether she expresses hostile feelings toward the child, also make a difference in children's adjustment (Hughes et al., 1998).

As mentioned previously in other chapters, proposed mechanisms to explain the impact of interparental violence that have been discussed include the direct mechanisms of modeling and stress. In addition, indirect mechanisms have also been proposed; these are basically related to interactions between parents and children (see Chapters 2, 3, and 4). Again, these mechanisms have been proposed for the most part based on investigations that were conducted with no distinction between majority and nonmajority families. Similarly, the samples upon which the above-mentioned results are based are almost entirely Anglo and low income. The majority of the families are recruited from shelters and therefore are very likely to be low SES families with few resources. We know little about higher income or non-Anglo families, and it is unclear whether the above mechanisms, moderators, mediators, or theories hold for them. However, we do know from Masten and Coatsworth (1998) that in studies of various samples, they found that the factors that are protective and lead to children's resilient outcomes are protective in both favorable and unfavorable environments.

Any conjecture about what the impact of exposure to family violence is likely to be on these diverse youngsters is just that: speculation and conjecture. Regarding the mechanisms through which the impact is seen, there does not seem to be any reason one would not see similar reactions in these youngsters to the problems noted in Anglo children, although some group-specific difficulties might be identified. It is likely that the mechanisms would still operate directly, through modeling and stress, and indirectly, through characteristics of the parent–child relationship and discipline. The associated features, often considered mediators or moderators or both, probably would be similar for nontraditional families and would include those factors that are both child-related and situational/contextual. Clearly, it will take time to see if the mechanisms operate in similar ways and whether the associated factors that function as mediators or moderators for minority children act in a comparable way as they do with children from the dominant culture. Regarding adjustment, it is also likely that one would see a similar impact on children of color as with youngsters from the dominant culture. Behavioral, emotional, social, and cognitive areas of functioning would conceivably be disrupted, although the problems could be more severe due to the greater adversity children from these diverse families encounter. Again, some group-specific difficulties might be expected, and some examples regarding various groups of children of color showing distress differently are discussed below.

African American Families

Interparental Conflict. Regarding the prevalence of family violence, Hampton and Gelles (1994) examined spousal violence in Black families. They found that, based on telephone interviews and using questions from the Conflict Tactics Scales, 17% of wives had at least one violent incident within the past year, and

7%had experienced severe violence. Black wives were found to be 1.23 times more likely to experience minor violence and 2.36 times more likely to experience severe violence than Anglo wives. Neff, Holamon, and Schluter (1995) also found in a community sample that African American females, in particular, were most likely to report being beaten up and beating a spouse. This finding remained after controlling statistically for demographic variables, financial stress, social desirability, and sex role traditionalism. Similarly, Sorenson, Upchurch, and Shen (1996) found that in Anglo, Latino, and African American families, being younger, an urban dweller, less educated, a low-income earner, and African American were risk factors for being more likely to be violent toward their spouse. Understanding some of the reasons for this greater risk among African American women would be very informative and needs to be a priority for investigation.

Culturally Specific Manifestations of Distress.   There are several types of problems one might see when these children are distressed, based on literature (Allen & Majidi-Ahi, 1989). Black American children are likely to experience behavioral and academic problems as well as emotional difficulties. Poor academic achievement often comes first, then learning problems and aggression. Conduct problems are common, and African American adolescents are hospitalized at rates 2 to 3 times higher than Anglos. Other important mental health issues include higher rates of depression among males and low income Blacks. Suicide rates are increasing, and it is now the third leading cause of death. In addition, school drop-out rates and substance abuse are high, according to Gibbs (1989).

Because service providers are likely to see more externalizing-type problems as well as school difficulties, rather than internalizing, it is important also to be aware of these latter problems because they are easier to overlook. Clearly, then, workers need to be especially watchful for signs of depression and suicide as well as acting out.

In terms of gender roles, both boys and girls are socialized to be aggressive and assertive, and also expressive and nurturing (Allen & Majidi-Ahi, 1989). Because African American children and adolescents likely have been raised with more egalitarian gender-role socialization models, both boys and girls might show both depression or anxiety and disobedience or aggression. Therefore, it might be likely that both sexes of children would manifest both externalizing and internalizing types of problems.

Moreover, according to Gibbs (1989), a major issue and stress for Black American adolescents is racism, with both working class and middle class Blacks having to deal with prejudice and discrimination. Therefore, these are the types of difficulties clinicians and others would be most likely to see if these children were distressed as a result of being exposed to interparental violence.

Special Considerations.   Given the cultural style of egalitarian relationships, and the types of difficulties one is likely to see among African American children, it would be helpful to include relevant topics in groups conducted for the children. In terms of dealing with stress, acknowledging the negative impact of racism and addressing children's concerns about it, and providing some suggestions regarding ways to cope with it could be beneficial. Tutoring for school difficulties and information or treatment regarding substance abuse would be helpful. In addition, because children of both genders are raised to be assertive and aggressive, it is important to teach nonviolent conflict resolution techniques to both boys and girls.

Latino Families

Interparental Conflict.   Regarding prevalence, Kantor, Jasinski, and Aldarondo (1994) found that, as a group, Latino families have similar rates of spouse abuse as Anglo families. This finding was replicated by Neff et al. (1995) among Mexican Americans and Anglos. However, considerable variation has been seen within different ethnic groups of Hispanic families. For example, about 20.4% of Puerto Rican wives reported husband-to-wife violence, 10.5% of Mexican wives, 17.9% of Mexican American wives, 2.5% of Cuban wives, and 9.9% of Anglo wives in their survey. The authors felt that power theories related to domestic violence explained these differences better than any cultural reasons. One evident difference was that men who had been born in the United States were more likely to abuse their wives.

Internationally, McWhirter (1999) reported similar prevalence among Chilean women, with 25% of women experiencing physical abuse at the hands of a male partner, whereas Ellsberg, Caldera, Herrera, Winkvist, and Kullgren (1999) found higher rates for Nicaraguan women, with 52% reporting partner physical abuse. Ferrer's (1998) results were somewhat in the middle, where she indicated that little information is available on Puerto Rican women, although surveys have revealed a lifetime prevalence rate that ranged from 33% to 60%.

Culturally Specific Manifestations of Distress.   Based on the literature, Mexican American children and adolescents seem to have problems at approximately the same rates as Anglos, and the difficulties are similar (Ramirez, 1989). Substance abuse, depression, anxiety, and conduct disorders are among the most frequent problems for Mexicans. M. K. Ho (1992) presented clinic-based data that indicate Mexican American girls showed more depressive features than Mexican American boys. Ho also stated that the literature strongly indicated a direct positive correlation between the Hispanic child's level of acculturation and behavior problems, with the closer the child's acculturation to Western values, the greater the difficulties. Bicultural children seemed to be the most well adjusted.

According to Arroyo (1997), discrimination and other environmental stressors, plus cultural identity and customs, are sources of stress for Mexican and Mexican American children. All of these stressors, combined with exposure to interparental violence, likely would result in the above-mentioned types of problems for the children. Due to the more highly proscribed gender roles in Latino families, it might be more usual to see internalizing-type problems among girls and externalizing-type difficulties among boys (M. K. Ho, 1992). Thus, based on the scant literature, it seems that Latino children's difficulties are rather similar to those of Anglos, although, as Arroyo (1997) points out, not much is known about these youngsters and how they manifest distress.

However, it seems that acculturation may play a role in occurrence of violence in the family. There is some evidence for more acculturated Latino men being more likely to abuse their women partners. Behavioral problems are seen in the children as well when family members' acculturation level is more Westernized. This is in line with literature that reports increased amounts of aggressiveness among the children when they are in families where there is more abuse.

Special Considerations.   For Latino youngsters, acculturation issues and cultural identity would be major topics to address. For boys especially, it would be important to discuss the role of men in the culture. Healthy male–female relationships would be crucial to address, as would nonviolent conflict resolution skills. Internalizing and externalizing problems would likely need attention.

Asian Families

Interparental Conflict.   C. K. Ho (1996) suggests that traditional Asian values of close family ties, harmony, and order may not discourage physical and verbal abuse in the privacy of one's home and may only support the minimization and hiding of such problems. Based on a feminist analysis, the author points out that the role of the cultural values of fatalism, perseverance, and self-restraint play a part in reducing the incentive of Asian American women to change their oppressive situation. While reported cases of domestic violence in Asian American communities may be low, it is unclear whether this low reported frequency reflects an actual lower rate, Asian Americans' lack of utilization of public assistance, inadequate mental health services available to Asian Americans, or some other reason. The author notes that, in general, Asian Americans tend to hide domestic violence problems within the family and avoid outside intervention to prevent "loss of face." However, there are some differences regarding family violence among Asian groups. In her research C. K. Ho (1996) found that physical discipline toward children was used among Chinese, Vietnamese, Korean, and Laotian families. Chinese women estimated that 20% to 30% of Chinese husbands hit their wives, although it is not sanctioned in Chinese culture. In contrast, Vietnamese and Laotians appeared to be more tolerant of physical violence in the home.

Similarly, M. Y. Lee and Au (1998) as well as Tang (1997) concluded that Chinese culture perpetuates exploitation of women. The latter author investigated three groups of Chinese families: those in shelters for battered women, discordant couples, and nonviolent couples. Both verbal and physical wife abuse were related to negative effects on women and children. The husband's abusive behavior toward wives and children was associated with children's aggressive behavior. Comparisons among the shelter, discordant, and intact groups showed that women in shelters experienced the most abuse by their husbands and were the most depressed and anxious. Women in the shelter and discordant groups experienced higher levels of general distress than intact families. Children in the shelter witnessed more interparental violence and experienced more abuse by their fathers than children in the other groups.

Similar to the values found among the Vietnamese regarding tolerance of physical abuse in the home, Yoshihama and Sorenson (1994) noted that at least 60% of the Japanese women they surveyed reported some type of physical abuse by a male partner, including being slapped or hit with a fist, or kicked or thrown around. This violence cut across all SES levels. Some of the children witnessed the father beating the mother, and some children were abused by the father as well. In addition, Yoshihama (1998) described some cultural-specific forms of domestic violence, including overturning the dinner table and throwing liquid at the woman. She concluded that, overall, Japanese men's use of violence against their partners was generally condoned and not recognized as a social problem.

Culturally Specific Manifestations of Distress.   Based on available literature, the types of problems one might see when Asian children are distressed varies with their acculturation (Huang & Ying, 1989). Several sets of authors note that as children become more acculturated, aggression rates rise, and there are also identity conflicts. Anxiety is often manifest in somatic concerns and complaints, sleep and appetite disturbances, and disruptions in school performance (Huang & Ying, 1989; Lung & Sue, 1997). In addition, according to Lung and Sue, the types of problems that might be seen when there are mental health issues include rates of suicide that are higher than Anglos.

Thus, difficulties seen in Asian children seem likely to be more somatic in nature, with sleep and appetite disturbances, as well as decreases in school performance. Acculturation may also play a role in the nature of the problems seen in the children, as well as attitudes toward violence held by specific Asian groups. Asian values in general lead to hiding any spousal abuse, and some Asian groups feel that some physical violence within the family is not out of the ordinary. Moreover, it would not be unusual to find that in more acculturated families, higher levels of aggressiveness would be noted, especially among boys.

Special Considerations. Very few resources for Chinese or other Asian families are available, although M. Y. Lee and Au (1998) described some of the services that are beginning to be accessible to battered women. Issues for children would include concerns regarding ethnic identity, particularly as acculturation levels change. For children from Asian groups that are used to physical violence being expressed within the family, extra care might be taken in working with them regarding nonviolent relationships. Again, learning about healthy male–female relationships and nonviolent conflict resolution would be helpful. Also, be on the lookout for depression and suicidal tendencies. Because many difficulties are manifested somatically, service providers would have to pay attention to headaches and stomachaches as well as school problems. Trauma symptoms also might be exhibited differently, so workers would need to be careful not to overlook them.

American Indian Families

Interparental Conflict. Chester, Robin, Koss, Lopez, and Goldman (1994) stated that, in general, prevalence of family violence among American Indians is very difficult to establish; it is made even more difficult because of the heterogeneity within American Indian tribes. Some tribes are matriarchal and some are patriarchal, for example. According to Chester et al., estimates ranged from 26% to 76%, with about 50% to 55% of women being physically abused by their partner. These estimates were as high as 80% in urban areas. In addition, high rates of alcoholism and depression are also seen in these families (Chester et al.). Norton and Manson (1995) point out that no community surveys are available that provide lifetime rates of interparental violence for American Indians. However, they asked women at an urban Indian health center to fill out a mental health needs assessment and found that approximately 56% reported their parents were violent toward each other. This percentage was the same for women regardless of whether they had experienced domestic violence in their current relationship.

Culturally Specific Manifestations of Distress. In general, little is known about the mental health of American Indians and even less about their children and the way they manifest distress. American Indian children face a variety of problems (M. K. Ho, 1992). Otitis media is common, resulting in mild to moderate hearing loss or difficulties with speech and language. In addition, due to the rampant alcoholism, children are born with Fetal Alcohol Syndrome and Fetal Alcohol Effects, and children of alcoholic parents are often neglected or abandoned. Developmental disabilities and learning disabilities are also common (M. K. Ho, 1992). Anxiety is the fourth most common mental health problem for children, and suicide is the second leading cause of death for adolescents. The suicide rate is four times higher than in the general population. Racism is also difficult to deal with, and many boys drop out of school early as a result (M. K. Ho, 1992).

According to LaFromboise & Low (1989), approximately 63% of American Indians reside in cities in the United States. The stressors they encounter include frequent relocation, poverty, chronic unemployment, and substantial levels of alcohol and drug abuse. These families are among the most "invisible" of all to mental health practitioners as well as shelter workers. These families are likely to have an especially high number of stressors with which to deal. As a result, perhaps a concomitantly large number of difficulties would be seen among the children.

Special Considerations. American Indian children in particular need services delivered in line with cultural expectations and in conjunction with a tribal healer (Paniagua, 1998). Because of the vast array of difficulties the children have, they must have access to services that can meet their developmental needs in as many areas as possible. Teenagers in particular especially need services regarding depression, substance abuse, and suicide.

In general, for children of color, some similarities in the youngsters' difficulties were noted, with some differences among the diverse groups as well (e.g., Asian children and somatic symptoms). Acculturation issues are clearly important to take into consideration, as are the differences in the way distress might be manifested in different cultures. The oppressive impact of racism may exacerbate the effect of other stressors, so that one may see more difficulties among children of color than among Anglos, especially if the former have had to contend with substantial amounts of racism. Special consideration for all groups include teaching nonviolent conflict resolution skills in ways that are culturally compatible. Similarly, teaching about male–female relationships and relationships in general must be done in a manner that fits with the child's world view.

Families Headed by Lesbians or Gay Men

Interparental Conflict. Regarding prevalence, in one of the first discussions of same-sex abuse, Renzetti (1992) indicated that the incidence of violence in same-sex couples ranged from 11% to 45%. Although these figures are not based on nationally representative samples, it appears that the extent of relationship violence in gay and lesbian couples is at least as high as violence in heterosexual couples. Also, it is not a rare, one-time event. Renzetti (1992) reported that of the 100 lesbians she interviewed, only 8% reported one or two incidents of violence, whereas 54% had experienced 10 or more incidents. The violence included physical as well as emotional and sexual abuse. One distinct aspect of emotional abuse includes "outing" the partner (Renzetti, 1995).

Researchers also believe that although the partners are of the same sex, there is no pattern of mutual violence in gay and lesbian relationships (Letellier, 1994; Renzetti, 1992). Although the literature on violence in lesbian and gay relationships is somewhat limited, it appears that power and power imbalances are what precipitate the occurrence of couple violence (Lockhart, White, Causby, & Isaac, 1994).

A number of other authors have recently provided prevalence estimates, and all surmise that the prevalence is likely to be similar to heterosexual couples. Wiehe (1998), as well as Island and Letellier (1991), estimate that approximately 11% to 20% of gay male couples experience physical violence, whereas Loulan (1987) estimated about 17% of lesbian couples also do. Other estimates for women couples range greatly from 15% to 70%, depending on the definition of physical abuse used (Renzetti, 1998). Waterman, Dawson, and Bologna (1989) provided an estimate for gay men as about 18%, whereas Harms (1995) estimated a prevalence rate of about 25% to 26%. Merrill (1998) also concluded that the prevalence rates are likely to be similar to heterosexual couples.

Special Considerations and Manifestations of Distress.   These children have some special concerns and in some ways are even more "invisible" than are ethnic minority children. One of the main reasons that these children have not been studied may be related to their "invisibility" in our society. There are many reasons why children living in a home where there is interparental violence between their same-sex parents may not be identified. First, the sexual identity of their parents may not be acknowledged either because the parents are assumed to be heterosexual or because the parents' actively hide their identities for fear of retribution (Patterson & Chan, 1996). Often gay or lesbian parents will conceal their sexual identities not only outside of the home, but also from their own children (Dunne, 1998). Even if the parents do not hide their sexual identity, they may conceal the fact that there is violence in their relationship. Similar to families of color, according to Renzetti (1995), interparental violence among same-sex partners may be hidden to prevent further stigmatization of the gay and lesbian community. Violence in gay and lesbian relationships may also remain unrecognized because of the stereotypical belief that only men are batterers and only women are victims of interparental violence, because same-sex relationships are believed to be egalitarian and immune to interparental violence and because of the homophobia in the legal system and in domestic violence shelters (Renzetti, 1995).

Although it is likely that the impact of battering on same-sex parents is similar to the impact on heterosexual parents, the effects may be exacerbated by issues specific to their identification as homosexual. According to Hammond (1988), gay men and lesbians that are victims of interparental violence often do not have access to the same services as battered women. For example, shelters are designed primarily for women, and the assumption is often that the women are heterosexual. Even if lesbians are welcomed into the shelter system, the staff may not be sensitive to the unique issues these women may face, and residents may not be receptive to sharing common living space with women who identify as lesbians. As a result, many lesbians may not take advantage of the shelters, and those who do often choose not to reveal their sexual identity and are therefore unable to obtain optimal services for themselves and their children. The situation is even worse for gay men who are often not even welcome within the shelter system.

Another issue raised by Hammond (1988) is that gay men and lesbians have very limited legal protection. Not only do the parents face the threat of custody disputes from former spouses, but they may also have no legal recourse with their current partner. For example, they may not be able to obtain orders of protection for either themselves or their children. Also, if the parent being abused is not the child's custodial parent, they have no right to take the child from the situation, and if they choose to leave, they may need to leave the child with the abusive partner.

Finally, Hammond points out that often same-sex partners share many of the same friends, and by addressing the issues of violence in the relationship, the recipients of violence may risk losing valuable friendships. They also may fear being ostracized by members of the gay community who do not want to admit that violence exists within same-sex dyads. In either case, there may be a threat or actual loss of significant social support as the result of addressing the violence. This is especially detrimental to gay men and lesbians, since many of them have already been rejected by their families because of their sexual identities.

According to longitudinal studies (Patterson,1997; Tasker & Golombok, 1997), no significant problems have been identified in the children of lesbians, with generally no differences between these children and children of straight parents. The research presented thus far suggests that the adjustment of, and the parenting received by, children of gay and lesbian parents is not much different than that of children of heterosexual parents. Furthermore, the interparental violence in gay and lesbian relationships appears to be similar to that found in heterosexual relationships. One may then tend to conclude that the effects of interparental violence on children of gay and lesbian parents would be similar to those found in children of heterosexual parents. More specifically, one may expect to find these children exhibiting difficulties in the four main areas of functioning that are problematic for children of battered women: psychological/emotional (or trauma symptoms), somatic/health, behavioral, and school-related (Hughes & Graham-Bermann, 1998). Although it is likely that these same difficulties appear in children of battered gay men and lesbians, several characteristics of these families may result in a differential impact on children. The reason that these families may differ from heterosexual families is related to the interaction between the oppression they face in a heterosexist society and the presence of the interparental violence.

At this point, more research is needed on homophobia and how these children cope with the stresses they encounter. There is anecdotal information regarding reports of teasing by peers. These children report some concerns regarding being harassed by peers (O'Connell, 1993; Tasker & Golombok, 1995). However, the balance of the literature to date says children are not affected (Patterson, 1995; Tasker & Golombok, 1995). Nevertheless, at this point there is only a handful of studies where investigators have examined teasing or homophobia or both that children might have encountered. A recent study indicated that college students attributed more problems to the hypothetical child of a divorced lesbian mother than the child of a heterosexual mother (King & Black, 1999). Thus, homophobia as a stress needs to be studied in more detail.

In addition, it must be remembered when investigating types of problems seen in these children that only middle-class, Anglo children have been studied, and in these Anglo families, most had incomes above $30,000, and 75% were college educated. The story might be different with less well educated families and those with fewer resources. Reflect on the stresses a Latina mother who is a lesbian, living below the poverty line, and being beaten by her partner would encounter. Greene (1994) considers lesbian women of color to be living with the "triple jeopardy" of sexism, racism, and homophobia. It is likely that her children might respond to the combination of stresses with discernable levels of problems.

All of the difficult issues that have been presented above as unique to gay men and lesbians who are victims of violence from their partners can lead to increased levels of stress for same-sex parents involved in violence from their spouse. As has been suggested by previous researchers, the level of stress in the household may be one of the mechanisms through which interparental violence exerts an impact on the children. The stress may affect the children directly or can be indirect, by influencing parent–child interaction and parental disciplinary practices. Although there have been no studies documenting that there is an increased level of stress in the households of battered gay men and lesbians relative to battered heterosexual women, as was previously mentioned, it could be that the homophobia inherent in our society may contribute to relatively higher stress levels in these homes. It remains to be seen whether these high levels of stress will have a more substantial impact on the children.

In summary, although there may be more than a million children who have witnessed interparental violence between same-sex parents, there has been no research conducted that documents the impact this exposure to the violence has had on these children. It appears that in nonabusive gay and lesbian households, the children experience parenting that is similar to that found in heterosexual households, and children of lesbian and gay parents are equally as well adjusted as children of heterosexual parents. Therefore, the impact of witnessing violence between same-sex parents may be expected to be similar to the impact of witnessing violence between heterosexual parents. Furthermore, if differences in the children's adjustment do exist, these differences may be related to the increased stress in same-sex households that result from a lack of support resources, poor legal protection, and diminished social support.

Overall, research is lacking in areas related to domestic violence and ethnic minority and gay and lesbian families. Currently the area is wide open, with any type of study welcome. Below are a number of suggestions aimed at providing a focus for investigations and improving the knowledge that is available regarding these families.

☐ Implications

Implications for Research

Probably the clearest implication for research is sorely evident, which is the need for more specific investigations of children from different backgrounds, taking into account individual factors, family and parenting variables, community factors, and societal variables. This certainly seems like a tall order, and, in order to begin, the general issues need to be broken down into smaller steps. Based upon information presented in Chapters 2, 3, and 4, it would be helpful to examine whether the mechanisms of impact, direct and indirect, operate similarly for children from the dominant and nondominant cultures. Along the same lines, it would be instructive to investigate whether the theories hypothesized to explain the impact would be borne out with families of diverse background. In addition, factors that are associated with better or worse adjustment need to be studied in terms of risk or protective factors that might mediate or moderate the impact of exposure to family violence.

Prevalence.   Another step in the right direction would be to include more accurate statistics on prevalence of family violence and types of family violence among the various families who are culturally and individually diverse. This would help researchers and clinicians alike in identifying families in need of assistance and assist with prevention efforts by allowing them to target the families who are especially at risk. Neff et al. (1995) provide us with a model for ways to begin this process.

Individual Diversity and Values.   In terms of cultural values that maintain family violence, it seems clear that some cultural values function to maintain the oppression of women (for example, hierarchical gender roles in Latino and Asian families, or Confucian philosophy among Chinese women) and enhance the chances that a woman will be controlled by her male partner through violent means. In addition, it seems for some groups, perhaps Latino men in particular, as they become more acculturated, the men are more likely to engage in violence against their wives. More egalitarian relationships between African American men and women may contribute to higher levels of violence among those couples. Thus, researchers need to pay closer attention to cultural values and acculturation issues and values as they relate to attitudes and behaviors toward domestic violence.

Resilience and Risk.   In keeping with the focus on stressors and impact of stress, it would be helpful to have research on children who are resilient as well as those who are distressed (Hughes & Graham-Bermann, 1998). The characteristics that might protect children from experiencing a negative impact when they are subject to adversity need to be investigated. Although protective factors for children have been delineated for Anglo children (e.g., Masten & Coatsworth, 1998), they have not yet been delimited specifically for families and children from the nondominant culture.

According to Masten and Coatsworth (1998), characteristics of resilient children and adolescents that have been identified are the following: (1) at the individual level—good intellectual functioning; appealing, sociable, easygoing disposition; self-efficacy, self-confidence, high self-esteem; talents; faith; (2) at the family level—close relationship with caring parent figure; authoritative parenting: warmth, structure, high expectations; socioeconomic advantages; connections to supportive family networks; and (3) within the extrafamilial context—bonds to prosocial adults outside the family; connections to prosocial organizations; attending effective schools. Due to the fact that Masten and Coatsworth feel the two most important protective factors are intelligence and good parenting, those factors need to be investigated specifically for each different cultural group in order to examine whether the protective factors apply equally to all culturally or individually diverse groups. In addition, it will be important to address the heterogeneity within the diverse groups and understand the limitations of our findings where appropriate.

Methodology.   In terms of methodology, qualitative methods of inquiry are ideal at the current stage of research and would include more interview and narrative approaches to collecting information. This would facilitate the process of gathering data that is in the women and children's own words and thus would not impose a structure on the information by the researcher (Strauss & Corbin, 1990). As more becomes known about diverse families through qualitative methodologies, more quantitative methods can be implemented. For example, standardized measures can be developed that are appropriate for the different groups of children.

Implications for Clinical Practice

Cultural Sensitivity.   This quality in workers and service providers will go a long way in helping to provide better assistance to families of color or gay and lesbian family members. Staff need to educate themselves about diverse families and understand how there is diversity within ethnic and culturally diverse groups as well. A number of good sources are available, including Dana (1993), Gibbs and Huang (1989), M. K. Ho (1992), Johnson-Powell and Yamamoto (1997), and Paniagua (1998).

Cultural Competence.   Within the past year or so, several resources have become available to assist with providing shelter and services to diverse families. See Ferrer (1998), Lee and Au (1998), or Valencia and Van Hoorn (1999). For an international example, see Fawcett, Heise, Isita-Espejel, and Pick (1999).

Clinicians and workers also need to keep in mind that there are difficulties in establishing what type of impact on children of exposure to interparental violence might be noted, because of the influence of culture. Culture influences the way people express pain, and people from different cultural backgrounds will thus manifest distress in diverse ways (McGoldrick & Giordano,1996). We need to be culturally competent when we gather descriptions of behavior in order to make diagnoses, such as PTSD. Any measures we might use to assess behavioral or emotional difficulty will need to be appropriate for use with that group (Paniagua, 1998).

We also need to provide services within shelters that meet the needs of these families. Where there are large populations of families of the same ethnic group, shelters have opened that provide services specifically to that group (e.g., Valencia & Van Hoorn, 1999). Where that is not possible, shelter staff members need to educate themselves about the cultures and the world view of the women they serve. Those values will influence how the women feel about themselves, as well as their customs and feelings regarding parenting. If possible, it would be helpful to have a staff member who is from the same culture as the women. Lesbian women face similar obstacles to receiving services as battered women, as do their children. Again, service providers must educate themselves about homophobia and understand the dynamics of battering in lesbian relationships.

☐ Conclusion

Changing demographics make it imperative that clinicians and researchers become more aware of the "invisible" families who also suffer from family violence. In addition to issues related to domestic violence with which these families must contend that are similar to mainstream families, there are some unique issues and additional stressors that these diverse families grapple with, related to oppression. It appears reasonable to conjecture that children in these individually and culturally diverse families are likely to have problems in the four areas mentioned above: behavioral, emotional, cognitive/ school, and social functioning, although culture influences how children manifest distress. For example, clinicians might see more somatic symptoms among Asian children. Currently, little if any information is available about the children where domestic violence and diverse families intersect. There is a clear need for more research examining risk and protective factors as unique to these groups. Given the nascent state of the literature, qualitative methodologies are currently recommended to ascertain the meaning of the experiences in the family members' own words. In general, the most important implication for clinical work with culturally and individually diverse women and children is to be both sensitive and competent. It is incumbent upon us all to educate ourselves in order to participate in research and clinical work that is relevant and appropriate for the unique needs of these families who experience domestic violence.

☐ References

Allen, L., & Majidi-Ahi, S. (1989). Black American children. In J. T. Gibbs & L. N. Huang (Eds.), *Children of color: Psychological interventions with minority youth* (pp. 148–178). New York: Jossey-Bass.

Aponte, J. F., & Crouch, R. T. (1995). The changing ethnic profile of the United States. In J. F. Aponte, R. Y. Rivers, & J. Wohl (Eds.), *Psychological interactions and cultural diversity* (pp. 1–18). Needham Heights, MA: Allyn & Bacon.

Arroyo, W. (1997). Children and families of Mexican descent. In G. Johnson-Powell & J. Yamamoto (Eds.), *Transcultural child development: Psychological assessment and treatment* (pp. 290–304). New York: Wiley.

Black, L. (1996). Families of African origin: An overview. In M. McGoldrick, J. Giordano, & J. K. Pearce (Eds.), *Ethnicity and family therapy* (pp. 57–65). New York: Guilford.

Chester, B., Robin, R. W., Koss, M. P., Lopez, T., & Goldman, D. (1994). Grandmother dishonored: Violence against women by male partners in American Indian communities. *Violence & Victims, 9,* 249–258.

Dana, R. H. (1993). *Multicultural assessment perspectives for professional psychology.* Needham Heights, MA: Allyn & Bacon.

Deater-Decker, K., Dodge, K. A., Bates, J. E., & Pettit, G. S. (1996). Physical discipline among African American and European American mothers: Links to children's externalizing behaviors. *Developmental Psychology, 32,* 1065-1072.

Dunne, G. D. (1987). *Lesbian lifestyles: Women's work and the politics of sexuality.* Toronto: University of Toronto Press.

Ellsberg, M., Caldera, T., Herrera, A., Winkvist, A., & Kullgren, G. (1999). Domestic violence and emotional distress among Nicaraguan women: Results from a population-based study. *American Psychologist, 54,* 30–36.

Emery, R. E., & Laumann-Billings, L. (1998). An overview of the nature, causes, and consequences of abusive family relationships: Toward differentiating maltreatment and violence. *American Psychologist, 53,* 121–135.

Falk, P. J. (1989). Lesbian mothers: Psychosocial assumptions in family law. *American Psychologist, 44,* 941–947.

Fawcett, G. M., Heise, L. L., Isita-Espejel, L., & Pick, S. (1999). Changing community responses to wife abuse. *American Psychologist, 54,* 41-49.

Ferrer, D. V. (1998). Validating coping strategies and empowering Latino battered women in Puerto Rico. In A. R. Roberts (Ed.), *Battered women and their families* (2nd ed., pp. 483–511). New York: Springer.

Garcia-Preto, N. (1996). Latino families: An overview. In M. McGoldrick, J. Giordano, & J. K. Pearce (Eds.), *Ethnicity and family therapy* (pp. 141-154). New York: Guilford.

Gelles, R. J. (1997). *Interparental violence in families* (3rd ed.). Thousand Oaks, CA: Sage.

Gibbs, J. T. (1989). Black American adolescents. In J. T. Gibbs & L. N. Huang (Eds.), *Children of color: Psychological interventions with minority youth* (pp. 179–223). New York: Jossey-Bass.

Gibbs, J. T., & Huang, L. N. (Eds.). (1989). *Children of color: Psychological interventions with minority youth.* New York: Jossey-Bass.

Gottman, J. S. (1990). Children of gay and lesbian parents. In F. W. Bozett & M. B. Sussman (Eds.), *Homosexuality and family relations* (pp. 177–196). New York: Harrington Park Press.

Greene, B. (1994). Lesbian women of color: Triple jeopardy. In L. Comas-Diaz & B. Greene (Eds.), *Women of color: Integrating ethnic and gender identities in psychotherapy* (pp. 389-427). New York: Guilford.

Hammond, N. (1988). Lesbian victims of relationship violence. *Women and Therapy, 8,* 89–105.

Hampton, R. L., & Gelles, R. J. (1994). Violence toward Black women in a nationally representative sample of Black families. *Journal of Comparative Family Studies, 25,* 105–119.

Harms, B. (1995). *Domestic violence in the gay male community.* Unpublished master's thesis, San Francisco State University, Department of Psychology. Cited in Merrill, G. S. (1998). Understanding violence among gay and bisexual men. In R. K. Bergen (Ed.), *Issues in interparental violence* (pp. 129-141). Newbury Park, CA: Sage.

Hatchett, S. J. (1991). Women and men. In J. S. Jackson (Ed.), *Life in Black America* (pp. 84–104). Newbury Park, CA: Sage.

Ho, C. K. (1996). An analysis of domestic violence in Asian American communities: A multicultural approach to counseling. In K. P. Monteiro (Ed.), *Ethnicity and psychology* (pp. 138–151). Dubuque, IA: Kendall-Hunt.

Ho. M. K. (1992). *Minority children and adolescents in therapy.* Newbury Park, CA: Sage.

Huang, L. N., & Gibbs, J. T. (1989). Multicultural perspectives on two clinical cases. In J. T. Gibbs & L. N. Huang (Eds.), *Children of color: Psychological interventions with minority youth* (pp. 351–374). San Francisco: Jossey-Bass.

Huang, L. N., & Ying, Y. W. (1989). Chinese American children and adolescents. In J. T. Gibbs & L. N. Huang (Eds.), *Children of color: Psychological interventions with minority youth* (pp. 30–66). San Francisco: Jossey-Bass.

Hughes, H. M. (1991, August*). Research concerning children of battered women: Clinical and policy implications.* In R. Geffner & M. Paludi (Cochairs), *State-of-the art research in family violence: Practical implications.* Paper presented at the annual meeting of the American Psychological Association, San Francisco.

Hughes, H. M. (1997). Research concerning children of battered women: Clinical implications. In R. Geffner, S. B. Sorenson, & P. K. Lundberg-Love (Eds.), *Violence and sexual abuse at home: Current issues, interventions, and research in spousal battering and child maltreatment* (pp. 225–244). Binghamton, NY: Haworth.

Hughes, H. M., & Graham-Bermann, S.A. (1998). Children of battered women: Impact of emotional abuse on adjustment and development. *Journal of Emotional Abuse, 1*(2), 23–50.

Hughes, H. M., & Luke, D. A. (1998). Heterogeneity in adjustment among children of battered women. In G. W. Holden, R. Geffner, & E. N. Jouriles (Eds.), *Children exposed to family violence: Theory, research, and applied issues* (pp. 185–222). Washington, DC: American Psychological Association.

Hughes, H. M., Luke, D. A., Cangiano, C., & Peterson, M. (1998, October). *Clinical implications of heterogeneity in psychological functioning among children of battered women.* Paper presented at the Fourth National Conference on Children Exposed to Family Violence, San Diego.

Hughes, H. M., & Marshall, M. (1995). Advocacy for children of battered women. In J. L. Edleson, P. G. Jaffe, & E. Peled (Eds.), *Ending the cycle of violence: Community responses to children of battered women* (pp. 121–144). Newbury Park, CA: Sage.

Island, D., & Letellier, P. (1991). *Men who beat the men who love them: Battered gay men and domestic violence.* New York: Haworth.

Johnson-Powell, G., & Yamamoto, J. (Eds.). (1997). *Transcultural child development: Psychological assessment and treatment.* New York: Wiley.

Kantor, G. K., Jasinski, J. L., & Aldarondo, E. (1994). Socioeconomic status and incidence of marital violence in Hispanic families. *Violence & Victims, 9,* 207–222.

Kanuha, V. (1997). Women of color in battering relationships. In L. Comas-Diaz & B. Greene (Eds.), *Woman of color: Integrating ethnic and gender identities in psychotherapy* (pp. 428–454). New York: Guilford.

King, B. R., & Black, K. N. (1999). College students' perceptual stigmatization of the children of lesbian mothers. *American Journal of Orthopsychiatry, 69,* 220–227.

Koss, M. P. (1990). The women's mental health agenda: Violence against women. *American Psychologist, 45,* 374–380.

Koss-Chioino, J. D., & Vargas, L. A. (1992). Through the looking glass: A model for understanding culturally responsive psychotherapies (pp. 1–22); Conclusion: Improving the prospects for ethnic minority children in therapy (pp. 300–309). In L. A. Vargas & J. D. Koss-Chioino (Eds.), *Working with children: Psychotherapeutic interventions with ethnic minority children and adolescents.* (pp. 1–22, 300–309). San Francisco: Jossey-Bass.

LaFromboise, T. D., & Low, K. G. (1989). American Indian children and adolescents. In J. T. Gibbs & L. N. Huang (Eds.), *Children of color: Psychological interventions with minority youth* (pp. 114–147). New York: Jossey-Bass.

Lee, E. (1996). Asian-American families: An overview. In M. McGoldrick, J. Giordano, & J. K. Pearce (Eds.), *Ethnicity and family therapy* (pp. 227–248). New York: Guilford.

Lee, M. Y., & Au, P. (1998). Chinese battered women in North America: Their experience and treatment. In A. R. Roberts (Ed.), *Battered women and their families* (2nd ed., pp. 448–482). New York: Springer.

Letellier, P. (1994). Gay and lesbian male domestic violence victimization: Challenges to feminist theory and responses to violence. *Violence and Victims, 9,* 95–106.

Lockhart, L. L., White, B. W., Causby, V., & Isaac, A. (1994). Letting out the secret: Violence in lesbian relationships. *Journal of Interpersonal Violence, 9,* 469–492.

Loulan, J. (1987). *Lesbian passion.* San Francisco: Spinsters/Aunt Lute.

Lung, A. Y., & Sue, S. (1997). Chinese American children. In G. Johnson-Powell & J. Yamamoto (Eds.), *Transcultural child development: Psychological assessment and treatment* (pp. 208–236). New York: Wiley.

Masten, A. S., & Coatsworth, J. D. (1998). Development of competence in favorable and unfavorable environments: Lessons from research on successful children. *American Psychologist, 53,* 205–220.

McGoldrick, M., & Giordano, J. (1996). Overview: Ethnicity and family therapy. In M. McGoldrick, J. Giordano, & J. K. Pearce (Eds.), *Ethnicity and family therapy* (2nd ed., pp. 1–27). New York: Guilford.

McLoyd, V. (1998). Socioeconomic disadvantage and child development. *American Psychologist, 53,* 185–204.

McRae, H. (1994). *The world in 2020: Power, culture, and prosperity.* Boston: Harvard Business School Press.

McWhirter, P. T. (1999). La violencia privada: Domestic violence in Chile. *American Psychologist, 54,* 37–40.

Merrill, G. S. (1998). Understanding violence among gay and bisexual men. In R. K. Bergen (Ed.), *Issues in interparental violence* (pp. 129–141). Newbury Park, CA: Sage.

Neff, J. A., Holamon, B., & Schluter, T. D. (1995). Spousal violence among Anglos, Blacks, and Mexican-Americans: The role of demographic variables, psychosocial predictors, and alcohol consumption. *Journal of Family Violence, 10,* 1–21.

Norton, I. M., & Manson, S. M. (1995). A silent minority: Battered American Indian women. *Journal of Family Violence, 10,* 307–317.

O'Connell, A. (1993). Voices from the heart: The developmental impact of a mother's lesbianism on her adolescent children. *Smith College Studies in Social Work, 63,* 281–299.

Paniagua, F. A. (1998). *Assessing and treating culturally diverse clients* (2nd ed.). Thousand Oaks, CA: Sage.

Parks, C. A. (1998). Lesbian parenthood: A review of the literature. *American Journal of Orthopsychiatry, 68,* 376–389.

Patterson, C. J. (1992). Children of lesbian and gay parents. *Child Development, 63,* 1025–1042.

Patterson, C. J. (1995). Lesbian mothers, gay fathers, and their children. In A. R. D'Augelli & C. J. Patterson (Eds.), *Lesbian, gay and bisexual identities over the lifespan: Psychological perspectives* (pp. 262–290). New York: Oxford University Press.

Patterson, C. J. (1997). Children of gay and lesbian parents. In T. H. Ollendick & R. J. Prinz (Eds.), *Advances in clinical child psychology* (Vol. 19, pp. 235–282). New York: Plenum.

Patterson, C. J., & Chan, R. W. (1996). Gay fathers and their children. In R. P. Cabaj & T. S. Stein (Eds.), *Homosexuality and mental health: A comprehensive textbook* (pp. 371–393). Washington, DC: American Psychiatric Association.

Prilleltensky, I., & Gonick, L. S. (1994). The discourse of oppression in the social sciences: Past, present, and future. In E. J. Trickett, R. J. Watts, & D. Birman (Eds.), *Human diversity: Perspectives on people in context* (pp. 145–177). San Francisco: Jossey-Bass.

Ramirez, O. (1989). Mexican-American children and adolescents. In J. T. Gibbs & L. N. Huang (Eds.), *Children of color: Psychological interventions with minority youth* (pp. 223–250). New York: Jossey-Bass.

Reinharz, S. (1994). Toward an ethnography of "voice" and "silence." In E. J. Trickett, R. J. Watts, & D. Birman, (Eds.), *Human diversity: Perspectives on people in context* (pp. 178–200). San Francisco: Jossey-Bass.

Renzetti, C. M. (1992). *Violent betrayal: Partner abuse in lesbian relationships.* Newbury Park, CA: Sage.

Renzetti, C. M. (1995). Violence in gay and lesbian relationships. In R. Gelles (Ed.), *Visions 2010: Families and violence, abuse, and neglect.* Minneapolis, MN: National Council on Family Relations.

Renzetti, C. M. (1998). Violence and abuse in lesbian relationships: Theoretical and empirical issues. In R. K. Bergen (Ed.), *Issues in interparental violence* (pp. 117–127). Newbury Park, CA: Sage.

Rutter, M. (1979). Protective factors in children's responses to stress and disadvantage. In M. W. Kent & J. E. Rolf (Eds.), *Primary prevention of psychopathology* (Vol. 3, pp. 49–74). Hanover, NH: University Press of New England.

Sorenson, S. B., Upchurch, D. M., & Shen, H. (1996). Violence and injury in marital arguments: Risk patterns and gender differences. *American Journal of Public Health, 86,* 35–40.

Strauss, A., & Corbin, J. (1990). *Basics of qualitative research: Grounded theory procedures and techniques.* London: Sage.

Sutton, C. T., & Broken Nose, M. A. (1996). American Indian families: An overview. In M. McGoldrick, J. Giordano, & J. K. Pearce (Eds.), *Ethnicity and family therapy* (pp. 31–44). New York: Guilford.

Tang, S.-K. C. (1997). Psychological impact of wife abuse: Experiences of Chinese women and their children. *Journal of Interpersonal Violence, 12,* 466–478.

Tasker, F. L., & Golombok, S. (1995). Adults raised as children in lesbian families. *American Journal of Orthopsychiatry, 65,* 203–215.

Tasker, F. L., & Golombok, S. (1997). *Growing up in a lesbian family.* New York/London: Guilford.

U.S. Bureau of the Census (1996). *Statistical abstract for the United States.* Washington, DC: Government Printing Office.

Valencia, A., & Van Hoorn, J. (1999). La Isla Pacifica: A haven for Mexican-American women. *American Psychologist, 54,* 62–63.

Waterman, C. K., Dawson, L. J., & Bologna, M. J. (1989). Sexual coercion in gay male and lesbian relationships: Predictors and implications for support services. *Journal of Sex Research, 26,* 118–124.

Wiehe, V. R. (1998). *Understanding family violence: Treating and preventing partner, child, sibling, and elder abuse.* Thousand Oaks, CA: Sage.

Yamamoto, J., Silva, J. A., Ferrari, M., & Nukarija, K. (1997). Culture and psychopathology. In G. Johnson-Powell & J. Yamamoto (Eds.), *Transcultural child development: Psychological assessment and treatment* (pp. 34–60). New York: Wiley.

Yoshihama, M. (1998). Domestic violence in Japan: Research, program development, and emerging movements. In A. R. Roberts (Ed.), *Battered women and their families* (2nd ed., pp. 405–447). New York: Springer.

Yoshihama, M., & Sorenson, S. B. (1994). Physical, sexual and emotional abuse by male intimates: Experiences of women in Japan. *Violence & Victims, 9,* 63–77.

Treatment and Prevention of the Impact of Exposure

Mark and Arthur S. are twins whose mother brought them to the clinic with concerns about their psychological adjustment. Both had been exposed to the violence that their father perpetrated against their mother repeatedly over the course of their 11-year-old lifetimes. Shortly before she left him, he had started being violent toward the boys as well, including throwing Arthur against a wall. She had obtained a divorce approximately 6 months prior to starting therapy. When she presented at the clinic, Ms. S. was concerned that Arthur was having difficulties in school and had become more disobedient at home recently. Mark did not have school problems, but he seemed to have many feelings bottled up inside. He tended to be quiet and keep things to himself; his mother was worried that he might "explode" one day and become violent like his father.

Interventions with Arthur, Mark, and their mother focused on the impact of the violence that they had witnessed and experienced, addressing their feelings and behaviors as well as their relationship. Over the course of a year with each in individual therapy, Arthur started doing better in school and was more obedient at home. In addition, he seemed to have a reasonably realistic view of his father and did not take it personally when the father did not show up to take them somewhere or left the boys at his mother's house while he went out with his new girlfriend. Mark was having a more difficult time, because he identified more strongly with his father. For example, he experienced much frustration over the father's lack of consistency and seeming lack of interest in him. In addition, being in therapy was problematic for him because his father insisted on telling him that they were going to a "nut doctor" and it was his mother who was "nuts," not him. Ms. S. was making good progress in her therapy focused on learning new parenting strategies. However, the most difficult part for her was being able to use the new strategies she was learning when she was upset or angry. Spanking or slapping the boys was her first response to frustration with them, which she attributed to her own upbringing, where there was much physical discipline imposed upon her and her siblings. In the last several weeks, she was finding that she was better able to stop and think about how she wanted to handle the situation before she reacted, using a cognitive technique she had practiced with her therapist.

In this chapter, the focus is on both treatment and prevention of exposure to family violence. First, we review interventions designed to ameliorate the detrimental impact of exposure to spouse abuse. These detrimental influences were discussed in Chapter 2, with research findings indicating that, in general, most children experience some degree of negative sequelae due to this exposure. In Chapters 3, 4, and 5, additional topics relevant for intervention were presented, including individual differences, models of how the impact takes place, and the impact of exposure in different family contexts. Recommendations regarding interventions are made in this chapter based on an integration of clinical writings with the theoretical literature discussed in previous chapters. In addition, because treatment is focused after the fact on reducing difficulties rather than on removing the cause of the distress, a discussion of the prevention of interparental violence is also included.

☐ Treatment Considerations

Clinical Focus

The following discussion in this chapter focuses on treatment provided to family members after the crisis phase has passed. For discussion of advocacy and crisis intervention more immediately after a battering incident, or when a family initially enters a shelter, see Arroyo and Eth (1995), Hughes and Marshall (1995), Lehmann and Carlson (1998), and Rosenberg and Rossman (1990). In addition, it must be noted that few approaches have been formally evaluated. Treatment strategies that will be discussed include those with and without evaluations and will be noted as such. In addition, some discussion of variations in children's need for interventions and of innovative programs will be included.

As Graham-Bermann and Hughes (1998) point out, most of the treatment approaches currently in use have primarily grown out of clinical necessity. Many of the initial intervention accounts were based on the needs of shelter staff for provision of support to children who were staying in shelters for battered women (e.g., Gentry & Eaddy, 1980; Hughes, 1982). These programs described comprehensive approaches to intervention with the women, including attention to the children, to the women as mothers, advocacy for the children with the schools, and training for shelter personnel related to children's needs (Hughes, 1982). In addition, clinicians often drew on other areas of literature when first planning interventions, for example, from the work available in the areas of child abuse and general child psychopathology (Hughes & Fantuzzo, 1994).

Also reflecting a comprehensive approach, recently Carlson (1996) in her review recommended 10 elements that would be included in an ideal program for children of battered women, either in a shelter or in a nonresident program: (1) individual assessment; (2) individual counseling; (3) referrals; (4) advocacy; (5) group work for children; (6) regular, structured recreational activities for children; (7) aftercare or follow-up services; (8) prevention services; (9) parenting education and support groups for mothers; and (10) evaluation of all aspects of the program. She also conducted a survey of 15 shelters for battered women in New York state and found that the average number of program components per shelter was 3.8, with a range of 1 to 7. The most common child-related program components were parenting education or support groups for mothers or both (50% of the shelters surveyed had these). Next most common were child care (33%), individual counseling (33%), and group counseling (33%).

The frequency of the above-mentioned program components is reflected in the literature as well. The following is a discussion of the types of programs that were developed out of clinical necessity and focused on alleviation of the negative behavioral and emotional impact seen among these children. In general, these components are applicable to children of battered women who were either still residing in shelters, were former residents of shelters, or were receiving services from a domestic violence nonresidential agency.

Approaches to Child-Oriented Intervention.
Overall in the literature, authors' approaches to intervention targeting the children generally are multifaceted, involve several family members as the focus, and are developmentally appropriate. Basically these strategies were developed based on clinical experience and theoretical formulations, rather than from empirical work. The techniques seemed face-valid at the time of development and for the most part remain to be tested empirically.

Multifaceted.   Most of the authors writing in this area recommend a multifaceted approach to the treatment of children exposed to partner abuse, one which frequently includes interventions with the children and the women in separate groups (Davies, 1991; Frey-Angel, 1989; Gentry & Eaddy, 1980; Gibson & Gutierrez, 1991; Grusznski, Brink, & Edleson, 1988; Hughes, 1982, 1986; Jaffe, Wolfe, & Wilson, 1990; Johnson & Montgomery, 1990; Peled & Davis, 1995; Peled & Edleson, 1992, 1995; Ragg, 1991; Ragg & Webb, 1992; Tutty & Wagar, 1994; Wagar & Rodway. 1995). In addition, as previously noted, in keeping with an ecological and comprehensive focus, Hughes (1982) recommended training for the shelter staff also to improve their ability to provide support to their resident children. Some programs also included outreach to men (e.g., Gentry & Eaddy, 1980; Grusznski et al., 1988; Potgieter, 1988), although there is controversy over to what extent and when to involve the abusive men in treatment with the women and children (to be addressed in more detail later). Peled and Edleson (1995) mentioned that they occasionally included the men in the parenting groups (not with their former partner) if safety was not a concern. Moreover, Matthews (1995) describes a model for parent training specifically for men who batter.

Approaches for Children: Group.   Because most of the clinical work and writings originated in shelters, intervention in a group format was an economical way in that setting to provide support to the children. Much of the group work that is conducted is based on models provided by Jaffe and his colleagues (Jaffe et al., 1990; Wilson, Cameron, Jaffe, & Wolfe, 1989) or Peled and Edleson and their colleagues (Grusznski et al., 1988; Peled & Davis, 1995; Peled & Edleson, 1992, 1995). Both sets of authors make clear that these groups are appropriate for children who are experiencing mild distress, not those having more major emotional and behavioral problems. Another example of an approach to children's groups is provided by Graham-Bermann (1992). She developed a "Kids Club" as a 10-week "preventive" intervention program that was designed to reduce the impact of domestic violence. The 10 sessions are focused on children's knowledge about family violence, emotions, and fears associated with domestic abuse, beliefs about families and gender roles, as well as the children's behavior in the group setting.

Children are seen in mixed-gender, similar-age groups, with children ranging in age from 6 to 12 years. Two facilitators lead each group. Graham-Bermann is also in the process of finishing an evaluation of this treatment (1998). The Peled and Davis (1995) publication in particular is very useful, consisting of a detailed manual describing the authors' groups for both children and mothers, complete with a description of the structure of the groups, notes to the group facilitators, and forms to use.

In general, the groups are most often time limited; are for children ages 8 to 13, although sometimes youngsters ages 3 to 7 are included also; are divided by age group; and are co-led by male and female counselors. Facilitators are often from an agency or one of the shelter staff. Groups are typically 10 to 12 weeks, and children may go through a group "cycle" more than once. Group meetings are usually 60 to 90 minutes in length and have 6 to 9 participants per group. A number of different topics are covered, typically including learning to do the following: (a) label feelings; (b) deal with anger; (c) acquire safety skills; (d) obtain social support; (e) enhance social competence and self-esteem; (f) understand issues of responsibility for the violence; (g) understand the dynamics of family violence; and (h) validate wishes the children have about their families. Often there is an introductory session and a review and wrap-up session at the end of the group. For older children and adolescents, sessions on love, sex, and sexuality are included (e.g., Alessi & Hearn, 1984, 1998).

A rather innovative study was recently carried out by Rossman (1999). They conducted a short-term intervention (four sessions) with currently single women who had experienced violence at the hands of their male partners. To date, 30 low-income, ethnic minority women and their children ages 7 to 11 years have participated. The psychoeducational intervention consisted of 6 to 7 children and their mothers and was conducted by graduate students. For each of the four group sessions there was a "theme" presented via the use of specially designed booklets (low self-esteem, poor emotion regulation, poor friendship skills, and understanding adult conflict). Half of each 90-minute session was spent with the children and the facilitator, and half of the session was spent with the mothers and children together with the facilitator. In addition, four similar content specific booklets were designed to be used by the mothers and children in their four subsequent at-home sessions. Evaluation of the intervention indicated that both children and women benefited from the training; in addition, women stated that they felt closer to their children as a result of the treatment.

A recently presented approach is from Roseby and Johnston (1997), who developed a theory-based, structured treatment program for school-age children in highly conflicted and violent divorcing families. The approach engages children in group activities that are specially designed to challenge rigid patterns of thinking and feeling. The authors present an innovative treatment model based in part on developmental object relations, which differs from the typical group work with exposed children that has been described in the literature above. The intervention focuses on the ways exposed children manage anxiety by narrowing their feelings and ideas about themselves and others into simple, rigid "internal scripts" (akin to what Rossman has noted as "leveling"). Through specific group activities, the intervention helps children access and change their internal scripts into more realistic and flexible interpersonal understanding. (For a more complete discussion of the developmental problems in high-conflict divorcing families, see Johnston & Roseby, 1997; Roseby & Johnston, 1998.)

Children aged 5 to 13 years participated, with interparental violence and parenting difficulties reported for approximately 70% of the sample. Groups were 90 minutes in length for approximately 10 weeks, with an average of 7 children per group. Children of similar grade level and age range were placed together, co-led by one experienced clinician and one clinical intern. School-referred families were predominantly Hispanic, whereas agency-referred families were primarily Anglo. The majority of families experienced serious stressful life events, including a history of unemployment and financial problems for almost 73% of the sample, health problems for 67%, and housing difficulties for 43%.

Johnston (1998) concluded that children who are the most troubled and at risk need more than one group intervention: they need a continuum of interventions to address their specific needs. They may need socialization experiences at first, so that they could feel comfortable talking with other children and adults in a group setting. Then these children could make deeper use of the curriculum to develop a language of emotion, rather than acting out their anger and frustration, and develop the capacity for empathy, which further promotes flexible coping and moral action. For children who have been severely traumatized (e.g., severe family violence, exposure to shootings, and other trauma), more time was needed to develop group trust and to allow their complex, often repressed feelings to emerge. The clinicians also found they needed to exchange the more cognitively advanced exercises when meeting with ethnic minority children for a greater focus on emotional understanding and expression. For children with behavioral problems, it was important to incorporate more socialization exercises into the curriculum (e.g., more discussion on how to make friends, inappropriate and appropriate behavior, how it feels to be bullied, etc.). For children who were exposed to serious domestic violence, pregang activities and racial hostilities, it was critical to incorporate discussion about safety and protection, both physically and psychologically. At the end of the group series, the clinicians evaluated what each child and parent needed next to reinforce the skills and knowledge they learned and strengthen their coping and then made the appropriate referrals for services.

Approaches for Children: Individual.   For children whose difficulties are more pronounced (e.g., are above a cutoff indicating a need for clinical services or showing considerable impairment in functioning, such as those youngsters described above), intervention on an individual basis is most often recommended. Sometimes this can be provided on a short-term basis in a shelter if trained personnel are available, although more often it is provided by referral to a clinician at an agency. Silvern, Karyl, and Landis (1995) present an approach they recommend when conducting individual therapy with children of battered women that employs a PTSD and trauma orientation in the interventions. For example, they recommend four strategies for a trauma-specific intervention, including (a) targeting the posttraumatic symptoms, (b) facilitating disclosure with "straight talk," (c) desensitization and cognitive restructuring, and (d) interpretation and symbolic symptoms. (See also Hughes & Marshall, 1995; Kerig, Fedorowicz, Brown, & Warren, 1997; and Rosenberg & Rossman, 1990). Kerig et al. discussed the two main goals of their approach: (1) reexposing the child to traumatic cues in a manner that is therapeutic and not retraumatizing, and (2) clearing up any cognitive distortions the child might have. These authors suggest using a variety of techniques, including systematic desensitization, psychodynamically oriented play therapy, and cognitive-behavioral play, as well as family therapy when appropriate. They also emphasize and provide suggestions for conducting these interventions in a developmentally appropriate fashion.

In addition, Jouriles and colleagues (1998) have recently presented a treatment approach appropriate for children of battered women who have behavioral difficulties. This approach consists of weekly home visits for families in which a boy between the ages of 4 and 9 years meets the diagnostic criteria for either Oppositional Defiant Disorder or Conduct Disorder. Children meet weekly with an undergraduate mentor who acts as a role model and plays with them in an "older sibling" capacity, providing them with positive attention and affection. Mothers are provided at the same time with training in child management skills by a therapist. These meetings occur weekly for up to 8 months.

Developmentally Appropriate.   Although children of all ages reside in shelters, frequently the majority are younger than 8 years (e.g., Hughes, 1997). In a domestic violence agency, Grusznski et al. (1988) found that the majority of children in their groups were between the ages of 5 and 9 (47%), the next largest group were in the 10 and above range (34.5%), and the smallest of the groups were for the 4 and under age range (18%). As a result of this range in age and the variation in developmental capabilities of the different ages, a number of authors discuss the need for developmentally appropriate activities and materials for the children participating in the groups. Generally the groups are divided roughly along age lines, approximately 8 to 10 and 11 to 13 years. Some of the clinicians also include younger school-age and preschool-age children (3 to 7), and discuss using materials designed for this age range (Alessi & Hearn, 1984; Gibson & Gutierrez, 1991; Johnson & Montgomery, 1990; Peled & Edleson, 1992; Ragg & Webb, 1992). For example, most of the authors who conduct groups for younger children discuss the use of specially designed coloring books for the youngsters.

One unique approach to providing group services to these children was advanced by Frey-Angel (1989). She recommends including children ages 3 to 12 years in the same group, with the rationale that the children who are siblings will be able to provide support to each other. However, there are several obstacles to conducting groups like this, all related to levels of development. Although the support of siblings would be helpful in theory, developmentally there would be differences in emotional maturity and functioning. In addition, there would also be topics that would be appropriate for discussion for adolescents, but not for younger children; some topics also likely would not be understood by younger children.

Approaches for Mothers.   The authors mentioned above also frequently recommend a parallel group for mothers of the children exposed to the spouse abuse, which is sometimes optional and at times mandatory. However, few authors discuss content or format of these groups in the same detail as they devote to the children's groups. Most recommend an education-oriented approach and include discipline in particular as an issue for the women. Several descriptions of parent education/training approaches for battered women exist. Peled and Edleson (1995) mention that the two goals for their groups with mothers are to (a) provide information as well as challenge attitudes, beliefs, values, and assumptions, and (b) develop the parent's child-rearing skills.

Bilinkoff (1995), with her emphasis on empowering battered women as mothers, presents a number of topics to be addressed as part of her therapeutic approach. These consist of (a) parenting issues, including using power and control, making up for the absent father, the mother's perceptions of her children's similarities to the father, and using the children as confidants or allies; (b) understanding the traditional parenting model; (c) understanding a feminist parenting model; (d) developing an empowered vision of mothering; (e) developing new family rituals; (f) handling economic changes; and (g) developing an extended family network. Her recommendations are designed to be handled with a battered woman on an individual basis. In addition, the author recommends that clinicians address the above parenting issues after the woman has ended the violent relationship and is starting to heal from it.

Levendosky and Graham-Bermann (1994) discuss an approach for battered mothers that they call empowerment through learned competence. Their 10-week group is designed for women out of shelters and accompanies the group for their children. Each group is 90 minutes and covers one topic per session. The group is co-led and the authors emphasize both the educational and supportive aspects of the group experience for the women. Including introductory and wrap-up sessions, topics covered consist of issues related to (a) parents' worries and concerns; (b) family of origin; (c) communication with their children; (d) child development information; (e) empathy; (f) discipline; (g) stress management for both parents and children; and (h) having fun together as parents and children. The authors include some anecdotal evidence for the group's efficacy, although they also have more systematically collected data on its effectiveness (Graham-Bermann, 1998).

Edelson and Hokoda (1996) discuss a similar approach to parent training. Their program is a 12-week education-oriented one that is open to women who are participating in a support group at a women's crisis agency, have children between the ages of 3 and 12 years, and are no longer in immediate crisis. Discussion, role play, group activities, and homework assignments are used. The authors divide the groups into four sections, including a focus on discipline, self-esteem, depression, and inappropriate control. Evaluation information is currently being collected.

The Jouriles et al. (1998) approach (as mentioned above) is one that is conducted on an individual basis, rather than as a group. Individual treatment is especially appropriate with women who have more severe difficulties with their children. This allows them to address individual concerns in more detail than would be possible in a group. The therapists who met with the mothers weekly in their homes for 8 months focused on teaching problem-solving skills and child management skills as well as providing instrumental and social support. This approach is likely to be important for a number of families who experience spouse abuse, due to the 35% to 50% of children who have difficulties within the clinical range. It can be beneficial for women too. Jouriles et al. found that after treatment the mothers' parenting skills were better, and they showed more warmth and nurturance. In addition, the mothers' stress levels, as assessed by a symptom checklist, decreased over time.

Approaches for Fathers. As mentioned above, Peled and Edleson (1995) sometimes included fathers in their groups when it was felt to be safe. In addition, Matthews (1995) discusses one approach to parent training groups for men who batter. First, the men attend two individual sessions, then a 12-week group course. Each session lasts 2½ hours. Frequently the men repeat the series of group sessions. Critical issues for the fathers' groups raised by the author include the following: (a) men's resistance; (b) limited knowledge of child development; (c) shame and how they cope with it; (d) ability to have empathy for their children's experience of violence; (e) stepparenting; and (f) willingness to make a commitment to nonviolent parenting. This latter approach is one that has been adopted by some men's treatment programs (J. Edleson, personal communication, April 9, 1997).

Evaluation. Evaluations of the interventions, for either children or mothers, have, with some exceptions, been mostly informal and anecdotal. Several authors have conducted evaluations of their groups, which included pre- and posttesting, and one study was conducted using a waiting-list comparison group. In addition, another series of authors have conducted an extensive qualitative evaluation of their children's groups. Jaffe et al. (1990) and Grusznski et al. (1988) both carried out informal evaluations of their group interventions with children in shelters. Pre- and postgroup interviews were conducted in Jaffe et al., and mothers and children also completed several paper-and-pencil measures. The authors' results were encouraging, although no comparison groups were included. According to Jaffe et al., mothers felt satisfied with the children's participation, and the children noted that they enjoyed the 10-week group as well as learned some safety skills. In addition, more positive perceptions of the parents were reported by the children.

Grusznski et al. (1988) had group leaders complete clinical rating scales for the children in their intervention program. Their results indicated that by the end of the sessions, a large majority of children had met each of the four program goals: they acknowledged that violence is an issue in their family and not their fault; their self-esteem increased; they learned about new resources for support and about new ways to protect themselves; and they learned nonviolent ways of problem solving.

Program evaluation results from the Rossman (1999) short-term intervention were generally positive. They obtained reports from both mothers and children, with responses from both indicating the program was useful. Mothers thought their children were using the ideas they learned in the classes to calm themselves down and were having fewer conflicts with friends. Children were reported to generally cope with adult conflict through withdrawal, and they were able now to generate more alternatives. In addition, there was a statistically significant increase in the children's self-esteem, according to the women. Based on children's responses, results were equally positive. The children felt that they had a number of ways to cope if they felt bad, and they also felt that they were able to generate more alternatives to problems. The author recommends using the mother–child joint participation as a useful component of intervention programs (Rossman, 1999).

Initial evaluation data have been collected on the implementation of Roseby and Johnston's (1997) group program. Children aged 5 to 13 years were recruited from a variety of referral sources, including from judges, mediators, teachers, school counselors, principals, family therapists, family advocates, and parents or legal guardians. Eligibility criteria for group intervention included children who had witnessed violence or had been the object of violence; those who had experienced highly conflictual marriages of their parents and litigated divorce; children who had suddenly lost a primary caregiver as a consequence of violence, abuse, or criminal behavior; or those who had been exposed to abusive and neglectful environments due to parental substance abuse. Domestic violence and parenting difficulties were reported for approximately 70% of the sample.

Children were assessed at intake, at the end of group intervention, and again for a 6-month follow-up by parents, teachers, and clinicians using standardized measures of adjustment. The overall findings indicate that children who received group intervention showed significantly increased social competence according to clinician, parent, and teacher ratings. Parents and clinicians perceived significantly fewer emotional and behavioral problems. Both boys and girls made similar gains in their adjustment even though boys were perceived to have more behavioral problems and to be less socially competent than girls before and after treatment. Teachers' ratings of behavioral and learning problems did not change significantly over the intervention period, but ratings of social competence did increase significantly. Preliminary correlational findings indicate that children who had been exposed to domestic violence, neighborhood violence, and separation and loss are more likely to have behavioral problems and difficulties getting along with peers. In addition, children whose primary caretaker perceives they have a network of supportive persons are buffered from stressful life events. Parents whose sources of support live nearby also reported fewer difficulties with their children, thus confirming the positive impact of local neighborhood supports.

In an interesting study using a waiting-list comparison group, Wagar and Rodway (1995) assessed the effectiveness of a group for 8- to 13-year-olds based on the Jaffe et al. (1990) 10-week format, employing the latter's evaluation instrument. The Child Witness to Violence Questionnaire was used to evaluate the program, which measures four areas: (a) children's knowledge of spouse abuse, (b) their responses and attitudes toward anger, (c) their problem-solving abilities in relation to safety skills, and (d) their attributions of responsibility for the violence and for their parents. Children were included only if they were beyond the crisis stage (3-month violence-free period). In addition, they were randomly assigned to groups. Assessment was conducted 2 weeks before and after the series of group sessions. Results indicated that there were significant differences between groups on attitudes and responses to anger as well as sense of responsibility for the violence and for their parents, with more positive findings for the treatment group. Moreover, an informal 6-month follow-up indicated that both children and parents could provide concrete examples of changes that had been maintained.

Some recommendations for program changes were made by the authors as well. Concurring with others that this approach is most helpful with children who are experiencing mild adjustment problems, they suggested that some children would benefit from going through the group again and recommended that parents of children with more serious difficulties seek longer-term treatment. In addition, the authors suggested that parents of the children participate in an educational group of their own. Other suggested changes for the program are included in their report.

Peled and Edleson (1992) also discuss their group in some detail and provide results of their qualitative investigation based on both process and outcome information. They chose to utilize this methodology based on the advantages afforded by this method over a more traditional quantitatively based approach. Qualitative methodologies are usually more appropriate when program goals are vague and general. Also, appropriate standardized instruments were unavailable; moreover, they would be likely to limit the breadth and depth of information obtained. Another advantage was that in-depth information regarding the processes as well as the content of the groups would be obtained and could improve the program. In addition, side effects and unintended consequences were also a focus of interest, and the context in which the program was conducted required the least intrusive approach possible; therefore, qualitative methods were employed.

In-depth semi-structured interviews and observations of group sessions were conducted. The authors discussed both the intended and unintended results of their group related to the four goals of (a) breaking the secret; (b) learning to protect oneself; (c) having a positive experience; and (d) enhancing self-esteem. For example, for the first goal, the children learned about defining violence, that it is not their fault, and that it is okay to express feelings and share personal experiences. However, as an unintended, but perhaps inevitable, consequence this learning process dealt with highly charged emotional issues and produced stress among all the family members, children and mothers alike. The authors point out that these unintended consequences are probably also an essential part of the healing process.

The authors concluded, based on the perspectives of the children, parents, and staff, that the goals of the groups had been attained. In addition, they pointed out that unintended consequences require careful attention on the part of group leaders. Recommendations were also provided that suggested that children's individual characteristics and needs be taken into account (e.g., abuse of the child) and that appropriate referrals for more intensive treatment if necessary be provided within the context of a comprehensive approach to intervention with these families.

A longitudinal study has been recently conducted by Rossman (1998b). She and her colleagues followed for almost a year over 100 5- to 14-year-old children from disadvantaged shelter and community families that were characterized by different levels of marital conflict and violence. Over 90% of the exposed children had been in violent homes since age 2 or before. Researchers assessed initial and ongoing levels of poverty, marital violence, family life stressors, and children's PTSD symptomatology. In general, trauma symptoms and behavior problems decreased across follow-up for all violence-exposed children. Exposed children who received 6 to 12 treatment sessions in the community during that year showed better school functioning at follow-up. Three factors were associated with greater declines in symptoms and problems and lesser declines in school performance: the absence of ongoing interparental violence; the fact that children attended 6 to 12 treatment sessions on an outclient basis at area mental health agencies; and being male, because boys showed a greater decline in PTSD symptoms.

Jouriles et al. (1998), as mentioned above, have implemented an intervention program for children with conduct disorder problems that started when the family leaves a shelter and continued with weekly in-home contacts from therapists for up to 8 months. Follow-up assessments were made at 4, 8, 12 and 16 months after the initial contact. Interventions were individualized to fit the needs of the particular family members. Typically child management skills and problem-solving skills were taught to the mothers; instrumental and social support were also provided. Preliminary evidence suggested good outcome results with a sample of quite low-income women from a variety of ethnic backgrounds. Treatment families were compared with a group of families who had randomly been assigned to existing services in the community and were visited monthly by the treatment team in their homes. Initial evaluation indicated that there were reductions in children's antisocial behavior compared with the other group. Overall, child externalizing behaviors were noted to have decreased over the course of 8 months of treatment. The researchers stated that there were still some problems noted, but they were reduced at least one standard deviation on the CBCL. Jouriles et al. found that after treatment the mothers' parenting skills were better, and they showed more warmth and nurturance. In addition, the mothers' stress levels, as assessed by a symptom checklist, decreased over time. These investigations support the positive role of both a violence-free environment and appropriate treatment.

Variations in Children's Intervention Needs and Innovations in Intervention.

Individualization of Treatment. As discussed in several places above, there are indications that children require different forms and types of interventions based on their different capabilities, strengths, and needs. In Chapter 2, it was pointed out that based on the findings of a number of researchers, there are at least two different groups of children in shelters: those who, according to their mothers, are above and those who are below a cut-off level indicating need for clinical services. This would imply that some children would benefit from the group approach discussed above, whereas others would need additional services. Moreover, as suggested by Hughes and Luke (1998), there may be as many as five different subgroups of children and mothers in shelters, each with different needs for support and intervention.

Hughes and Luke (1998) hypothesized that children ages 6 to 12 years who were residing in a shelter for battered women would show a range in adjustment, varying from little to substantial distress. Cluster analysis was used to identify subgroups of children, based on similarities and differences among their behavior problems, internal distress, and self-esteem scores, which resulted in the identification of five distinct patterns in adjustment. The two largest clusters contained children who were at most only slightly distressed, accounting for approximately 60% of the children. Shelter and community services that include psychoeducational groups for the children and advocacy for the women were recommended for these families.

The other three clusters included children who experienced behavior problems, internal distress, and low self-esteem. Families in these latter three groups differed in mothers' depression and verbal aggressiveness levels as well as in duration of abuse of the mother. Additional attention to the individual needs of both the women and children in these groups, beyond the standard shelter services, was suggested. Recommendations for differential interventions based on different patterns of distress were provided (Hughes & Luke, 1998), similar to suggestions made later in this chapter. These findings of individual differences in families were replicated in a later study with an ethnically diverse sample, and the authors again made differential recommendations for clinicians and shelter workers who assess clinical needs and plan interventions (Hughes, Luke, Cangiano, & Peterson, 1998).

Innovations. Although the group approach for children either in or outside of shelters for battered women is the most typical, several other innovative approaches have been developed. These include outreach to women and children, with contacts continuing with the families post-shelter-stay, as well as in transitional housing. For example, Jouriles et al. (1998) used a treatment approach in which they employed home visits rather than expected the families to come to the agency. In addition, their treatment was rather lengthy, lasting at least 8 months, although this is quite appropriate given the nature of the conduct problems among the boys to whom they have been providing services. Rossman (1999) provided groups as "classes" in low-income housing areas. Some shelters and domestic violence programs currently have outreach services. For example, the shelter in Fayetteville, Arkansas, has an outreach worker who provides follow-up contacts and services to families after they leave the shelter. St. Martha's Hall, in St. Louis, Missouri, also has an outreach worker, as does the program for former residents conducted by the shelter in Boulder, Colorado. Although no formal evaluations of these services have been conducted, it is the workers' impression that when families are provided with additional support and resources, it helps them remain violence-free.

Summary. Overall, the programs discussed above take a multifaceted, ecologically oriented approach to providing support and intervention to children of battered women and their mothers. Typical support services provided are psychoeducationally focused groups for the women and the youngsters that are designed to alleviate current distress and prevent future difficulties. Many researchers and clinicians acknowledged that these support services were appropriate for the children experiencing mild to moderate problems, with attention on an individual basis needed for more serious difficulties. Authors have also shown a sensitivity to the need for developmentally appropriate services for the children. The majority of services offered are short-term groups for either children or women, and they most often have no evaluation other than anecdotal information. Gaps in the literature are prominent here, with a clear need for evaluation of the treatment programs.

Theoretical Focus

Although clinical needs initially guided the development of the majority of the intervention programs in use with children of battered women, more recently research and theory have become available that can also provide clinicians with guidance for treatment. As discussed in previous chapters, one place to start is with an understanding of the potential moderators of behavioral and emotional outcomes discussed above as well as of likely mechanisms of impact. This understanding has important implications for clinical intervention. Once some of the mechanisms by which spouse abuse exerts an impact are delineated, better treatment and prevention programs can be implemented. Recently a number of researchers have proposed models based on theory and research to help explain the psychological and behavioral consequences for the children, as was discussed in Chapter 4.

Mechanisms of Impact.   As discussed in previous chapters, mechanisms of impact likely work in both direct and indirect ways.

Direct Mechanisms.   Related to the fact that both boys and girls exhibit externalizing symptoms, the aggressiveness on the part of both likely has been acquired through social learning and modeling, with children copying what they see their father doing. Grych and Fincham (1990) point out that children tend to imitate their parents and learn about interpersonal relationships from them. In addition, Cummings and Davies (1994) suggest that children learn "scripts" from parents, these are general strategies for using aggressive behavior since they see their father being reinforced for using aggression to obtain what he wants.

Moreover, not only do children learn to be aggressive by watching others act in that fashion, there is a "disinhibitory" impact as well. Watching someone use physical force gives one permission to also be aggressive (Cummings & Davies, 1994; Grych & Fincham, 1990). Because children are more likely to imitate a model they view as powerful and successful in achieving goals (Bandura, 1973; Pagelow, 1984), modeling in the case of spouse abuse can be especially influential.

The second direct mechanism, stress, operates through the fact that the violent family environment is very stressful for the children (e.g., Cummings & Davies, 1994; Jaffe et al., 1990; Jouriles, Norwood, McDonald, Vincent, & Mahoney, 1996). Cummings and Davies describe typical responses to stress on the part of children as ones of physiological arousal and emotional dysregulation. Thus, being subject to chronic stress depletes the resources of the children over time and reduces the quality of the child's functioning. Therefore, the anxiety and depressive-type symptoms experienced by children are apt to be a result of the family stress created by the spouse abuse. In addition, Jouriles et al. (1996) emphasize that the physical violence occurs in a context of other marital aggression. Moreover, as Jaffe et al. (1990) point out, many of the signs of distress in children of battered women are very similar to PTSD symptoms in youngsters, such as nightmares; exaggerated startle responses; intense, perhaps phobic, fears of people or places; or "spacing out" (Kerig et al., 1997).

Indirect Mechanisms.   Indirect mechanisms have been discussed in Chapters 2 and 3; a brief review is offered here to tie this information to the treatment approaches discussed below.

Regarding characteristics of the mother–child relationship, abuse of the mother can be indirectly related to children's behavior problems since it can lead to a deterioration in the mental health of the mother and the quality of the parent–child relationship. For example, Wolfe, Jaffe, Wilson, and Zak (1985) investigated the extent to which shelter mothers' physical and mental health influenced children's adjustment. They found that maternal stress variables predicted child adjustment better than physical violence between parents and suggested that the impact on the child of observing spouse abuse may be partially a function of the mother's impairment following specific events, such as being beaten, as well as the accompanying disruption and uncertainly in the family. Graham-Bermann, Levendosky, Porterfield, and Okun (in press) and Hanson and Hughes (1998) also found evidence for indirect impact on the child mediated through the mental health of the mother.

Moreover, a likely outcome of being beaten is to become depressed (e.g., Carmen, Rieker, & Mills, 1984; Hughes & Rau, 1984). Depending on the length of time the women have experienced depressive symptoms and the severity of their dysfunction, the parent–child relationship could be negatively affected. Research indicates that children of depressed women are at risk for adjustment difficulties (Jaenicke et al., 1987; Lee & Gotlib, 1989).

In addition, hostility and aggression expressed during the marital conflict can "spill over" to the parent–child relationship (Fincham, Grych, & Osborne, 1994). Similarly, negative emotionality experienced by the parent(s) as a result of the conflict could result in responses to those feelings of either overt hostility toward the child or withdrawal and neglect of the child.

Stress related to parenting has also been found to be a potential influence on the parent-child relationship. Holden and Ritchie (1991) found that battered women who report greater parenting stress are more likely to have children who are experiencing adjustment problems. In addition, in that study, mothers' parenting stress level was one of two significant predictors of child behavior problems.

As additional support for the importance of the parent–child relationship, Rossman and Rosenberg (1997) present a model in which they delineate how marital conflict can interfere with parenting, resulting in caregiving that is insufficient for meeting a child's developmental needs. Through parenting that does not meet the youngsters' developmental needs, disruption of children's personality and psychological functioning occurs, resulting in difficulties for the children in the areas of competence, autonomy, and relatedness.

Moreover, Cummings and Davies (1994) propose a model based on Attachment Theory in which they present evidence for their hypothesis that marital conflict causes children to have concerns about their emotional security. The authors suggest that marital conflict undermines the children's feelings of emotional security, leading to adjustment problems in children. According to this hypothesis, emotional security is a central mediating mechanism, a link between parents' destructive styles of conflict and children's behavioral/emotional outcomes. Thus, this aspect of parenting, relationship between the parent and child, is seen as an important, although indirect, mechanism in the development of children's difficulties.

Concerning disciplinary practices as an indirect mechanism, a number of variables are important to consider. Inadequate parenting in the form of inconsistent or negative (or both) discipline puts children at especially high risk for aggressiveness through modeling. With that type of ineffective parenting, much aggressiveness occurs among family members within the home (e.g., Fauber, Forehand, Thomas, & Wierson, 1990; Patterson, De Baryshe, & Ramsey, 1989). Similarly, Cummings and Davies (1994) also point out that interparental conflict can lead to ineffective child management, inconsistent discipline, and lax monitoring of the children. Not only can there be inconsistent parenting, but disagreements over childrearing can be the source of some disputes (Grych & Fincham, 1990). Chew and Hughes (1996) completed a qualitative study of the parenting of battered women and found that the women described their parenting as rather inconsistent and often lax. Holden, Stein, Ritchie, Harris, and Jouriles (1998) also found inconsistency in parenting and lessened emotional availability to be very typical among battered women.

Summary.   The above review indicates that the direct mechanisms of modeling and stress, plus the indirect mechanisms of quality of the parent–child relationship and nature of discipline, all play a role in children's functioning. In addition, the direct and indirect mechanisms likely interact to produce the impact seen among the exposed youngsters. Clearly these mechanisms can be quite important for clinical intervention, and the implications for service provision based on these mechanisms are discussed in the following section.

Implications of Empirical, Conceptual, and Theoretical Work for Intervention

Drawing upon the findings delineated in Chapters 2, 3, and 4, as well as those discussed above, common threads among the recommendations for treatment based on empirical studies, clinical experience, and theoretical writings are evident. It is apparent that there are a number of consistent areas in which children experience symptoms as a result of exposure to spouse abuse. These include behavioral, cognitive, emotional, physiological or somatic as well as social areas. One strategy then would be that of taking a symptom-focused approach to child treatment. However, several important underlying issues also need to be addressed, including concerns related to attachment and emotional security. Thus relational aspects of intervention with the child must be included in comprehensive treatment.

It is apparent also, again from both clinical and theoretical perspectives, that addressing a woman's parenting abilities is crucial, both in terms of her relationship with her child, and her disciplinary strategies. Clearly a comprehensive approach is called for, with specific recommendations suggested by the current literature and by extrapolation from other areas of related child-treatment-focused literature. In addition, an individualized approach to each family, given each family members' functioning, would be the most effective.

Goals of Interventions.

Based on research discussed above, it is clear that children's distress can be alleviated by reducing their PTSD-related symptoms as well as their externalizing and internalizing behaviors. In addition, based on theory, children's needs to feel emotionally secure must be met, and improvements in their competence, autonomy, and ability to relate to people must be seen. Friedrich (1996) outlined a general, comprehensive approach to intervention with children who have experienced any type of maltreatment; thus it would be appropriate for youngsters who have been exposed to interparental violence. Friedrich discusses three main areas of development that are negatively influenced, which consist of attachment, self-perceptions, and behavioral/emotional dsyregulation. These problems underlie, and occur along with, all other difficulties that children might be experiencing.

According to Friedrich, attachment problems include relationship-based issues related to rejection, role reversal, boundary problems, distrust, or poor social skills. The main vehicle for change for these concerns is the treatment alliance. Self-perception difficulties include problems with understanding self-attributes and emotion and a need to concentrate on the accuracy of self-perceptions. Treatment focus would include an increase in one's sense of self-efficacy, better understanding of feelings, and changing one's "personal fable." Behavioral/emotional dysregulation is evidenced when children have difficulties inhibiting and controlling strong feelings, have problems calming themselves down after they have been upset, and generally are not able to organize themselves very well, either behaviorally or emotionally. The intervention focus that Friedrich recommends for these types of problems includes anxiety reduction techniques and keeping the treatment structured and predictable.

Therefore, it is likely that each child will have multiple areas of development that could benefit from intervention. For example, they might have PTSD-type symptoms and depression as well as have attachment issues. Shirk and Russell (1996) point out that one of the therapist's jobs during the initial evaluation for treatment planning is to assess which areas of difficulty would be most amenable to treatment first, and which should be targeted later on, thus prioritizing intervention strategies. For example, it might be that for one child, her nightmares and phobic reactions to bedtime would need to be considered first, then her attachment issues addressed in longer-term, relationship-oriented therapy (see Gil, 1991, for examples).

Thus, interventions clearly need to be tailored to the individual child and her or his situation. Group interventions for children as delineated above seem to be the best approach for those children exhibiting mild symptoms of distress. This approach could also be secondary prevention, preventing distress from becoming more pronounced, and hopefully providing the children with enough support and an understanding of the dynamics of family violence for them to be in nonviolent relationships as adults. Additional recommendations are made below for children whose level of distress and behavioral difficulty is high enough to warrant referrals and interventions beyond that of the group treatment approaches described.

Recommendations Based on Direct Mechanisms: Child Symptoms.

Regarding interventions for exposed children, focusing on the impact issues would include addressing both externalizing and internalizing behavior, cognitive processing and attributions, and trauma-specific symptoms, plus social competence and social problem solving. For readers who are interested in more detail than is possible to include here, consult Hughes and Luke (1998), Hughes et al. (1998), Hughes and Marshall (1995), Jaffe et al. (1990), Rosenberg and Giberson (1991) and Rosenberg and Rossman (1990) for more information about assessment and intervention issues for children of battered women.

As noted above, behaviors likely to result from the mechanism of social learning and modeling are usually externalizing-type problems, especially aggressiveness, for both boys and girls. Trauma-related and other PTSD-type symptoms, those that are more internalizing, are the kinds of difficulties likely to result from the mechanism of stress, again for both boys and girls. Several sources indicate that cognitive-behavioral techniques can be quite effective with both internalizing and externalizing behaviors (e.g., Finch, Nelson, & Ott, 1991; Kendall & Panichelli, 1995). Trauma-focused treatment can include the approach advocated by Kerig et al. (1997) and Silvern et al. (1995).

Modeling and Social Learning. As mentioned above, externalizing-type symptoms have been linked with modeling. For intervention with aggressiveness, empirical support has been obtained for the efficacy of training older children and adolescents on a group or an individual basis in problem-solving skills (e.g. Kazdin & Crowley, 1997) and anger control (Feindler, 1991; Feindler & Guttman, 1994). Kazdin and Crowley point out that treatment methods depend on the age and severity of the aggressive behavior, with the most evidence for success achieved with treatment of younger children and with oppositional and noncompliant behaviors. Options for intervention include parent management training, especially for younger children; and, for older children, anger management and the development of prosocial skills, such as social perspective-taking or empathy training, have been found to be effective. Feindler presents anger control strategies for aggressive youth, primarily older children and adolescents (Feindler, 1991; Feindler & Guttman, 1994). Finch, Nelson, and Moss (1993) also provide additional strategies for intervention with aggressiveness. In addition, Polyson and Kimball (1993) discuss social skills training for aggressive children.

Although these approaches have been shown to reduce aggressiveness among youngsters in a number of different populations, to date those techniques have not been evaluated specifically related to children who have been exposed to interparental abuse. Clearly additional treatment outcome research is needed with this population of youngsters. However, given the similarities in presenting problems and the range of backgrounds among the children studied, extrapolating from the studies in which effectiveness has been demonstrated seems to be quite reasonable.

Stress and Trauma-Related Symptoms. As mentioned above, internalizing-type symptoms have been linked with stress and trauma. Related to children's emotional distress, a cognitive-behavioral approach to treating both anxious and depressive symptoms has been shown to be helpful (Kaslow & Thompson, 1998; Ollendick & King, 1998). For example, with children of battered women, Wilson (1991) suggests treating negative cognitive errors and other characteristic thought patterns that seem to be conducive to depression, as well as intervening with their attributions and locus of control. Specific to children experiencing anxiety-related distress, Forman (1993) provides a good resource for clinicians focused on stress and coping. She discusses relaxation training, social problem-solving, decreasing irrational beliefs, and learning stress-reducing thought patterns. Kendall et al. (1991) also supply suggestions for treating anxiety disorders in children and adolescents, while Rehm and Sharp (1996) discuss treating depression. See also Grace, Spirito, Finch, and Ott (1993) for coping skills for anxiety and Carey (1993) for depression. Kerig et al. (1997) and Silvern et al. (1995) present their treatment focused on trauma symptoms in some detail, as noted above.

Cognitive deficits in processing have been noted by Rossman (1998a), as discussed in previous chapters. She found that, as trauma victims, children of battered women evidenced use of the strategy of "leveling," which is reducing the amount of input from the environment they receive in order to help them cope with their situation. The author pointed out that an important clinical implication of this strategy is that, regardless of therapeutic approach, clinicians may have to repeat instructions or interpretations several times before a child actually takes in the information.

Since children of battered women also show difficulties in social problem solving, enhancing those skills as well as children's empathy would be beneficial and will assist in reducing aggressiveness as well (see Dubois & Felner, 1996; LeCroy, 1994). Working on the skills deficits that are seen in the areas of social problem solving can also help with these emotionally based symptoms (Forman, 1993).

Play therapy (either nondirective or focused) to deal with interpersonal relationship and intrapersonal self-esteem issues is also likely to be beneficial with many children ages 12 years and younger. Silvern et al. (1995) provide some guidance in this area, as do Shirk and Harter (1996), who describe the treatment of low self-esteem. Children's problems with emotional security, feelings of competence, and ability to relate to people would be appropriate to treat with such an approach. This approach is likely to be longer term (e.g., 12 to 18 months), rather than 16 to 20 sessions.

Recommendations Based on Indirect Mechanisms: Parenting. Similar to the heterogeneity seen in children, the mothers also vary in their parenting skills and types of distress they might be experiencing. Hughes et al. (1998) found that although a number of women reported feeling stress related to parenting and occasionally using harsher parenting styles, a portion (approximately one-third) did not experience parenting difficulties. Thus, clinicians must individualize their approaches to the women also, depending on the mothers' needs.

If women are in need of intervention related to their parenting, research from other areas in psychology plus the models and mechanisms presented above and in previous chapters suggest that clinicians need to concentrate on parenting in a number of ways. One direction is to focus on characteristics of the women that influence the parent–child relationship. For example, clinicians would want to help the mothers reduce the "spillover" of hostility and negative affect toward the children, as well as to improve the mothers' mental health. Second, clinicians need to attend to and treat the women's depression or trauma. Doing so with an empowerment focus (Bilinkoff, 1995) will not only relieve depression but will also improve a mother's ability to be attached to her children and meet their emotional needs. Several sources suggest that intervention needs to be provided to the women for their depression before any other focus for intervention is introduced (e.g., Webster-Stratton & Hammond, 1988). Another major positive outcome would be for mothers to be able to learn ways to make the time they spend with their children more pleasurable, although this is difficult to bring about in the short term.

Another important aspect of parenting is assistance for a mother to decrease her discipline problems. She can be a much happier and more successful parent with more adequate disciplinary techniques, and she will feel empowered by her efficacy as a mother. Blechman (1981, 1984) provides an excellent discussion of a comprehensive approach to parenting, one which addresses the individual needs of the women as well as their parenting skills. Webster-Stratton and Herbert (1994) also suggest a number of strategies for therapists to help battered women learn new skills and improve the effectiveness of their discipline. In regard to conduct problems in particular, Brestan and Eyberg (1998) discuss the effectiveness of various types of parent training techniques, while Hanish, Tolan, and Guerra (1996) provide an example of a treatment program. Moreover, as mentioned previously, Jouriles et al. (1998) have good evidence for the effectiveness of their 8-month-long home-based program.

Specifically for formerly battered women, Hokoda, Edelson, Tate, Carter, and Guerrero (1998) describe a distinctive example of a parenting program. This is a 12-week program designed for women who have left the batterer, are no longer in crisis, have a child between the ages of 6 and 12 years, and agree to the evaluation component. The "Moms Helping Kids" (MHK) curriculum addresses a number of issues, including trauma symptoms and coping strategies, safety and warmth in the mother–child relationship, mothers' depression and negative distorted beliefs, plus social problem-solving skills, building self-control, and anger management. In addition, it is designed to be culturally sensitive to the needs of the primarily Spanish-speaking Mexican and Mexican American women. An especially noteworthy aspect of the program is the authors' evaluation of its effectiveness. They are using a pre- and posttest as well as 12-week follow-up test design and are randomly assigning women to either the treatment or waiting-list comparison group. Assessment is conducted using a number of scales obtained through mother and child reports, as well as a videotaped observation, which is then coded. The results of this evaluation will be very interesting and instructive. This is the kind of evaluation that is necessary to advance knowledge in this area.

Most interventions are designed for women who do not go back to live with the batterer again. The primary issue for women who do return is safety; so far no parenting programs have been designed for women who plan to go back. Parenting for women who return is likely to be much more ambiguous due to the input of the man, because women often report that they change their parenting styles when their partner is present, becoming either more lax or more strict (Chew & Hughes, 1996; Holden et al. 1998).

Summary.   The integration of clinically based literature and theoretical findings suggests a number of interventions for the women and children. Gaps between theory and intervention are all too evident, as are the needs for evaluation. Techniques discussed above that have been found to be effective in other populations must be tested out with these children exposed to interparental violence. Evaluation of the treatment approaches that are extrapolated from other samples is crucial. Although it is likely that interventions for conduct problems, depression, anxiety, PTSD symptoms, or social skills would be successful with this population as well, whether they are effective is an empirical question and remains to be assessed. Similarly, more interpersonally oriented interventions focused on increasing emotional security and improving self-esteem must be evaluated for effectiveness.

Needs in the Intervention Literature

There are a number of areas in which the literature relevant to intervention can be improved. Two areas in which the needs seem especially evident are in follow-up contacts and evaluation of treatment success. A third area of need is for more innovative interventions to be conducted, which are designed to enhance the parent–child relationship. This could be done by having time in each parenting program for some structured activity or discussion time with mothers and children. Staff could model interactions with the children for the mothers, and the mothers would be able to experience a relaxed, pleasurable time with their children.

Follow-Up.   Only a few follow-up studies after children leave shelters are available. Emery, Kraft, Joyce, and Shaw (1984) reported on a 4-month follow-up of children who had been residents in a shelter for battered women. They found that with a small sample of 16 children, a significant improvement was seen in internalizing behaviors, although the scores were still one standard deviation above the mean of the standardization sample. No change was seen in externalizing scores. When adjustment was examined relative to whether the family had returned to the batterer, few differences were noted. Scores for all of the children had declined slightly, although the children whose mothers did not return were slightly higher at the time they were in the shelter and remained so at the 4-month follow-up.

That same author conducted a 12-month follow-up of children's functioning after they left the shelter and found that the most important factor in their adjustment 12-months postshelter stay was whether their mothers returned to the batterer or remained violence-free (Emery, 1996). Children's internalizing and externalizing behaviors decreased over time if the family did not return to the batterer, as did the mothers' depression levels. If the family returned, increases in all three (mothers' depression and children's internalizing and externalizing behavior problems) were noted.

Another recently reported study followed the families for 6 months after they left the shelter (and did not return to the batterer). Holden et al. (1998) found that the mothers' punitiveness decreased substantially, and the relationship between maternal stress and violence toward the child also was no longer seen. In addition, based on the mothers' reports, the children's behaviors improved, from 63% of the children above a cutoff score for needing clinical services to 22% above that cut-off after 6 months.

These follow-up studies indicate that shelter residence is a time of transition for family members and that some of the symptoms seen may be transitory. It is important to know that returning to a violent situation worsens adjustment and that treatment hastens and improves recovery. Moreover, follow-up contacts would be very valuable in monitoring the functioning of the children and mothers, which is essential to understanding this transition process. Better understanding leads to improved treatment.

Evaluation.

Group and Individual Approaches.   Continued treatment evaluation is very important. These types of assessments, when conducted, need to be done with a specific focus, with the appropriate goals measured. Researchers must make sure that they are measuring the actual goals of a group and design the curriculum of the group accordingly. Waiting-list comparison groups seem to be the most ethical way to conduct these types of evaluations. Follow-ups of various lengths can then be obtained after the groups have been completed. Initial indications from the group treatment sessions mentioned above are that the groups are effective in their goals of increasing knowledge in certain areas. We also need evaluations of individual approaches targeting more severe difficulties. It would be helpful to know whether other areas of children's difficulties—behavioral, emotional, social, trauma-related—change. These problems also need to be assessed; then intervention focused upon them can be evaluated. A comprehensive evaluation would include standardized measures, behavioral observations, and qualitative interviews with children and mothers.

Evaluation of the parenting groups for the mothers also needs to be conducted. Most of the groups had educationally oriented goals, including the mothers' increased understanding of the impact of spouse abuse on the children and increased understanding of appropriate methods of discipline. In addition, the groups often served a supportive function; thus the women's feelings of being supported could be measured. A more difficult task would be to ascertain whether the mother's actual disciplinary practices changed, although this would be a very important goal. Similar to Hokoda et al. (1998), women and children could be observed interacting together; this could be accomplished at the same time they are receiving an assessment of their psychological functioning.

Cultural Diversity.   Tailoring interventions based on the cultural diversity of the families involved would also be important. Hokoda et al. (1998) provide a good example of such an approach, as does Silvern et al. (1995). Paniagua (1998) is a good resource for obtaining information related to culturally diverse families, as is McGoldrick, Giordano, and Pearce (1996). For example, Paniagua discusses the importance of clinicians being aware of their own biases and educating themselves about the appropriate cultural expectations and world view of any diverse families with whom they interact. He suggests a number of behaviors of which clinicians should be aware, such as particular ways to interact that are helpful for building rapport. In another good source, Koss-Chioino and Vargas (1992) point out differences one might see in the ways that trauma symptoms might be manifested in children from different cultures, or that children vary in their levels of trust for professionals, or people outside the family, with some more reluctant to reveal details than others. See also the suggestions made in Chapter 5. Clearly, families would need to receive culturally competent and culturally sensitive interventions for maximum benefit.

Program Evaluation.   Another area that would be very beneficial to assess comes under the heading of program and treatment evaluation. Currently, of the 800 or so children's programs in operation in shelters for battered women across the country, few evaluations of their programs have been conducted. It would make sense to conduct evaluations of these programs as they currently operate. It would be helpful to know whether women who stayed longer seemed to be less distressed when they left and at follow-up than women who stayed in the shelter for a shorter time. It would also be helpful to know which other variables influence postshelter adjustment, especially if those factors could be tied to shelter stay. Given that a number of shelters allow residents to remain for 8 to 10 weeks, an interesting study would be to examine adjustment and distress soon after shelter entrance and compare that with their functioning just before the family leaves after having stayed 60 to 70 days in the shelter. The interventions received by the families could also be documented in order to begin to evaluate which components of the shelter programs seemed to be most helpful. Then treatment can be tailored to the individual shelter as well as the individual child and his or her family.

Appropriate Methodologies.   Several different types of methodological approaches for program and intervention evaluation need to be employed. This would include both qualitative and quantitative methodologies. Each has its advantages and disadvantages. As Peled and Edleson (1992) point out, a qualitative approach is often good in situations when research in an area is at the preliminary stages. They suggest that this could include situations such as when the following occur: (a) program goals are vague and general; (b) appropriate standardized instruments were unavailable as well as were likely to limit the breadth and depth of information obtained; (c) in-depth information regarding the processes as well as the content of the groups would improve the program; (d) side effects and unintended consequences were also a focus of interest; and (e) the context in which the program was conducted required the least intrusive approach possible. Quantitative approaches lend themselves to the next stage of research, when the participants have been heard from in their own words. This way the researcher does not impose her or his structure upon the participants (Strauss & Corbin, 1990). The development of standardized instruments for specific populations, such as culturally diverse samples, could be conducted based upon information gained through narrative means.

Summary.   A number of approaches to providing clinical services to children and their mothers have been developed, some appropriate for children with mild difficulties, others for children with more severe problems. Underlying most of the behavioral, cognitive, emotional, somatic, or social problems children experience are issues related to attachment problems, self-perception difficulties, and behavioral/emotional dysregulation. Individual, relationship-based therapy was discussed as appropriate for these types of problems. In addition, approaches for women were discussed; these focused mainly on alleviating their depression and improving their disciplinary techniques.

Overall, it seems clear that much remains to be done in this area. Although a number of programs for children and women have been developed based on clinical writings and theoretical considerations, very few have been evaluated in a formal manner. This is the next, very vital step in this area, which is to assess and evaluate the effectiveness of current programs. Overall shelter programs as well as specific treatments and interventions need to be examined. It is incumbent upon researchers and clinicians to be creative in their approaches to intervention and evaluation.

☐ Prevention Considerations

In an old fable, villagers are faced with the task of rescuing women and children who have disappeared while in the forest and reappear later as they float, some half-drowned, down the stream near the village. Much time and effort goes into pulling them out of the stream. Quite a bit later, several of the villagers venture upstream and discover that there is a monster grabbing the children and women while they are in the forest and throwing them into the water. It is not until the monster is vanquished that no other villagers disappear and the women and children are finally safe.

Clearly the moral of this story is that one must do more than merely respond, after the fact, to a tragedy. Prevention of the traumatic events through eradication of the cause is what makes the most sense. However, for a number of reasons, clinicians and researchers in the field of family violence have been slow and reluctant to put effort into prevention endeavors. Partially this is a result of lack of resources available for anything except responding after the traumatic event has occurred. When workers are stretched thin, both in terms of person power and funding, it is difficult to take time or focus away from the immediate needs of children and women for safety and shelter. This reluctance has also been related to the fact that in general, prevention efforts are difficult to sell to agencies, the government, or to funding sources, due to insufficient resources, person power, or research evidence for their cost effectiveness (Braden & Hightower, 1998).

Perspectives on Prevention

Willis, Holden, and Rosenberg (1992) describe prevention efforts as taking place before the occurrence of a disorder in order to "either prevent the disorder itself or prevent some manifestation of the disorder" (p. 5). Prevention efforts that are conducted at the primary level change the rate of occurrence of the disorder, in this case, family violence. The authors also point out that effective prevention requires knowledge of etiology or of risk factors for woman abuse. As discussed earlier in this chapter and in previous chapters, neither the causes nor the risk factors have been clearly delineated, although more information is available currently than a decade ago.

Most authors describe three levels upon which prevention efforts can be made: primary, secondary, and tertiary. At the primary level, an intervention is aimed at an entire population, before there are evident difficulties, to reduce the incidence of new cases. Secondary prevention efforts are focused on an at-risk population and focus on early identification of individuals who are at risk. These interventions are designed to reduce the overall prevalence of a disorder. Then tertiary prevention is planned to reduce the distress associated with the disorder, similar to treatment interventions.

Gordon (1983) provided an alternative classification system, which he labeled "universal intervention," "selected intervention," and "indicated intervention." His main point was that with mental health difficulties and other problems in functioning, it is important to specify who receives the intervention. With "universal intervention," it is clear that everyone in a population receives this kind of treatment. In order to accomplish this, the treatment must be simple and not terribly expensive. Universal interventions to prevent family violence would include providing education regarding nonviolent relationships to everyone in a given population. "Selected interventions" are applied to children who are at risk for problems; "indicated interventions" are useful for those who are already showing signs of difficulties. Examples of the latter—indicated interventions—for children exposed to interparental violence would be treatment directed at the women to reduce their distress, intervention focused on batterers to reduce the chances that they will use violence in relationships again, or treatment for children who are showing substantial difficulties. Selected interventions or secondary prevention would be aimed at exposed children who have not yet developed serious problems; they would receive interventions designed to help them learn conflict resolution and negotiation skills.

Generally, prevention practitioners and researchers emphasize that the most effective preventive interventions are those that are conducted at all three levels simultaneously (Braden & Hightower, 1998). In order to prevent children from being exposed to interparental violence, one solution might be to attempt to keep youngsters from being in close proximity when parents are fighting. However, this would not really be enough to prevent distress, because of the dynamics of battering, which involve psychological coercion and verbal abuse as well as physical aggression, to which the children would be exposed every day. The only way to completely prevent exposure of children is to prevent the coercive, violent dynamics from developing. As Wekerle and Wolfe (1998) put it, prevention and intervention efforts include those that are intended to "promote healthy, nonviolent relationships ... and to ameliorate violence-promoting relationships. The overall goal is to facilitate a positive, nonaversive interactional style across all salient partners" (p. 341).

Service Delivery.   Braden and Hightower (1998) describe service delivery as occurring on three levels: individual, interpersonal, and organizational. Most often, services are targeted at individuals, although ecological perspectives on causal factors are important. An ecological approach includes considering causal factors at the level of the individual plus at the family, community, and culture levels (Willis et al., 1992). When incidence of disorders is considered on an individual level, it is seen as a function of both risk factors (such as one's genetic endowment, and environmental stressors, as well as an interaction between one's genes and the environment) and protective factors (e.g., social/coping skills, self-esteem, or social support). Prevention programs are usually focused on either reducing stressors or increasing skills, self-esteem, and social support or both (Braden & Hightower).

Researchers and clinicians have proposed a variety of family violence prevention ideas that address each of the components of the equation delineated above. For example, Swift (1988) suggests programs designed to reduce stress (GED programs, job training for those who are unemployed); to reduce risk status (support and respite for battered women); and programs designed to increase social support, self-esteem, social/coping skills, or all of these. Straus and Smith (1990) proposed that family problem-solving workshops or problem-solving courses be offered through high schools, religious organizations, or other community groups, in order to teach skills for resolving interpersonal conflict through negotiation, compromise, and reciprocity. Although these types of programs seem like they would be full of promise, as Willis et al. (1992) point out, they have not yet been tested empirically.

Promising Programs

Recently, Wolfe and Jaffe (1999) discussed several promising programs that have potential to reduce family violence across a person's lifetime. In their words, "learning to relate to others, especially intimates, in a respectful, nonviolent manner, is a crucial foundation for building effective prevention strategies for related forms of relationship violence and abuse across the lifespan" (p. 1). Moreover, the goal of prevention is "to promote attitudes and behaviors that are incompatible with violence and abuse, and that encourage the formation of healthy relationships" (p. 2). The authors describe prevention efforts across the lifespan as involving every aspect of social ecology: social, community, and neighborhood forces, schools and peer groups, family processes, and individual strengths and weaknesses. At every level efforts are made to strengthen protective factors and reduce risk factors.

Infants and Preschool Children. In terms of a lifespan approach, infants and preschool children have needs for being raised in a way that promotes physical and psychological health. In their review, Wolfe and Jaffe (1999) point out that home visitor programs have been shown to be effective in promoting healthy child development and in reducing and preventing crime. The home visitor concept was originally developed by Olds to prevent child maltreatment and has since then been applied to other social problems, such as preventing antisocial behavior (Olds & Henderson, 1989). In this context, Olds, Kitaman, Cole, and Robinson (1997) have shown that this approach can be used with good success with high-risk young mothers. According to Wolfe and Jaffe, this arrangement shows great promise for preventing interparental violence as well. As a primary prevention approach, this service could be provided to all mothers with their first child. Home visitors would be able to provide education regarding the baby, and they would also be able to stay in touch with the women regarding the state of their couple relationship as well. This approach also would be appropriate and more feasible as a "selected intervention," with family members who are high risk for interparental violence due to stress or personal history factors as the reasons for selection for the home visitation program. In terms of tertiary prevention, outreach workers are often used by shelters for battered women and other domestic violence programs. Similar to the home visitor concept, outreach workers provide support to the women regarding more effective, nonviolent, parenting as well as related to continued safety of the women and children. Tharp (1991) also recommends this strategy with children and families of diverse cultural and ethnic backgrounds, especially African American families. Locating the focus of the preventive intervention within the family supports the strong family link that African American and Latino families often have, which contributes to the intervention's success.

School-Age Children. School is an ideal setting in which to reach large numbers of children, some of whom are at risk for difficulties due to interparental violence. Youngsters this age can benefit from learning positive messages about relationships and about family roles and boundaries (Wolfe & Jaffe, 1999). Several recent projects have been undertaken to promote violence awareness and safety skill development, including one implemented by the Minnesota Coalition for Battered Women (Gamache & Snapp, 1995). The goals of the curriculum for children in kindergarten through sixth grade were to raise awareness of the influence of family problems; define violence and its impact; develop safety plans; learn to express feelings and opinions based on the values of equality, respect, and sharing of power; learn nonviolent conflict resolution; and gain a sense of worth regardless of family difficulties. According to Wolfe and Jaffe, one of the key tenets of these types of programs is the emphasis that every student needs to know about domestic violence and other forms of abuse. This awareness then allows them to assist peers or neighbors, even if they are never involved in family violence personally. Thus, this type of approach takes place on a community and social level as well as on an individual basis.

Adolescents.   According to Wolfe and Jaffe (1999), midadolescence is an ideal time to learn healthy ways to form intimate relationships because it is a time of important cognitive and social development. In terms of primary prevention, messages regarding relationships aimed at teens are able to take advantage of adolescents' interest in romantic partners and the influence of peer opinion. In addition, teens are more able to think rationally and hypothetically, which allows them to explore possibilities regarding relationships. Teens, especially those who grew up with family violence, benefit from the education and skills presented regarding healthy relationships and alternatives to violence and abuse. The early phases of social dating create an excellent opportunity for adolescents to become knowledgeable regarding ways in which violent and abusive behavior toward intimate partners may occur, patterns that occasionally develop somewhat by accident. This seems to be an opportune time for learning, regardless of whether the teens were from violent or nonviolent family backgrounds (Gray & Foshee, 1997).

As secondary prevention, programs can be organized in schools (e.g., Gray & Foshee, 1997) or be community based. Intended for a more select population, such as teens who are at risk due to family violence in their background, these programs can be implemented in various settings. An example of a community-based program is the Youth Relationships Project (Wolfe et al., 1996), which was developed to help teens understand the dynamics of power and abuse of power in relationships and relate that understanding to their own social and dating relationships. This program involves teens from ages 14 to 17 years who have been referred from active caseloads of child protection service agencies because they experience violence and abuse in their family background. This program has been evaluated and found to result in positive changes in attitudes and knowledge, as well as decreases in self-reported initiation of dating violence (Wekerle & Wolfe, 1998).

Adults.   With a lifespan focus, adults would be the target of public service announcements and other advertisements for primary prevention. The purpose of these ads would be to promote awareness of family violence and the specialized resources that are in place to address the needs of family members. Wolfe and Jaffe (1999) emphasize that these ads are not "one size fits all", but rather they contain different types of information that are modified to fit the particular target group. For example, men and women would need different messages because they have different levels of awareness as well as commitment to the issue. In addition, information would need to be addressed to specific communities, such as different ethnic or cultural groups, for the reasons delineated in Chapter 5.

Secondary prevention would include identifying at-risk groups of adults, or identifying battered women at the earliest stage possible, and providing them with resources in order to relieve distress and prevent additional trauma.

Summary

Prevention approaches show great promise for reducing the likelihood of interparental violence, although the impact of these programs would not be seen immediately. The values of prevention work fit nicely with those of many domestic violence programs. For example, many shelters provide speakers to interested groups in order to educate people, to identify people in need of assistance, and possibly ultimately to prevent interparental violence. However, there are a number of obstacles to prevention efforts becoming widespread. Partially the paucity of prevention programs is due to lack of training on the part of individual service delivery personnel; partially it is due to systemic obstacles such as funding mechanisms. Fee-for-service treatment and insurance reimbursement do not lend themselves easily to a prevention model. In addition, providing evidence for the effectiveness of prevention programs is very difficult, due to the fact that results are seen years, and often decades, later.

Nevertheless, there are a number of promising programs that have been developed as appropriate across the lifespan. Home visitors seem to be helpful for infants and preschool children and their parents, while school-based programs reach school-age children. For adolescents, a relationship-based focus seems to be rather effective at a primary or secondary level. Public service announcements could be effective at the primary prevention level for adults. In general, we need evaluations of all of the above programs, evidence that indicates that over the long term, prevention is less costly, financially and socially, than waiting to treat psychologically and physically injured children and women.

☐ Conclusions

Treatment and prevention together can assist in reducing the negative impact and the amount of interparental violence to which children are exposed. It is evident that most of the intervention approaches in use today grew out of clinician's needs, although many of the treatment programs now are more grounded in theory and empirical work. As a result in this area, an understanding of associated factors as well as direct and indirect mechanisms now provides us with some guidance regarding treatment. However, currently there are very few studies of the effectiveness of interventions, although the results from the few that are available (Graham-Bermann, 1998; Jouriles et al., 1998; Rossman, 1999) are indeed encouraging.

The tertiary prevention, or treatment, approaches differ according to the severity of the problems the children experience. Milder difficulties are appropriate for group approaches, while more severe problems are more effectively addressed individually. Individualized intervention is available for children and for the women, with very little known about parenting approaches for abusive men. Treatment goals for children are focused on helping them deal with behavioral and emotional symptoms as well as with low self-esteem and attachment-based problems. There is no doubt that we also need more evaluation of the effectiveness of these interventions. The same could be said of approaches for mothers, where the programs are focused on the women's depression and parenting skills. Similar to groups for children, groups are an alternative for women whose difficulties are mild; more intensive programs are more effective for more severe levels of problems.

There is a definite need for more follow-up studies examining the transition and healing process. In addition, general program evaluations to assess the effectiveness of shelters' children's programs would be very useful. Moreover, treatment programs are not enough; we must use primary and secondary prevention also to reduce and ideally eliminate interparental violence.

☐ References

Alessi, J. J., & Hearn, K. (1984). Group treatment of children in shelters for battered women. In A. R. Roberts (Ed.), *Battered women and their families* (pp. 49–61). New York: Springer.

Alessi, J. J., & Hearn, K. (1998). Group treatment of children in shelters for battered women. In A. R. Roberts (Ed.), *Battered women and their families* (2nd ed., pp. 159-173). New York: Springer.

Arroyo, W., & Eth, S. (1995). Assessment following violence-witnessing trauma. In E. Peled, P. G. Jaffe, & J. L. Edleson (Eds.), *Ending the cycle of violence: Community responses to children of battered women* (pp. 27–42). Newbury Park, CA: Sage.

Bandura, A. (1973). *Aggression: A social learning analysis.* Englewood Cliffs, NJ: Prentice–Hall.

Bilinkoff, J. (1995). Empowering battered women as mothers. In E. Peled, P. G. Jaffe, & J. L. Edleson (Eds.), *Ending the cycle of violence: Community responses to children of battered women* (pp. 97–105). Newbury Park, CA: Sage.

Blechman, E. A. (1981). Toward comprehensive behavioral family interventions: An algorithm for matching families and interventions. *Behavior Modification, 5,* 221–235.

Blechman, E. A. (1984). Competent parents, competent children: Behavioral objectives of parent training. In R. A. Polster & R. F. Dangel (Eds.), *Parent training: Foundations of research and practice* (pp. 34–66). New York: Guilford.

Braden, J. P., & Hightower, A. D. (1998). Prevention. In R. J. Morris & T. R. Kratochwill (Eds.), *The practice of child psychotherapy* (3rd ed., pp. 510–539). Boston: Allyn & Bacon.

Brestan, E. V., & Eyberg, S. M. (1998). Effective psychosocial treatments of conduct-disordered children and adolescents: 29 years, 82 studies, and 5,272 kids. *Journal of Clinical Child Psychology, 27,* 180–189.

Carey, M. P. (1993). Child and adolescent depression: Cognitive-behavioral therapy strategies and interventions. In A. J. Finch, Jr., W. M. Nelson, III, & E. S. Ott (Eds.), *Cognitive-behavioral procedures with children and adolescents* (pp. 289–314). Boston: Allyn & Bacon.

Carlson, B. E. (1996). Children of battered women: Research, programs, and services. In A. R. Roberts (Ed.), *Helping battered women: New perspectives and remedies* (pp. 172–187). New York: Oxford University Press.

Carmen, E., Rieker, P., & Mills, T. (1984). Victims of violence and psychiatric illness. *American Journal of Psychiatry, 141,* 387–383.

Chew, C., & Hughes, H. M. (1996, June). *Parenting of battered women: A preliminary investigation.* Paper presented at the second Conference on Children Exposed to Family Violence, Austin, TX.

Cummings, E. M., & Davies, P. (1994). *Children and marital conflict: The impact of family dispute and resolution.* New York: Guilford.

DuBois, D. L., & Felner, R. D. (1996). The quadripartite model of social competence: Theory and applications to clinical interventions. In M. A. Reinecke, R. M. Dattilio, & A. Freeman (Eds.), *Cognitive therapy with children and adolescents* (pp. 124–152). New York: Guilford.

Edelson, M. G., & Hokoda, A. (1996, March). *Moms Helping Kids: Teaching moms to help their children cope with the effects of domestic violence.* Paper presented at the 21st Annual Association for Women in Psychology Conference, Portland, OR.

Emery, R. (1996, June). *A longitudinal study of battered women and their children: One year following shelter residence.* Paper presented at the Second Conference on Children Exposed to Family Violence, Austin, TX.

Emery, R. E., Kraft, S. P., Joyce, S., & Shaw, D. (1984). *Children of abused women: Adjustment at four months following shelter residence.* Paper presented at the annual meeting of the American Psychological Association, Toronto.

Fauber, R., Forehand, R., Thomas, A. M., & Wierson, M. (1990). A mediational model of marital conflict on adolescent adjustment in intact and divorced families: The role of disrupted parenting. *Child Development, 61,* 1112–1123.

Feindler, E. L. (1991). Cognitive strategies in anger control interventions for children and adolescents. In P. C. Kendall (Ed.), *Child and adolescent therapy: Cognitive-behavioral procedures* (pp. 66–97). New York: Guilford.

Feindler, E. L., & Guttman, J. (1994). Cognitive-behavioral anger control training. In C. W. LeCroy (Ed.), *Handbook of child and adolescent treatment manuals* (pp. 170–199). New York: Lexington.

Finch, Jr., A. J., Nelson, III, W. M., & Moss, J. H. (1993). Childhood aggression: Cognitive-behavioral therapy strategies and interventions. In A. J. Finch, Jr., W. M. Nelson, III, & E. S. Ott (Eds.), *Cognitive-behavioral procedures with children and adolescents* (pp. 148–205). Boston: Allyn & Bacon.

Finch, Jr., A. J., Nelson, W. M., III, & Ott, E. S. (1991). (Eds.), *Cognitive-behavioral procedures with children and adolescents.* Boston: Allyn & Bacon.

Fincham, F. D., Grych, J. H., & Osborne, L. N. (1994). Does marital conflict cause child maladjustment? Directions and challenges for longitudinal research. *Journal of Family Psychology, 8,* 128–140.

Forman, S. G. (1993). *Coping skills interventions for children and adolescents.* San Francisco: Jossey-Bass.

Frey-Angel, J. (1989). Treating children of violent families: A sibling group approach. *Social Work with Groups, 12,* 95–107.

Friedrich, W. N. (1996). An integrated model of psychotherapy for abused children. In J. Briere, L. Berliner, J. A. Bulkley, C. Jenny, & T. Reid (Eds.), *The APSAC handbook on child maltreatment* (pp. 104–118). Thousand Oaks, CA: Sage.

Gamache, D., & Snapp, D. (1995). Teach your children well: Elementary schools and violence prevention. In E. Peled, P. G. Jaffe, & J. L. Edleson (Eds.), *Ending the cycle of violence: Community responses to children of battered women* (pp. 209–231). Newbury Park, CA: Sage.

Gentry, C. E., & Eaddy, V. B. (1980). Treatment of children in spouse abusive families. *Victimology, 5,* 240–250.

Gibson, J. W., & Gutierrez, L. (1991). A service program for safe-home children. *Families in Society: The Journal of Contemporary Human Services, 72,* 554–562.

Gil, E. (1991). *The healing power of play: Working with abused children.* New York: Guilford.

Grace, N., Spirito, A., Finch, A. J., Jr., & Ott, E. S. (1993). Coping skills for anxiety control in children. In A. J. Finch, Jr., W. M. Nelson, III, & E. S. Ott (Eds.), *Cognitive-behavioral procedures with children and adolescents* (pp. 257–288). Boston: Allyn & Bacon.

Graham-Bermann, S. A. (1992). *"Kids' Club": An approach to supporting children of battered women.* (Available from S. A. Graham-Bermann, Dept. of Psychology, University of Michigan, Ann Arbor, MI 48109-1109.)

Graham-Bermann, S. A. (1998, October). *An evaluation of "Kids' Club."* Paper presented at the Fourth International Conference on Children Exposed to Family Violence, San Diego.

Graham-Bermann, S. A., & Hughes, H. M. (1998). The impact of domestic violence and emotional abuse on children: The intersection of research, theory, and clinical intervention. *Journal of Emotional Abuse, 1*(2), 1–22.

Graham-Bermann, S. A., Levendosky, A. A., Porterfield, K., & Okun, A. (in press). The impact of woman abuse on children: The role of social relationships and emotional context. *Journal of Clinical Child Psychology.*

Gray, H. M., & Foshee, V. (1997). Adolescent dating violence: Differences between one-sided and mutually violent profiles. *Journal of Interpersonal Violence, 12,* 126–141.

Grusznski, R. J., Brink, J. C., & Edleson, J. L. (1988). Support and education groups for children of battered women. *Child Welfare, 67,* 431–444.

Grych, J. H., & Fincham, F. D. (1990). Marital conflict and children's adjustment: A cognitive-contextual framework. *Psychological Bulletin, 108,* 267–290.

Hanish, L. D., Tolan, P. H., & Guerra, N. G. (1996). Treatment of Oppositional Defiant Disorder. In M. A. Reinecke, F. M. Dattilio, & A. Freeman (Eds.), *Cognitive therapy with children and adolescents* (pp. 62–78). New York: Guilford.

Hanson, K. L., & Hughes, H. M. (1998, August). *Children of battered women and adjustment problems: A proposed causal model.* Paper presented at the annual meeting of the American Psychological Association, San Francisco.

Hokoda, A., Edelson, M. G., Tate, D., Carter, A., & Guerrero, G. (1998). *Moms Helping Kids (MHK): An educational program to help children cope with the effects of domestic violence.* Paper presented at the Fourth International Conference on Children Exposed to Family Violence. San Diego.

Holden, G. W., & Ritchie, K. L. (1991). Linking extreme marital discord, child rearing, and child behavior problems: Evidence from battered women. *Child Development, 62,* 311–327.

Holden, G. W., Stein, J. D., Ritchie, K. L., Harris, S. O., & Jouriles, E. N. (1998). The parenting behaviors and beliefs of battered women. In G. W. Holden, R. Geffner, & E. N. Jouriles (Eds.), *Children exposed to marital violence: Theory, research, and intervention* (pp. 289-334). Washington, DC: American Psychological Association.

Hughes, H. M. (1982). Brief interventions with children in a battered women's shelter: A model preventive program. *Family Relations, 31,* 495–502.

Hughes, H. M. (1986). Research with children in shelters: Implications for clinical services. *Children Today, 15,* 21–25 (DHHS Publication No. 86–30014).

Hughes, H. M. (1991, August). Research concerning children of battered women: Clinical and policy implications. In R. Geffner & M. Paludi (Cochairs), *State-of-the-art research in family violence: Practical implications.* Paper presented at the annual meeting of the American Psychological Association, San Francisco.

Hughes, H. M. (1997). Research concerning children of battered women: Clinical implications. In R. Geffner, S. Sorenson, & P. Lundberg-Love (Eds.), *Violence and sexual abuse at home: Current issues in spousal battering and child maltreatment* (pp. 225–244). New York: Haworth.

Hughes, H. M., & Fantuzzo, J. W. (1994). Family violence: Child. In R. T. Ammerman, M. Hersen, & L. Sisson (Eds.), *Handbook of aggressive and destructive behavior in psychiatric patients* (pp. 491–508). New York: Plenum.

Hughes, H. M., & Graham-Bermann, S. A. (1998). Children of battered women: Impact of emotional abuse on adjustment and development. *Journal of Emotional Abuse, 1*(2), 23-50.

Hughes, H. M., & Luke, D. A. (1998). Heterogeneity in adjustment among children of battered women. In G. W. Holden, R. Geffner, & E. N. Jouriles (Eds.), *Children exposed to marital violence: Theory, research, and applied issues* (pp. 185–222). Washington, DC: American Psychological Association.

Hughes, H. M., Luke, D. A., Cangiano, C., & Peterson, M. (1998, October). *Clinical implications of heterogeneity in psychological functioning among children of battered women.* Paper presented at the Fourth International Conference on Children Exposed to Family Violence, San Diego.

Hughes, H. M., & Marshall, M. (1995). Advocacy for children of battered women. In E. Peled, P. G. Jaffe, & J. L. Edleson (Eds.), *Ending the cycle of violence: Community responses to children of battered women* (pp. 121–144). Newbury Park, CA: Sage.

Hughes, H. M., & Rau, T. J. (1984, August). *Psychological adjustment of battered women in shelters.* Paper presented at the annual meeting of the American Psychological Association, Toronto.

Jaenicke, C., Hammen, C., Zupan, B., Hiroto, D., Gordon, D., Adrian, C., & Burge, D. (1987). Cognitive vulnerability in children at risk for depression. *Journal of Abnormal Child Psychology, 15,* 559–572.

Jaffe, P. G., Wolfe, D. A., & Wilson, S. K. (1990). *Children of battered women.* Newbury Park, CA: Sage.

Johnson, R. J., & Montgomery, M. (1990). Children at multiple risk: Treatment and prevention. In *Aggression, family violence, and chemical dependency* (pp. 145–163). New York: Haworth.

Johnston, J. R. (1998). Biennial report for group interventions for children and parents at-risk from abuse and violence. Unpublished manuscript.

Johnston, J. R., & Roseby, V. (1997). *In the name of the child: A developmental approach to understanding and helping children of conflicted and violent divorce.* New York: Free Press.

Jouriles, E. N., McDonald, R., Stephens, N., Norwood, W., Spiller, L. C., & Ware, H. S. (1998). Breaking the cycle of violence: Helping families departing from battered women's shelters. In G. W. Holden, R. Geffner, & E. N. Jouriles (Eds.), *Children exposed to marital violence: Theory, research, and applied issues* (pp. 337–370). Washington, DC: American Psychological Association.

Jouriles, E. N., Norwood, W. D., McDonald, R., Vincent, J. P., & Mahoney, A. (1996). Physical violence and other forms of marital aggression: Links with children's behavior problems. *Journal of Family Psychology, 10,* 223–234.

Kaslow, N. J., & Thompson, M. P. (1998). Applying the criteria for empirically supported treatments to studies of psychosocial interventions for child and adolescent depression. *Journal of Clinical Child Psychology, 27,* 146–155.

Kazdin, A. E., & Crowley, M. (1997). Moderators of treatment outcome in cognitively-based treatment of antisocial behavior. *Cognitive Therapy and Research, 21,* 185–207.

Kendall, P. C., Chansky, T. E., Friedman, M., Kim, R., Kortlander, E., Sessa, F. M., & Siqueland, L. (1991). Treating anxiety disorders in children and adolescents. In P. C. Kendall (Ed.), *Child and adolescent therapy: Cognitive-behavioral procedures* (pp. 131–164). New York: Guilford.

Kendall, P. C., & Panichelli, S. M. (1995). Cognitive-behavioral treatments. *Journal of Abnormal Child Psychology, 23,* 107–124.

Kerig, P. K., Fedorowicz, A. E., Brown, C. A., & Warren, M. (1997, June). *Assessment and intervention with PTSD in children exposed to violence.* Paper presented at the Third International Conference on Children Exposed to Family Violence, London, Ontario, Canada.

Koss-Chioino, J. D., & Vargas, L. A. (1992). Conclusion: Improving the prospects for ethnic minority children in therapy. In L. A. Vargas & J. D. Koss-Chioino (Eds.), *Working with children: Psychotherapeutic interventions with ethnic minority children and adolescents* (pp. 300–309). San Francisco: Jossey-Bass.

Le Croy, C. W. (1994). *Handbook of child and adolescent treatment manuals.* New York: Lexington.

Lee, C. M., & Gotlib, I. H. (1989). Maternal depression and child adjustment: A longitudinal analysis. *Journal of Abnormal Psychology, 98,* 78–85.

Lehmann, P., & Carlson, B. E. (1998). Crisis intervention with traumatized child witnesses in shelters for battered women. In A. R. Roberts (Ed.), *Battered women and their families* (2nd ed., pp. 99-128). New York: Springer.

Levendosky, A., & Graham-Bermann, S. A. (1994, August). *A parenting group for battered women: Empowerment through learned competence.* Paper presented at the annual meeting of the American Psychological Association, Los Angeles.

Matthews, D. J. (1995). Parenting groups for men who batter. In E. Peled, P. G. Jaffe, & J. L. Edleson (Eds.), *Ending the cycle of violence: Community responses to children of battered women* (pp. 106–120). Newbury Park, CA: Sage.

McGoldrick, M., Giordano, J., & Pearce, J. K. (Eds.). (1996). *Ethnicity and family therapy.* New York: Guilford.

Olds, D., & Henderson, C. (1989). The prevention of maltreatment. In D. Cicchetti & V. Carlson (Eds.), *The handbook of child maltreatment* (pp. 722–763). Cambridge: Cambridge University Press.

Olds, D., Kitaman, H., Cole, R., & Robinson, J. (1997). Theoretical foundations of a program of home visitation for pregnant women and parents of young children. *Journal of Community Psychology, 25,* 9–25.

Ollendick, T. H., & King, N. J. (1998). Empirically supported treatments for children with Phobia and Anxiety Disorder: Current status. *Journal of Clinical Child Psychology, 27,* 156–167.

Pagelow, M. D. (1984). *Family violence.* New York: Praeger.

Paniagua, F. A. (1998). *Assessing and treating culturally diverse clients* (2nd ed.). Thousand Oaks, CA: Sage.

Patterson, G. R., De Baryshe, B. D., & Ramsey, E. (1989). A developmental perspective on antisocial behavior. *American Psychologist, 44,* 329–335.

Peled, E., & Davis, D. (1995). *Group work with child witnesses of domestic violence: A practitioner's manual.* Thousand Oaks, CA: Sage.

Peled, E., & Edleson, J. L. (1992). Multiple perspectives on groupwork with children of battered women, *Violence & Victims, 7,* 327–346.

Peled, E., & Edleson, J. L. (1995). Process and outcome in small groups for children of battered women. In E. Peled, P. G. Jaffe, & J. L. Edleson (Eds.), *Ending the cycle of violence: Community responses to children of battered women* (pp. 77–96). Newbury Park, CA: Sage.

Peled, E., Jaffe, P. G., & Edleson, J. L. (1995). *Ending the cycle of violence: Community responses to children of battered women*. Newbury Park, CA: Sage.

Polyson, S., & Kimball, W. (1993). Social skills training with aggressive children. In A. J. Finch, Jr., W. M. Nelson, III, & E. S. Ott (Eds.), *Cognitive-behavioral procedures with children and adolescents* (pp. 206–232). Boston: Allyn & Bacon.

Potgieter, R. (1988). A comprehensive, centrally coordinated, cost-effective family violence counseling program for small communities. *Canadian Journal of Community Mental Health, 7,* 137–145.

Ragg, D. M. (1991). Differential group programming for children exposed to spouse abuse. *Journal of Child and Youth Care, 5,* 59–75.

Ragg, D. M., & Webb, C. (1992). Group treatment for the preschool child witness of spouse abuse. *Journal of Child and Youth Care, 7,* 1–19.

Rehm, L. P., & Sharp, R. N. (1996). Strategies for childhood depression. In M. A. Reinecke, F. M. Dattilio, & A. Freeman (Eds.), *Cognitive therapy with children and adolescents* (pp. 103–122). New York: Guilford.

Roseby, V., & Johnston, J. R. (1997). *High-conflict, violent, and separating families: A group treatment manual for school age children*. New York: Free Press.

Roseby, V., & Johnston, J. R. (1998). Children of Armageddon: Common developmental threats in high-conflict divorcing families. *Child and Adolescent Psychiatric Clinics of North America, 7,* 295–309.

Rosenberg, M. S. (1987). Children of battered women: The effects of witnessing violence on their social problem-solving abilities. *The Behavior Therapist, 4,* 85–89.

Rosenberg, M. S., & Giberson, R. S. (1991). The child witness of family violence. In R. T. Ammerman & M. Hersen (Eds.), *Case studies in family violence* (pp. 231–254). New York: Plenum.

Rosenberg, M. S., & Rossman, B. B. R. (1990). The child witness to marital violence. In R. T. Ammerman & M. Hersen (Eds.), *Treatment of family violence* (pp. 183–210). New York: Wiley.

Rossman, B. B. R. (1998a). Descartes' Error and Posttraumatic Stress Disorder: Cognition and emotion in children who are exposed to parental violence. In G. W. Holden, R. Geffner, & E. N. Jouriles (Eds.), *Children exposed to marital violence: Theory, research, and applied issues* (pp. 223–256). Washington, DC: American Psychological Association.

Rossman, B. B. R. (1998b, October). *Time heals all: How much and for whom?* Paper presented at the Fourth International Children Exposed to Family Violence Conference, San Diego.

Rossman, B. B. R. (1999). *Frost Foundation final report*. Unpublished manuscript, University of Denver.

Rossman, B. B. R., Hughes, H. M., & Hanson, K. L. (1998). Victimization of school-aged children. In B. B. R. Rossman & M. S. Rosenberg (Eds.), *Multiple victimization of children: Conceptual, developmental, research, and treatment issues* (pp. 87–106). Binghamton, NY: Haworth.

Rossman, B. B. R., & Rosenberg, M. S. (1997). Psychological maltreatment: A needs analysis and application for children in violent families. In R. Geffner, S. B. Sorenson, & P. K. Lundberg-Love (Eds.), *Violence and sexual abuse at home: Current issues in spousal battering and child maltreatment* (pp. 245–262). Binghamton, NY: Haworth.

Shirk, S., & Harter, S. (1996). Treatment of low self-esteem. In M. A. Reinecke, F. M. Dattilio, & A. Freeman (Eds.), *Cognitive therapy with children and adolescents* (pp. 175–198). New York: Guilford.

Shirk, S. R., & Russell, R. L. (1996). *Change processes in child psychotherapy*. New York: Guilford.

Silvern, L., Karyl, J., & Landis, T. Y. (1995). Individual psychotherapy for the traumatized children of abused women. In E. Peled, P. G. Jaffe, & J. L. Edleson (Eds.), *Ending the cycle of violence: Community responses to children of battered women* (pp. 43–76). Newbury Park, CA: Sage.

Stark, K. W., Rouse, L. W., & Livingston, R. (1991). Treatment of depression during childhood: Cognitive-behavioral procedures for the individual and the family. In P. C. Kendall (Ed.), *Child and adolescent therapy: Cognitive-behavioral procedures* (pp. 165–208). New York: Guilford.

Straus, M. A., & Smith, C. (1990). Family patterns and primary prevention of family violence. In M. A. Straus & R. J. Gelles (Eds.), *Physical violence in American families: Risk factors and adaptation to violence in 8,145 families* (pp. 507–528). New Brunswick, NJ: Transaction Publishers.

Strauss, A., & Corbin, J. (1990). *Basics of qualitative research: Grounded theory, procedures and techniques*. London: Sage.

Swift, C. F. (1988). Stopping the violence: Prevention strategies for families. In L. A. Bond & B. M. Wagner (Eds.), *Families in transition: Primary prevention programs that work* (pp. 252–285). Beverly Hills, CA: Sage.

Tharp, R. G. (1991). Cultural diversity and treatment of children. *Journal of Consulting and Clinical Psychology, 59,* 799–812.

Tutty, L. M., & Wagar, J. M. (1994). The evolution of a group for young children who have witnessed family violence. *Social Work with Groups, 17,* 89–104.

Wagar, J. M., & Rodway, M. R. (1995). An evaluation of a group treatment approach for children who have witnessed wife abuse. *Journal of Family Violence, 10,* 295–305.

Webster-Stratton, C., & Hammond, M. (1988). Maternal depression and its relationship to life stress, perceptions of child behavior problems, parenting behaviors and child conduct problems. *Journal of Abnormal Child Psychology, 16,* 299–315.

Webster-Stratton, C., & Herbert, M. (1994). *Troubled families, problem children*. New York: Wiley.

Wekerle, C., & Wolfe, D. A. (1998). Windows for preventing child and partner abuse: Early childhood and adolescence. In P. K. Trickett & C. J. Schellenbach (Eds.), *Violence against children in the family and community* (pp. 339–370). Washington, DC: American Psychological Association.

Willis, D. J., Holden, E. W., & Rosenberg, M. S. (1992). *Prevention of child maltreatment: Developmental and ecological perspectives*. New York: Wiley.

Wilson, S. K. (1991, March). *Improving social problem-solving skills in children from violent homes*. Paper presented at the annual meeting of the American Orthopsychiatric Association, Toronto, Canada.

Wilson, S. K., Cameron, S., Jaffe, P., & Wolfe, D. (1989). Children exposed to wife abuse: An intervention model. *Social Casework: The Journal of Contemporary Social Work, 70,* 180–184.

Wolfe, D. A., & Jaffe, P. G. (1999, February). *Prevention of domestic violence: Emerging initiatives*. Paper presented at the Asilomar Conference on Children and Intimate Violence. Pacific Grove, CA.

Wolfe, D. A., Jaffe, P., Wilson, S., & Zak, L. (1985). Children of battered women: The relationship of child behavior to family violence and maternal stress. *Journal of Consulting and Clinical Psychology, 53,* 657–665.

Wolfe, D. A., Wekerle, C., Gough, R., Reitzel-Jaffe, D., Grasley, C., & Pittman, A. (1996). *The Youth Relationships Manual: A group approach to ending woman abuse and promoting healthy relationships*. Newbury Park, CA: Sage.

7

CHAPTER

Children and Youth Exposed to Interparental Violence and the Courts

Children and youth exposed to interparental violence may come into contact with the court system in a variety of ways. Consider the following examples. In the first situation, parents with a long history of father-perpetrated domestic violence decide to separate and divorce, and a contested custody battle ensues in family court. Although child physical abuse has not been an issue in this particular family, the mother is concerned that her husband's rage will be displaced from her onto their children, or will erupt when he becomes involved in another intimate relationship or both. Moreover, she and her attorney argue that exposing children to interparental violence represents psychological maltreatment and indicates poor parenting skills. The child is then subjected to multiple interviews and a psychological evaluation in a process to determine the best custody arrangement for this family. In a second situation, an adolescent who has grown up in a high-conflict, violent family since childhood has now come into contact with the juvenile court for aggressive behavior toward his teachers and peers, substance-related crimes, and truancy. The court will make a decision about community-based treatment, residential placement, or possibly referral to a secure corrections facility, depending on the nature and frequency of the offenses.

In this chapter, we will address the relevant psychological and forensic issues that arise when children who have been exposed to interparental violence come into contact with varying aspects of our court system. Clinical case examples and research will be incorporated into our discussion, with the goal of describing what is known about these issues in the literature and what is available to inform practitioners who work with these children and their families.

☐ Child Custody Issues with Exposed Children

Astrid and Mark

Astrid and Mark, both of European American descent, dated in high school and decided to marry after graduation. They had their first child one year later, a daughter, whom they named Amelia. When Amelia was 6 years old, her parents separated and later divorced. A psychologist was appointed to conduct the custody evaluation in the bitter contested battle for Amelia that followed. Astrid told the psychologist that Mark had "thrown her around" when she was pregnant with Amelia and had "pushed and slapped" her on several occasions. She also mentioned he continued to call and harrass her after they separated and had threatened to kill her and kidnap Amelia. When confronted by the psychologist, Mark acknowledged "slapping and shoving Astrid around on several occasions" but denied threatening his wife. Mark portrayed Astrid as physically abusive and mentally unstable when they were together, stating that she was often angry and provocative with him, threatening to stab him in the middle of the night. He denied abusing alcohol, contradicting Astrid's report of Mark's excessive drinking, often in front of their daughter. Amelia, during her interview, was reticent about her feelings and thoughts: she was noncommittal about her parents' relationship or her father's drinking, wanted to live with her mother if possible, and admitted it was hard sometimes for her mother to get her to school on time. The psychologist noted that the child looked disheveled, had numerous school tardies, and according to her teacher, appeared fatigued and had difficulty concentrating.

Psychological testing revealed both parents had emotional difficulties that would likely interfere with parenting. Mark's low tolerance for stress and emotional discomfort contributed to frequent bursts of anger and irritability that often escalated into physically abusive behavior. He tended to externalize and blame problems on Astrid or Amelia and had limited psychological insight into his contribution to conficts. Although he liked to think of himself as a competent, compassionate, strong (i.e., aggressive), and independent man, personality testing revealed him as inadequate, emotionally dependent, hypersensitive to others' opinions, and easily wounded by perceived slights. He was at high risk for using alcohol or other substances or both to mute his emotional pain. His empathic understanding of Amelia and the concerns she might have living with him and away from her mother was quite limited. The psychologist did find that a positive factor in favor of Mark's situation was the close proximity to his mother (Amelia's grandmother), who could provide her son with support and her granddaughter with a positive female influence. Contrary to the psychologist's perception, Amelia herself did not feel close with her grandmother, feeling that she treated her like a much younger child.

Astrid's psychological evaluation revealed longstanding depression, anxiety, somatization, and low self-worth. She was easily overwhelmed by stress, preferring to withdraw and isolate rather than seek help. Astrid tended to be impulsive, could be unpredictable, and had wide mood swings. She presented to the examiner as uncertain, vague, and somewhat inarticulate about her relationship with Mark and her parenting abilities, with great difficulty maintaining an independent life. Because she was not receiving child support from Mark and had problems keeping regular employment, she relied primarily on her parents for financial backing. The psychologist noted that she did not keep Amelia clean and appropriately dressed, nor did she provide adequate supervision. Because the psychologist discounted and failed to follow up on the comments Astrid made about Mark's violence toward her, no attempt was made to further evaluate for PTSD or to view several of Astrid's psychological symptoms in the context of a traumatic reaction to interparental violence and psychological abuse. The psychologist did note that Astrid was empathic with her daughter and could put Amelia's needs in front of her own.

The psychologist recommended that physical custody be given to Mark, and an appropriate visiting schedule be set up for Astrid and her daughter. Apart from noting superficially the incidents of physical violence between Astrid and Mark, the psychologist did not pursue further assessment of the couple's relationship dynamics to determine whether these incidents were the "tip of the iceberg," and more extensive physical and psychological violence lay underneath. In fact, the psychologist discounted Asrid's accounts of violence and abuse in light of her psychological test results and portrayed her as a histrionic, emotionally unstable, and potentially dangerous woman and neglectful mother who would latch onto any reason to slander her former husband.

Under the best of circumstances, child custody evaluations are extraordinarily difficult to conduct, but the issues become even more thorny with the addition of interparental violence to the equation. Until very recently, psychologists, other mental health professionals, attorneys, and judges who were involved with contested custody evaluations did not always understand the dynamics involved with interparental violence or their impact on children and parenting. A common assumption was that interparental violence occurred between adult partners and if physical child abuse was not involved, then children were not affected (Walker & Edwall, 1987). Or if children were considered in the equation, then the court assumed that the violence would stop once the adults separated and, therefore, there was no need to factor that information into the custody decision making process. Mental health professionals involved in custody decision-making were not always trained in domestic violence and did not know how to assess for it or factor it into their recommendations.

When Astrid decided to challenge the court's custody findings, she hired an attorney who was sensitive to the issues involved with domestic violence. A second psychologist was appointed to review the case and determine whether additional information about domestic violence and its effects on Asrid and Amelia were relevant to the custody determination. After reviewing Astrid's medical and psychiatric records; Amelia's complete set of school and medical records; police records; and interviews with Mark, Astrid, Amelia, and both sets of grandparents; the second psychologist had findings that differed from the first evaluator and recommended physical custody be given to the mother. Additional therapy and parenting classes were also recommended for both parents, and an alcohol treatment program was recommended for the father.

Detailed questioning about the couple's relationship revealed a lengthy, violent history that began during dating and escalated over time in the marriage. Astrid described numerous incidents of being smacked, pushed, and shoved into furniture and doors; being punched while holding Amelia; having her arm twisted; being kicked in the head; choked; had large objects thrown at her such as a telephone or redwood table; was repeatedly threatened to be murdered; and feared for her life. Both parents stated they were unable to talk with each other without screaming, yelling, or insulting the other. The police were twice called to the home by neighbors, but Astrid declined to press charges (these incidents occurred prior to the state's mandatory arrest law). Once separated, Astrid reported that Mark continually harrassed her with threatening phone calls, some of which she taped, and that he waited for her outside of her job. Mark reported incidents where Astrid pushed him, threatened to kill him, and was "emotionally out of control." Upon further questioning and confrontation with police and the telephone tapes, Mark admitted that he was more often the aggressor, although "she drove me to it," he said. He denied alcohol has ever been a problem.

Amelia reported feeling frightened of her father's angry temper and was nervous about telling the first evaluator much information because she did not want to be held responsible as the informant about her parents' problems and further risk her father's anger. For example, in asking open-ended questions about her parents' use of alcohol and drugs, a different picture emerged than the one she told the first psychologist. Amelia was extremely concerned about her father's past and present alcohol use, recognizing that he often became belligerent and unpredictable when he drank. She reported taking the initiative to talk with him about stopping drinking and he "did it for awhile," but started again when he had a new girlfriend. It became apparent that Amelia was monitoring her father's drinking and was quite anxious whenever he did drink. Amelia described her relationship with her mother as closer, and she said her father did not play with her or pay her much attention when she was with him. Amelia wanted to live with her mother and felt well cared for by Astrid.

☐ Interparental Violence and the Parent–Child Relationship

Studies investigating maternal psychological impairment in the context of battering and its effects on children have found that the mother–child relationship suffers. (See Chapter 2 for additional research on the topic, only some of which will be discussed here.) Margolin (1995) points out that the many roles played by parents (e.g., providers of emotional support, models of emotion regulation, instructors, disciplinarians) could be undermined by interparental violence and that any of these roles could be disrupted in battered women who experience depression, are distracted by basic safety concerns, or who live with fear in their own homes. Mothers in violent relationships who are preoccupied with feelings of fear, guilt, depression, or low self-esteem may be psychologically unavailable for their children or unable to provide them with a safe, nurturing family environment (Aguilar & Nightingale, 1994; Elbow, 1982; van der Kolk, 1987). In fact, failure to protect children from exposure to battering and the physical abuse that may accompany interparental violence has been used against the mother in child protection allegations and proceedings (Magen, 1999). In failure-to-protect cases, the burden is placed on the mother to control and predict the violence, rather than on the father's abusive behavior.

Mothers who are living with violent mates also report feeling significantly less able to cope with the ordinary parenting demands in contrast to nonvictimized mothers. In one study of battered and nonbattered mothers (Holden & Ritchie, 1991), maternal parenting stress levels were correlated positively with paternal irritability (i.e., frequent anger and fault finding) and the degree to which mothers changed their behavior toward children in the presence of fathers (i.e., they became more lenient or harsh). In addition, parental irritability was related significantly to maternal ratings of their children's behavior. Fathers who are violent with their mates also appear to have difficulty relating to their children. They are rated by their partners as emotionally uninvolved, inconsistent, with a greater tendency to use power control tactics with their children (Holden & Ritchie). In fact, one study of battered women and their children found highest rates of child abuse with fathers (50% of children), compared with mothers abusing 35%, and both parents abusing 15% (Stark & Flitcraft, 1988).

When women and men separate after being involved in a battering relationship, many have difficulty with the aftermath of the violence and its effects on their ability to establish a healthy parenting relationship with their children. Rosenberg, Giberson, Rossman, and Acker (in press) describe several types of these problems including (1) helping the custodial parent and children gradually decrease the guarded, crisis atmosphere that tends to pervade the home even after the batterer leaves; (2) helping to repair troubled parent–child relationships, which entails assisting the children and custodial parent (and, if appropriate, the noncustodial parent in separate sessions) to air their experiences of violence and vulnerability, encourage productive communication and problem solving, and rebuild a foundation of trust and nurturance; (3) changing inadequate or destructive disciplinary tactics to setting healthy limits and increasing the repertoire of constructive disciplinary strategies; (4) helping children and parents cope with traumatic memories; and (5) promoting emotion regulation and appropriate emotional expression. Clearly, the postseparation/divorce parental and family tasks can be a considerable but gratifying undertaking for clinicians and families alike.

Variations in Interparental Violence and Its Effects on Custody Decision Making

Recent research on men who batter have identified different typologies of men and different contexts in which interparental violence occurs (e.g., Dutton, 1998; Hamberger, Lohr, Bonge, & Tolin, 1996; Holtzworth-Munroe & Stuart, 1994). Although the specific typologies vary somewhat across studies, three general profiles have emerged that consider dimensions of violence severity, generality of violence beyond intimate relationships, and personality disorder or psychopathology of the perpetrator. In their proposed typology, Holtzworth-Munroe and Stuart identify batterers who are violent only within their families, antisocial batterers who are violent both within and outside the family, and batterers described as dysphoric/borderline, with high dependency needs and depressive affect. In an empirical test of Holtzworth-Munroe and Stuart's model, Hamberger et al. identified three similar profiles, including batterers described as nonpathological, antisocial, and passive aggressive dependent. Dutton identified three batterer typologies including those who are overcontrolled, psychopathic, or borderline. However, the question in custody decision making is whether these different types of battering men do or do not make good fathers. We are not aware of any research that relates specific profiles of battering men with demonstrated parenting capacities and skills. In fact, the research on battering men and observed parenting skills is essentially nonexistent.

However, the initial findings reported above do have implications for intervention and custody decision making and suggest the need for careful assessment of violent incidents in the context of the marital or intimate relationship and divorce process. Johnston and Roseby (1997) are one of the few research teams who have related typologies of domestic violence perpetrators (both men and women) to child outcomes, parent–child relationships, and suggestions for custody decision making. Based on their study of interparental violence among divorcing families, Johnston and Campbell (1993a, 1993b) identified five profiles of violence in 140 custody-disputing couples with 175 children. In their sample, three-fourths of the separating/divorced couples had a history of physical aggression: 41% revealed high violence (beating up the other, threats of or use of a weapon), 23% admitted moderate violence (slapped, kicked, bit, or hit the other), 10% described low violence (threw or smashed objects, pushed, grabbed, or shoved the other), and 26% reported no violence. Based on clinical and qualitative data, the five violence profiles were (1) ongoing/episodic male battering, which most closely resembles the battering spouse/battered wife syndrome; (2) female-initiated violence, in which the woman always initiates the physical assault; (3) male-controlling interactive violence, in which the man exercises physical domination and control as a legitimate way of resolving interpersonal conflict; (4) separation-engendered or postdivorce trauma, where violence is typically uncharacteristic of the marital relationship but is precipitated by the relationship's dissolution; and (5) psychotic and paranoid reactions, where violence results from disordered thinking and serious distortions of reality. These distortions may be a consequence of severe psychopathology, substance abuse, or both.

Given the different manifestations of interparental violence across families, Johnston and Roseby (1997) make specific recommendations in the areas of mediation, visitation, and custody arrangements when interparental violence is involved. First, they suggest a careful evaluation of violence within the context of the marital relationship, with each party interviewed separately. In California, and in other states across the country, there is now mandated training on domestic violence for professionals involved in family court and custody determinations (e.g., mediators, judges, attorneys, clinicians, etc.), so that professionals have information about the dynamics of interparental violence and its effects. During interviews, data about violent incidents are gathered, including precipitating factors, who initiates and who responds with violence, patterns of violence frequency and severity over time, and each person's psychological response. In addition, we suggest reviewing documentation of violent incidents through police reports and medical records if available; assembling corroborative accounts from others such as friends, family, and neighbors; and assessing for psychologically abusive behavior such as intimidation, control, degradation, isolation, and so on in addition to physical violence (see Pence & Paymar, 1993, and Sonkin, 1995, for details about gathering data on psychological abuse). Further discussion of evaluating psychological abuse in intimate relationships is found in the section on exposed youth and the juvenile justice system. Finally, information about parenting capacities of each parent and the quality of the parent–child relationship are crucial elements to integrate into the evaluation.

In their recommendations about mediation, Johnston and Roseby (1997) argue against including the ongoing/episodic batterer and the psychotic-paranoid batterer in confidential mediation. Mediation can be successful when parents demonstrate the capacity to contain their emotional distress and focus on the needs of their children. Mediation is inappropriate for men who have histories of serious battering, whose distortions of reality seriously impair their psychological functioning, and who cannot make good use of a rational decision-making process. Both profiles of men are potentially quite dangerous, and they can use the mediation process to manipulate or frighten the participants (including the mediator) into making unfair agreements that suit their needs, or fail to follow through on agreements perceived as biased against them. Thus, the women in these situations often need the court's authority to support their custody and visitation arrangements.

Johnston and Roseby (1997) recommend adapting mediation and family counseling services for individuals who fit the other three violence profiles. Ensuring physical safety, rebuilding trust, and creating a balance of power between the parties are the guiding principles of intervention. Setting the frame for mediation or family counseling is the first step in working with domestically violent couples. This includes addressing the limits of confidentiality if threats of violence or violent incidents reoccur (i.e., the court will be informed without consent of either party) and ensuring that restraining orders are in place as well as adequate security procedures on court premises. Separate mediation and counseling sessions are recommended for victim and perpetrator to work out custody and visitation plans. Victims are encouraged to seek out a support person (i.e., friend, mental health professional) to help them through the process and to make use of community resources to support family members.

Regarding custody and visitation arrangements, Johnston and Roseby (1997) caution that sole or joint physical custody is contraindicated with fathers who have engaged in episodic or ongoing battering and who are psychotic or have paranoid delusions. Supervised visitation or suspension of visitation are options for parents who continue to stalk or harass their partners, threaten violence, or commit new violent acts against their partners. Resuming unsupervised visits should be dependent on the parent's complete cessation of physical violence and psychological abuse as well as successful completion of relevant interventions, such as a batterers' program, alcohol or substance abuse treatment, parenting classes, or psychiatric treatment. Court orders need to be specific about dates, times, and places of child transfer, and the exchange of children may need to be supervised by or done solely by a neutral third party. The court needs to be quick and forceful in response to parent violations of court orders, including restraining orders. In states with mandatory arrest laws and intensive supervision for domestic violence, a parent is charged with a criminal offense. The court then has more intervention options for parents who violate court orders.

In California, similar to many other states across the country, new domestic violence laws require men (and women) arrested for domestic violence to participate in a 52-week intervention program, perform community service hours, be supervised on probation for 3 years, and follow through on the attached regulations (e.g., chemical testing for alcohol or drugs, random search and seizure, no weapons, no contact with the victim or only peaceful contact, etc.), pay relevant fines and fees, and come to court regularly for progress reports. If defendants are terminated unsuccessfully from their batterers' program or from probation or both, they could be sentenced up to a year in jail. Some counties have created domestic violence courts, where a judge (in addition to probation) monitors the progress (or lack thereof) of defendants over their entire probationary period until it is completed successfully or until they are sent to jail to finish out their sentence.

Those men and women who are on probation for interparental violence and who are also in the midst of custody or visitation disputes potentially have access to resources that could help them with family-related concerns outside the context of family court. Since the 52-week group intervention is focused on stopping physical and psychological violence, there is a forum for discussion and confrontation on batterers' use of abusive power and control tactics to get back at their partners directly or through their children during visitation or other aspects of the custody process. For example, men may continue to harass a (former) wife by making abusive phone calls, pumping the children for information, refusing to pick up or return the children at the designated time and place, and demanding frequent court appearances to alter visitation arrangements (Walker & Edwall, 1987). In contrast to family court arrangements, men and women on probation for domestic violence may address these issues if group facilitators or probation officers or both are made aware of them. Men and women are often referred for collateral services such as parenting classes, individual therapy, and other support groups. In family court, counseling may be recommended, but a family court judge does not have the same legal mandate that a domestic violence court judge does if one or the other party declines to participate in counseling.

Psychological evaluations are recommended for parents with suspected mental illness and include a risk assessment for homicide and suicide (Johnston & Roseby, 1997). In addition, evaluations to determine parenting capacities are needed for women who initiate violence, since their behavior places children at greater risk for abuse and neglect. Women arrested for interparental violence may be involved in mutually combative relationships, or were caught for striking their partner in the context of being battered themselves, or fall into Johnston and Campbell's (1993a) typology of women-initiated violence. Making this distinction has implications for custody arrangements, since the father may be a more appropriate custodial choice. Successful completion of parenting education and anger management programs may be indicated for both the violent woman and her partner. In many communities, there are now anger management groups designed specifically for abusive women, including those with related substance abuse problems.

In summary, the variations in domestically violent families make it impossible to recommend a unitary procedure or policy to cover all circumstances and families. These cases are extremely difficult, time consuming, and anxiety provoking for mental health professionals and families alike. It is imperative that a detailed evaluation of physical violence and psychological abuse be conducted in each situation to help guide appropriate interventions for these families. In the past, mental health and legal professionals involved in custody decisions have not been adequately trained and educated about the dynamics of interparental violence, their different effects on the parent–child relationship, the range of child psychological outcomes that vary by gender and developmental period, and the issues involved in the aftermath of separation and divorce. More research on the parenting capacities of victimized parents and their battering partners is needed to help guide these difficult decisions. Extremely little is known, for example, about the parenting capacities of different types of violent men and women and how these may or may not change over time and with intervention. Now, many courts are amenable to working with mental health professionals and other disciplines on the issue of interparental violence and the custody decision-making process. We are witnessing an exciting time to make changes in the ways courts handle these cases and in helping the children and families who struggle to recover and heal from these traumatizing experiences.

☐ Exposed Youth and the Juvenile Justice System

Clyde

Clyde, a bright, engaging, African American young man was exposed to an extraordinary amount of violence in his nuclear family, between his relatives, and in his community. His mother and stepfather were involved in a mutually combative, dangerous, and savage relationship, fighting with whatever objects were available to them, including glass items such as ashtrays; baseball bats; kitchen utensils; and weapons such as knives, pistols, and shotguns. Clyde also witnessed or was aware of several incidents where his mother viciously attacked women in the neighborhood with razors and knives or was attacked herself and sustained critical injuries. Relatives, with whom he spent considerable time during his childhood, were similarly brutal. At 8 years old, he observed his aunt's death at the hand of his uncle, followed immediately by the police shooting his uncle in the head and killing him. At 10 years old, he was playing basketball when he observed another uncle gunning down his wife.

Tragically, Clyde grew up in a community with rampant violence, fueled by poverty, substance abuse and easy access to guns and other weapons. To protect himself from his mother's dangerous unpredictability, Clyde withdrew emotionally, hid under his bed, and "shut people out" as a child. Then, later, he began to stay away from home as much as possible and found his neighborhood was even more dangerous than his family. It was commonplace for him to observe dead bodies in alleys, gang fights with weapons, and, later on, drive-by shootings. With the juxtaposition of long-standing family and social problems against a dearth of community services and programs, it was not surprising that Clyde and most of his friends ended up in the juvenile justice system as the first step to extended criminal involvement.

At 13 years old, Clyde and several older friends were charged with robbery, which was later dismissed. One year later, Clyde and two companions were charged with burglary. He was then placed on probation until he and another friend were arrested for driving a vehicle without authorized consent, whereupon Clyde was made a ward of the court and sent to a juvenile court youth camp. Clyde did well in the structured camp, and his probation officer predicted he would continue his "outstanding adjustment" after he returned home. Not surprisingly, Clyde was soon caught up in the neighborhood life again. At 17 years old, Clyde and three codefendants were charged and convicted of murdering a drug dealer while in the commission of a robbery.

Clyde, and others like him, who grow up in a labyrinth of violent relationships without adequate intervention or substantive protective factors are at high risk of becoming involved in the juvenile justice system. As discussed in prior chapters, exposure to marital violence has been linked to a range of problem behaviors and impaired skills that may increase the potential for getting in trouble at school and in the community. For example, children and youth exposed to interparental violence tend to exhibit increased externalizing behavioral problems such as aggression (Holden & Ritchie, 1991), alcohol and substance use (Dembo, Williams, Wothke, Schmeidler, & Brown, 1992), and delinquency (Rosenberg, 1987). Poor problem-solving and conflict resolution skills (Jaffe, Wolfe, & Wilson, 1990; Moore, Pepler, Mae, & Kates, 1989; Rosenberg, 1987) coupled with low social competence (Hughes, 1988; Rossman et al., 1993; Wolfe, Zak, Wilson, & Jaffe, 1986) and limited empathy (Rosenberg, 1987) can leave children and youth vulnerable to making improper peer choices or using flawed judgment in difficult situations. Getting caught for illegal behavior or status offenses (i.e., behaviors that are illegal given the youth's age, such as truancy, incorrigibility, promiscuity) brings the youth into contact with a system that, ostensibly, has the youth's interests in mind and may be able to provide a point of positive intervention for the family. However, until relatively recently, domestic violence in the absence of physical or sexual abuse and neglect has not been recognized as a significant contributor to a minor's psychological and legal problems.

As extreme as Clyde's situation is, he tends to exemplify a subpopulation of youth who are inundated by multiple risk factors and victimization experiences simultaneously, such as marital violence; poverty or low income; parental psychopathology; parental alcoholism and substance abuse; loss through separation, divorce, or death; stressful and traumatic life events; neighborhood violence; and direct experiences of physical, sexual, and psychological maltreatment (Rossman & Rosenberg, 1998). Potentially any one of these risk factors can be associated with developmental impairments and behavioral problems, but the sheer accumulation of adverse factors can be overwhelming to the youth and families involved, as well as those attempting to intervene with this population.

Paul

In contrast to Clyde, there is another subgroup of youth and families who come into contact with juvenile justice but who, on the surface, may present to the outside world as considerably less disturbed. Paul A. was in his last year of high school when he came to the attention of the juvenile authorities for truancy. Paul was the oldest of three siblings in a middle-class family of European American descent. Throughout his childhood and adolescence, he and his siblings were exposed to their father's rampant alcoholism, his tortuous physical and psychological abuse of their mother, and incessant verbal cruelty. Paul observed his father regularly push, kick, choke, and punch his mother interspersed with more severe beatings, and he heard threats to kill her, her relatives, himself, the children, and strangers. Mr. A. routinely made hateful racist remarks that typically ended with threats to blow up various groups of people he despised, including Mexicans, Catholics, Democrats, Asians, and anyone else that did not share his ethnic, religious, and political background. Whenever Mrs. A. contemplated leaving her husband, Mr. A. intensified his drinking and murderous threats to kill his wife, to sever her spine, to kill Paul in front of his wife, or to kill innocent people at a mall. These threats were most terrifying and credible to the family, since Mr. A.'s unpredictability and countless demonstrations of physical cruelty to family members and pets indicated that he was capable of almost anything. The lethality potential was especially high in the A. family, because since Mr. A. hunted and had a ready supply of guns and ammunition in the home.

Both parents held respectable jobs and were perceived as pillars of their church and community, and the children participated actively in social groups (e.g., Boy and Girl Scouts, religious youth groups, and sports teams). With the exception of several parents of the children's friends commenting occasionally that Mr. A. appeared "controlling" or "moody," especially when he had too much to drink, no one knew the depths to which Paul, his mother, and siblings struggled with Mr. A.'s aggressive, terrifying behavior. When Paul was reported for truancy and vandalism to juvenile authorities, his situation did not raise suspicion nor was an individual or family evaluation recommended by the court or the school. Both systems dismissed his behavior as "just being an adolescent," rather than a cry for help. However, within a family that required absolute obedience, Paul's actions were tantamount to mutiny. He was seriously beaten by his father, necessitating a week at home to recover from the bruises and swelling.

Three months after his case was dismissed without any referrals for academic or psychological intervention, Mr. and Mrs. A. had a particularly frightening argument on Easter morning, which ended with Mr. A.'s threat to kill his wife. That evening, after Mr. A.'s regular drinking binge, he fell asleep in the living room chair. It was common

for Mr. A. to drink in his chair, start a verbal fight with his wife that sometimes intensified into an injurious attack, and then go back to his chair to drink and start the cycle
again. Over the last 3 months, with his father's increasingly disturbed behavior, esca-
lating threats to kill, and lack of outside intervention by the courts, school, relatives, or
police, Paul came to believe that his father would win in the end and not only kill his
mother but kill them all. As an act of desperate protection of his mother and family,
Paul took a gun and shot his father in the head. He was tried and convicted of volun-
tary manslaughter and sent to a treatment-oriented correctional youth program for 2
years.

☐ Clinical and Forensic Issues

Mental health professionals are often asked to evaluate children and youth who come
into contact with the juvenile justice system. The purpose of these evaluations may
vary, from those that are clinical in nature to those whose goals are chiefly forensic.
Examples of issues included in clinical evaluations are diagnostic information (e.g.,
depression, organic brain damage, PTSD, substance abuse, and psychosis), whether
medication is warranted, psychological testing results, and a description of the
defendant's psychological dynamics and functioning. In forensic evaluations, the above
information may also be included but oriented toward legal issues. Examples of forensic concerns in juvenile criminal matters include whether the child or youth is competent to stand trial (i.e., whether the defendant understands the charges and can cooper-
ate with the attorney in the proceedings); whether the child or youth should be tried
in juvenile court or held to answer as an adult in criminal court; the child or youth's
state of mind at the time of the crime; and extenuating mental health, family, or contextual factors that could further illuminate the crime itself or circumstances surrounding
the crime or status transgression (Grisso, 1986; Melton, Petrila, Poythress, & Slobogin,
1997).

Developing social histories. As part of the evaluation process, attorneys often ask
mental health professionals to prepare a social history of the child or youth charged
with a violent crime. A social history is similar to, although much more thorough than,
the typical clinical evaluation. In a social history, the social historian (i.e., mental health
professional) assembles and relies on multiple sources of information from different
facets of the defendant's life to provide the judge or jury with an expanded explanation
of how the child or youth came to be in the present circumstance (Rosenberg & Liebert,
1997). This type of information is legally permitted and serves not to excuse the defendant but to provide a bio-psycho-social context from which to view his or her behavior.
Included in a social history is an analysis of the life events, traumas, and other critical
factors that have influenced the defendant's psychological functioning, including behavior, emotional life, social and family relationships, cognitive abilities, and sense of
identity. Understanding the dynamics of domestic violence, along with other direct
and indirect experiences of physical, sexual, and psychological maltreatment and their
impact on the individual's psychological functioning are critical components of a social
history.

The social historian gathers data from available documents such as medical and
academic records, juvenile justice history, prior psychological and educational evaluations, psychiatric history, child protective service records, and family-related documents

and information such as parental and other family members' psychiatric history, criminal involvement, alcoholism and substance abuse, and so on. Multiple interviews are conducted with the defendant as well as with family members and significant others (e.g., teachers, coaches, neighbors, religious leaders, friends, intimate partners, therapists, probation officers, etc.), who could provide developmental or current or both perspectives on the defendant's and family's lives. A defendant's social history is often entered through live testimony during the guilt or sentencing or both phases of a trial if the defendant is tried as an adult. In situations where the defendant remains under juvenile court jurisdiction, the judge may ask for testimony or a written report in order to inform intervention or out-of-home placement decisions.

In over a decade of one author's experience (M.S. Rosenberg), it is typical that a social history represents the first time a comprehensive, inclusive analysis has been conducted with this population of highly conflictual, violent families whose children wind up in the court system. Although hindsight is 20/20, it is possible to see missed opportunities for intervention when reviewing defendants' social histories, which can better inform us about recognizing signs of danger and contribute to thinking about early intervention or prevention efforts.

Evaluation of Domestic Violence. In the past, mental health and court personnel have failed to evaluate for the presence and extent of domestic violence and its psychological effects on juveniles. Although the climate in juvenile justice is to make judges, attorneys, mental health professionals, and others who work closely with children and youth acutely aware of domestic violence and its effects, it has been our and others' experience that until very recently, legal and mental health professionals have not conducted the type of thorough domestic violence assessments similar to those documenting sexual or physical abuse, nor have they understood the psychological implications of exposure (Jaffe et al., 1990; Kenning, Merchant, & Tomkins, 1991). In fact, due to court constraints of time and money, or professionals' lack of specific training, it is not unusual for juveniles to have relatively brief (i.e., 1 to 2 hours) psychological or psychiatric assessments, if they are evaluated at all. These evaluations typically fail to identify even the most basic traumatic experiences. Given that children and adolescents often have mixed feelings about revealing personal and incriminating information about their families to anyone, let alone to a stranger (Femina, Yeager, & Lewis, 1990), it is not uncommon that brief interviews fail to reveal an accurate accounting of the defendant's traumatic history and its effects on current functioning.

Questionnaires focusing on domestic violence and other traumatic experiences should be incorporated into the evaluation process for juveniles coming into contact with the courts. Whether the information is gathered for purposes of a clinical evaluation, a social history, or a presentence report, thorough data gathering about domestic violence, child maltreatment, and other stressful and traumatic influences on the defendant's behavior presents the judge or jury or both with a comprehensive assessment of the defendant's behavior.

Even those defendants who are relatively forthcoming about the quality of their parents' relationship or the extent of physical and psychological maltreatment experienced personally can benefit from structured questions. These questions may reveal additional information not recalled previously, or experiences that have become so "normalized" that they are not considered atypical, or experiences not easily put into words. For example, Clyde initially described his parents' relationship as "madness that wouldn't end," "like being on a roller coaster," "like drowning in fear." It was difficult for him to say exactly what he observed, because the sheer frequency, severity, and terror associated with the violence was far too overwhelming and had occurred from such a young age. After talking generally about his own emotional reactions during his childhood and adolescence, he was able to respond to specific behavioral questions related to domestic violence (Sonkin, 1998) that helped him organize and communicate his experiences to the interviewer. Paul, on the other hand, tended to minimize and understate his father's violence and control over the family. Without asking specific questions that elicited the obvious and subtle forms of violence and intimidation perpetrated by Mr. A., the interviewer could have easily misrepresented Paul's experience and the historical elements that contributed to his fearful perception of his father's behavior on the night of his death.

There are several questionnaires available to help clinicians and social historians elicit detailed information about domestic violence. The CTS (Straus, 1979) is one of the most frequently used research instruments to gather data about a range of behaviors used to resolve interpersonal conflict and can also be used as an interview tool. Rosenberg (1987) modified the CTS to ask children as young as 5 years old whether they observed (i.e., saw or heard or both) their parents using the various conflict resolution strategies when they argued, with good results. Sonkin's (1998) Spouse Abuse History Form is based loosely on the CTS but was expanded considerably to include a broader range of physically abusive behaviors, sexual abuse, psychological violence, and injuries resulting from domestic violence. Although the form was developed initially as a data gathering tool for adult respondents, it has been used successfully with adolescents as young as 13 years old. During the evaluation process, the clinician asks the youth whether he or she has been exposed to the following types of situations and, if so, to describe what happened and their behavioral and emotional response.

Often it is easier to gather information about the physical aspects of domestic violence and more difficult to elicit information on specific incidents of psychological abuse. Sonkin's (1998) Spouse Abuse History Form has a separate section for psychological violence, with categories based on Amnesty International's definition of psychological abuse composed of items tailored specifically to domestically violent relationships. The categories are somewhat similar to those of APSAC (see Chapter 1) and include isolation (e.g., observed parent who refused to let the other socialize with family or friends; prohibited use of the telephone), induced debility-producing exhaustion (e.g., observed parent who forced the other to clean house or work excessively long hours; other not allowed to sleep), monopolization of perceptions (e.g., observed parent who was pathologically jealous and controlled activities such as money and socializing), threats (e.g., observed parent who made threats to kill spouse or children; threats to kill others), degradation (e.g., observed parent who belittled or publicly humiliated spouse), alcohol or drug administration (e.g., observed parent who forced other to use alcohol or drugs), denying other's reality (e.g., observed parent who told or convinced other that he or she was mentally ill; lying and manipulating), and occasional kindness (e.g., observed parent who promised that abuse would stop and showed remorse). The limitation of questions about psychological abuse is that children and youth may be unsophisticated regarding the subtleties in adult relationships unless they overhear blatantly abusive remarks (e.g., threats or degrading comments) or are made aware of them by one of the parents. Certainly, children and youth are likely to experience similar types of psychological abuse and manipulation in their personal relationships with parent(s), which should also be explored by the interviewer. Brassard, Hart, and Hardy (1993) offer clinicians a parent–child interaction rating scale of psychologically abusive interactions that could be used for that purpose.

William

William J., a 16-year-old African American male, illustrates how critical it is to understand and document the scope and effects of psychological abuse observed between parents and between parent and child when conducting a social history or clinical evaluation or both for the court. William and two codefendants (who were actually family members) were arrested for first degree murder of their distant cousin. All three young men were under 18 years of age but were tried as adults in superior court. William was the third child of five, raised by his mother and stepfather, who became part of the family when William was 2 years old. Mr. J. had been extraordinarily violent toward his wife during the early and middle years of their marriage, which included incidents of choking her to unconsciousness, punching with fists and beating her with an extension cord, burning her arm with an iron, and once holding a pillow in front of her face in an attempt to suffocate her. When Mr. J. stopped drinking and using methamphetamines, his physical violence became intermittent, but his psychological terrorizing and domination continued unabated. He threatened Mrs. J. and William with knives ("don't talk back to me or I'll come after you"), with a bat, and threatened to kill if anyone fought back with him ("that will be the day that you die"). Although neighbors often called the police, William followed his stepfather's instructions not to reveal any information to outsiders, and no further investigation was done.

When William was 9 years old, he witnessed a particularly gruesome homicide of a relative's boyfriend committed by his stepfather and mother, when both were high on methamphetamine. William's stepfather stabbed the man, and extracted his eye from the socket, while William's mother continued to stab him numerous times. William had been friendly with the boyfriend, sometimes watching television with him or playing games. Shockingly, the parents spent little time in jail since their actions were ruled as self-defense. From that time onward, Mr. J. terrorized William and the other children with fabricated stories about atrocities he had committed as a soldier in Vietnam (in fact, he was never in Vietnam). The combination of exposure to his stepfather's prior brutality, observing the gruesome death of a "friend" at the hands of his own parents, and being fed horrifying details about death and torture contributed to a myriad of psychological problems for William, including PTSD, depression, withdrawal, and significantly impaired cognitive functioning. Although his IQ placed him in the bright normal range of intellectual functioning, William failed third grade once and had to repeat seventh grade three times before he was expelled from school for violent outbursts.

William was referred for several psychological evaluations as he went through the juvenile system, and none of them mentioned a hint of the extreme domestic violence that permeated his childhood and adolescence nor understood the traumatic implications of witnessing a homicide committed by his parents. After he was released from a court-ordered placement, he returned home to "work with his family on a new business." Mr. J. was developing a "family business" in which he gathered relatives and associates around him to help create a nationwide credit card scam. As Mr. J. envisioned his enterprise, he demanded unquestioned compliance from everyone. When a cousin did not show the proper respect, Mr. J. ordered his execution to be carried out by two other family members and his son or risk a similar fate. William had no intent to murder his cousin but was too terrified to go against his stepfather's will directly. His muddled idea to somehow distract the others and save his cousin was unsuccessful, and his cousin was killed.

At the trial, one psychologist presented William's social history, which identified the extent of domestic violence and other trauma to which William was exposed and its effects on William's behavioral, social, emotional, and moral development. A second psychologist presented William's clinical evaluation, which included current psychological testing and results and a discussion of how previous clinical and school findings should have raised concern about his family situation. The jury wanted to acquit William of the charges, but because the judge did not allow instructions that provided for that opportunity, he was convicted of a lesser charge.

☐ Multiple Victimization and Sources of Adversity

We have already addressed the fact that domestic violence is frequently associated with other forms of child maltreatment and sources of adversity (see Barnett, Miller-Perrin, & Perrin, 1997; Rossman & Rosenberg, 1998). Children and youth who commit violent crimes, and those who come into contact with the juvenile system for status offenses, need to be evaluated for the range of potential trauma and stressors that may be contributing to their current life situations. Lewis and colleagues (Lewis, Mallouh, & Webb, 1989; Lewis, Shanok, Grant, & Ritvo, 1984; Lewis, Shanok, Pincus, & Glaser, 1979) and others (e.g., Fagan & Wexler, 1987; Mones, 1991; Widom, 1992) have noted the association between child maltreament and subsequent violent behavior. Even with all the heightened attention to child maltreatment during the past two decades, it is shocking how often children, youth, and their families fall through the cracks until a tragedy occurs and investigation uncovers previously blatant, yet undocumented, problems.

Various measures are available to assess for child maltreatment experiences during an interview, although many have been used for research rather than clinical purposes (see Briere, 1997, for a review of adult instruments with child history components). Some instruments also include additional sources of adversity and trauma such as exposure to neighborhood violence, natural disasters, serious illnesses, other situations involving serious injury, and so on. Although many of these instruments were developed for adults reporting on current and retrospective experiences, some may be suitable for adolescents or, at the very least, guide the clinician/evaluator in asking questions about the types of situations and experiences that need to be assessed. One example of such an instrument is the Traumatic Events Scale (Elliott, 1992, 1997), which includes 30 operationalized definitions of interpersonal and environmental traumas, 10 of which are childhood events. These events include the following: exposure to disasters, witnessing school and neighborhood violence, peer sexual and physical assault, exposure to interparental violence, and the range of child maltreatment experiences, including physical abuse, psychological abuse, and sexual abuse. Clinicians and social historians then integrate the information learned about the child or adolescent with psychological testing, if possible, to come to an understanding of how the various factors have contributed to his or her present circumstances, which could inform the court about intervention options.

☐ Intervention with Multiproblem Youth and Their Families

Juvenile justice systems are often quite limited in the types of intervention they could recommend for multiproblem youth and their families, due to the restricted range of community services available, especially alternatives to traditional mental health treatment, the costs, and the seriousness of the youth's offense. Much has been written about the problems in developing effective treatment for serious juvenile offenders and the necessity to recognize and incorporate multiple determinants of antisocial behavior (e.g., Kazdin, 1996; Mulvey, Arthur, & Reppucci, 1990). Henggeler (1989) has argued that the primary reason for poor treatment outcomes with delinquent youth may be the failure to address the ecological complexity of factors contributing to a youth's criminal behavior. Typical interventions are short term, narrow in scope, or are holding environments without treatment components or follow-up, so that youth are returned to the same family and environment that might have contributed initially to their legal problems. It has been our experience that youth who come from families with interparental violence and are sent away from home to residential placements are frequently returned to their families without the court's recognition of domestic violence or its effects. Clyde, in fact, is a good example of that practice. After placement at a juvenile court youth camp, he returned to live in his violent family and community and was soon rearrested for a more serious crime.

Henggeler and colleagues (Henggeler & Borduin, 1990) have created an ecologically oriented treatment approach to working with multiproblem youth and families called multisystemic therapy (MST), which would be an excellent choice of treating at-risk youth from domestically violent families. MST is a highly individualized family and home-based treatment that intervenes with systems and processes known to be related to youth antisocial behavior, such as family affective relations, parental disciplinary strategies, peer relationships, and school performance. Previous research has found MST effective in treating inner-city juvenile offenders (Henggeler et al., 1986) child abuse and neglect (Brunk, Henggeler, & Whelen, 1987), adolescent sex offenders (Borduin, Henggeler, Blaske, & Stein, 1990), and chronic juvenile offenders (Mann, Borduin, Henggeler, & Blaske, 1990).

In a study of MST effectiveness with 84 serious juvenile offenders and their families compared with youth who received the usual services delivered by a Department of Youth Services (Henggeler, Melton, & Smith, 1992), the MST group had fewer arrests and self-reported offenses and spent an average of 10 fewer weeks incarcerated. Families in the MST condition reported increased family cohesion and decreased youth aggression in peer relationships. Usual services for comparison group youth entailed one or more of the following monitored by probation officers: curfews, school attendance, referral to an outside agency for mental health or other services. Although treatment referrals were frequently made to agencies, few youth and families actually complied or followed through for any period of time due to resistance, family difficulties, and the passive nature of traditional mental health treatment. In contrast, MST services were delivered in the home, varied in frequency as needed (from daily to once a week, depending on crises), and incorporated family systems, ecological, and behavioral models. MST was found equally effective with youths of different gender, ethnic background, and level of family cohesion. Moreover, MST is a relatively inexpensive, although intensive, intervention in contrast to institutional placement. A 3-month course of MST treatment per client cost $2,800 compared with $16,300 for an average cost of institutional placement in North Carolina (Henggeler et al., 1992).

Although this study did not address specifically the types of family problems encountered or the extent to which interparental violence was present, it was clear from the youths' behaviors that interparental violence and other forms of child maltreatment would not be unexpected. Youth averaged 3.4 prior arrests, 8.1 weeks of previous incarcerations, and 59% of the sample had at least one arrest for a violent crime. MST presents an excellent alternative to traditional mental health and probation services for youth and families who face multiple problems, including legal involvement. For many of these families, intervention with the juvenile justice system represents an opportunity for multiple problems, including interparental violence and child maltreatment, to be identified and treated. Therefore, it is imperative that juvenile court personnel and associated mental health professionals take advantage of training on domestic violence and come to understand how it may be an important contributing factor to these youths' legal problems.

☐ Conclusion

We have discussed two common situations in which exposed children are likely to come into contact with the court system: children involved in custody and visitation arrangements in postseparation/divorcing domestically violent families and youth involved in the juvenile justice system as a result of status offenses or criminal behavior. Each situation demands a complex response from professionals across several disciplines and points of view (e.g., law, mental health, policy, advocates, victim services, batterer programs, etc.) and a coordinated community response if we are truly to address the myriad of children's, youths' and families' needs. Throughout this chapter, we have stressed the importance of conducting in-depth evaluations of interparental violence, including both the physical and psychological manifestations, in order to help guide decision making about intervention, whether it is related to family or juvenile court matters. Recent mandates to provide training on domestic violence to those legal and mental health professionals involved in custody evaluations and other court processes is an important step toward educating individuals, who hold enormous power over these families' lives, about the subtle dynamics of intimate violence and control. Children and parents do not need to be further victimized by our lack of knowledge and understanding about their complicated lives.

A second theme throughout the chapter is the need to create an individualized response to children, youth, and families struggling with interparental violence and its effects. As we are coming to realize, there are different profiles of abusive men and women and that a careful analysis of the context of violence, specific incidents, patterns, and psychological reactions could help guide intervention efforts and tailor what is needed for a particular family at a particular point in time. In fact, researchers, clinicians, and the legal system are finally beginning to recognize the complexity of interparental violence and are thinking about a continuum of services for children and families rather than short-term, narrow interventions without adequate follow-up. Interventions will be more effective when they are ecologically based, taking into account the variety of systemic forces, community and family dynamics, and individual processes that contribute to this complex psychosocial problem.

☐ References

Aguilar, R. J., & Nightingale, N. N. (1994). The impact of specific battering experiences on the self-esteem of abused women. *Journal of Family Violence, 9,* 35–45.

Barnett, O. W., Miller-Perrin, C. L, & Perrin, R. D. (1997). Children exposed to marital violence. *Family violence across the lifespan: An introduction.* (pp. 133–157). Thousand Oaks, CA: Sage.

Borduin, C. M., Henggeler, S. W., Blaske, D. M, & Stein, R. (1990). Multisystemic treatment of adolescent sexual offenders. *International Journal of Offender Therapy and Comparative Criminology, 34,* 105–113.

Brassard, M. R., Hart, S. N., & Hardy, D. B. (1993). The Psychological Maltreatment Rating Scales. *Child Abuse and Neglect, 17,* 715–729.

Briere, J. (1997). *Psychological assessment of adult posttraumatic states.* Washington, DC: American Psychological Association.

Brunk, M., Henggeler, S. W., & Whelen, J. P. (1987). Comparison of multisystemic therapy and parent training in the brief treatment of child abuse and neglect. *Journal of Consulting and Clinical Psychology, 55,* 171–178.

Dembo, R., Williams, L., Wothke, W., Schmeidler, J., & Brown, C. H. (1992). The role of family factors, physical abuse, and sexual victimization experiences in high-risk youths' alcohol and other drug use and delinquency: A longitudinal model. *Violence and Victims, 7,* 245–266.

Dutton, D. G. (1998). *The abusive personality: Violence and control in intimate relationships.* New York: Guilford.

Elbow, M. (1982). Children of violent marriages: The forgotten victims. *Social Casework, 63,* 465–471.

Elliott, D. M. (1992). *Traumatic Events Survey.* Unpublished test, University of California, Los Angeles, School of Medicine.

Elliott, D. M. (1997). Traumatic events: Prevalence and delayed recall in the general population. *Journal of Consulting and Clinical Psychology, 65,* 811–820.

Fagan, J., & Wexler, S. (1987). Family origins of violent delinquents. *Criminology, 25,* 643–669.

Femina, D. D., Yeager, C., & Lewis, D. O. (1990). *Violence and Victims.*

Grisso, T. (1986). *Evaluating competencies.* New York: Plenum.

Hamberger, L. K., Lohr, J. M., Bonge, D., & Tolin, D. F. (1996). A large sample empirical typology of male spouse abusers and its relationship to dimensions of abuse. *Violence and Victims, 11*(4), 277–292.

Henggeler, S. W. (1989). *Delinquency in adolescence.* Newbury Park, CA: Sage.

Henggeler, S. W., & Borduin, C. M. (1990). *Family therapy and beyond: A multisystemic approach to treating the behavior problems of children and adolescents.* Pacific Grove, CA: Brooks/Cole.

Henggeler, S. W., Melton, G. B., & Smith, L. A. (1992). Family preservation using multisystemic therapy: An effective alternative to incarcerating serious juvenile offenders. *Journal of Consulting and Clinical Psychology, 60,* 953–961.

Henggeler, S. W., Rodick, J. D., Borduin, C. M., Hanson, C. L., Watson, S. M., & Ulrey, J. R. (1986). Multisystemic treatment of juvenile offenders: Effects on adolescent behavior and family interaction. *Developmental Psychology, 22,* 132–141.

Holden, G. L., & Ritchie, K. L. (1991). Linking extreme marital discord, child rearing, and child behavior problems: Evidence from battered women. *Child Development, 62,* 311–327.

Holtzworth-Munroe, A., & Stuart, G. L. (1994). Typologies of male batterers: Three subtypes and the differences among them. *Psychological Bulletin, 116,* 476–497.

Hughes, H. M. (1988). Psychological and behavioral correlates of family violence in child witnesses and victims. *American Journal of Orthopsychiatry, 58,* 77–90.

Jaffe, P. G., Wolfe, D. A., & Wilson, S. K. (1990). *Children of battered women.* Newbury Park, CA: Sage.

Johnston, J. R., & Campbell, L. (1993a). A clinical typology of interparental violence in disputing custody divorces. *American Journal of Orthopsychiatry, 63,* 190–199.

Johnston, J. R., & Campbell, L. (1993b). Parent-child relationships in domestic violence families disputing custody. *Family and Conciliation Courts Review, 31,* 282–298.

Johnston, J. R., & Roseby, V. (1997). *In the name of the child: A developmental approach to understanding and helping children of conflicted and violent divorce.* New York: Free Press.

Kazdin, A. E. (1996). *Conduct disorders in childhood and adolescence,* (2nd ed.). Thousand Oaks, CA: Sage.

Kenning, M., Merchant, A., & Tomkins, A. (1991). Research on the effects of witnessing parental battering: Clinical and legal policy implications. In M. Steinman (Ed.), *Women battering: Policy responses* (pp. 237–261). Cincinnati, OH: Anderson.

Lewis, D. O., Mallouh, C., & Webb, V. (1989). Child abuse, delinquency, and violent criminality. In D. Cicchetti & V. Carlson (Eds.), *Child maltreatment: Theory and research on the causes and consequences of child abuse and neglect* (pp. 707–721). New York: Cambridge University Press.

Lewis, D. O., Shanok, S., Grant, M., & Ritvo, E. (1984). Homicidally aggressive young children: Neuropsychiatric and experimental correlates. In R. Mathias, P. DeMuro, & R. S. Allison (Eds.), *Violent juvenile offender: An anthology* (pp. 71–82). San Francisco: National Council on Crime and Delinquency.

Lewis, D. O., Shanok, S., Pincus, J., & Glaser, G. (1979). Violent juvenile delinquents: Psychiatric, neurological and abuse factors. *Journal of the American Academy of Child Psychology, 18,* 307–319.

Magen, R. H. (1999). In the best interests of battered women: Reconceptualizing allegations of failure to protect. *Child Maltreatment, 4,* 127-135.

Mann, B. J., Borduin, C. M., Henggeler, S. W., & Blaske, D. M. (1990). An investigation of systemic conceptualizations of parent-child coalitions and symptom change. *Journal of Consulting and Clinical Psychology, 58,* 336–344.

Margolin, G. (1995, January). *The effects of domestic violence on children.* Paper presented at the Conference on Violence Against Children in the Family and the Community, Los Angeles.

Melton, G., Petrila, J., Poythress, N. E., & Slobogin, C. (1997). *Psychological evaluations and the courts* (2nd ed.). New York: Guilford.

Mones, P. A. (1991). *When a child kills: Abused children who kill their parents.* New York: Pocket Books.

Moore, T., Pepler, D., Mae, R., & Kates, M. (1989). Effects of family violence on children: New directions for research and intervention. In B. Pressman, G. Cameron, & M. Rothery (Eds.), *Intervening with assaulted women: Current theory, research and practice.* Hillsdale, NJ: Lawrence Erlbaum.

Mulvey, E. P., Arthur, M. A., & Reppucci, N. D. (1990). *Review of programs for the prevention and treatment of delinquency* (Office of Technology Assessment). Washington, DC: U.S. Government Printing Office.

Pence, E., & Paymar, M. (1993). *Education groups for men who batter.* New York: Springer.

Rosenberg, M. S. (1987). Children of battered women: The effects of witnessing violence on their social problem solving abilities. *Behavior Therapist, 4,* 85–89.

Rosenberg, M. S., Giberson, R., Rossman, B. B. R., & Acker, M. (in press). The child witness to family violence. In R. T. Ammerman & M. Hersen (Eds.), *Clinical casebook in family violence* (2nd ed.). New York: Plenum.

Rosenberg, M. S., & Liebert, D. (1997, April). *Developing life histories for use in mitigation: Ethical, clinical and practical concerns.* Paper presented at the 13th Annual Symposium of the American College of Forensic Psychology, Vancouver, British Columbia.

Rossman, B. B. R., Bingham, R. D., Cimbora, D. M., Dickerson, L. K., Dexter, R. M., Balog, S. A., & Mallah, K. (1993, August). *Relationships of trauma severity to trauma symptoms for child witnesses.* Paper presented at the Annual Meeting of the American Psychological Association, Toronto, Canada.

Rossman, B. B. R., & Rosenberg, M. S. (Eds.). (1998). *Multiple victimization of children: Conceptual, developmental, research and treatment issues.* Binghamton, NY: Haworth.

Sonkin, D. J. (1995). *The counselor's guide to learning to live without violence.* Volcano, CA: Volcano.

Sonkin, D. J. (1998). *Domestic violence: The perpetrator assessment handbook.* Sausalito, CA: Self-published.

Stark, E., & Flitcraft, A. H. (1988). Women and children at risk: A feminist perspective on child abuse. *International Journal of Health Services, 18,* 97–118.

Straus, M. A. (1979). Measuring intrafamily conflict and violence: The Conflict Tactics (CT) Scale. *Journal of Marriage and the Family, 41,* 75–88.

van der Kolk, B. A. (1987). The psychological consequences of overwhelming life experiences. In B. A. van der Kolk (Ed.), *Psychological trauma* (pp. 1–30). Washington, DC: American Psychiatric Association.

Walker, L. E. A., & Edwall, G. E. (1987). Domestic violence and determination of visitation and custody in divorce. In D. J. Sonkin (Ed.), *Domestic violence on trial: Psychological and legal dimensions of family violence* (pp. 127–152). New York: Springer.

Widom, C. S. (1992, October). *The cycle of violence.* (Research in brief, Document #NCJ 136607). Washington, DC: National Institute of Justice.

Wolfe, D. A., Zak, L., Wilson, S., & Jaffe, P. G. (1986). Child witnesses to violence between parents: Critical issues in behavioral and social adjustment. *Journal of Abnormal Child Psychology, 14,* 95–104.

CHAPTER

Needs and New Directions

It is apparent from the foregoing chapters that there are a number of areas in which progress has been made. At the same time, it is also evident that much remains to be done related to children exposed to interparental violence. In this concluding chapter we will briefly summarize the areas in which progress has been made and discuss needs for the future. Some suggestions for funding priorities and policy initiatives will be offered as well.

☐ Progress

Myriad of Factors that Interact

One of the areas in which progress has been made is in identifying factors that influence the impact of exposure to interparental violence. We understand that there are child-related factors as well as family/situational/contextual factors and the fact that they need to be considered together. This new cognizance of the myriad of factors that influence the impact of exposure has been beneficial. We now are aware that individual differences are seen in impact, and the impact varies widely, depending on different combinations of factors, characteristics, and circumstances. It is clear that the answer to questions of whether there is negative impact of exposure and how serious it might be is, "It depends." For example, there may be a number of interactions among characteristics that influence the impact, including those of age and gender. Moreover, that impact is made much more complicated by interactions with dozens of other factors, including characteristics of the children themselves, such as temperament or of the family or the situation and context, such as the severity of the violence, the types of violence in the family, or the availability of social support.

Models and Theories

Another area of progress is the identification of theories and models that have relevance for understanding the impact seen on children. Behaviorally oriented and relationship-focused theories as well as theories from child development, trauma studies, and developmental psychopathology all make important contributions. Models that had been previously developed in these other areas can be extrapolated to fit the situations of these children and the mechanisms of action proposed. There is some consensus on the fact that the mechanisms of action take place both directly and indirectly. There is also some consensus on which factors are considered direct and which are indirect. Beyond that, many questions remain.

Diversity

We have also made progress in beginning to understand the important role diversity plays in contributing to individual differences in impact; thus, individual and cultural diversity must be taken into account and their influences understood. For example, the context of growing up in a lesbian family that is also African American, in which there is also interparental violence, contains a number of particularizing attendant conditions that must be considered. Each separate factor contributes in a synergistic fashion such that each family lives in a clearly unique context. As previously mentioned, all of these factors must be taken into account for an adequate understanding of the impact on the children of exposure as well as to provide culturally sensitive and relevant interventions.

Appropriate Interventions

Regarding interventions, we have made some progress in identifying several treatments, such as psychoeducational groups, that seem appropriate for children with mild to moderate problems. In addition, we have been able to describe other treatment approaches that are more appropriate for severe difficulties, using theories and literature from other areas as guidance. Also, we have been making progress in being able to distinguish, at least in a preliminary fashion, among important individual differences in children and match the youngsters with appropriate types of interventions based on several of those characteristics. Progress has been made, too, in proposing interventions for women in relation to their roles as caretakers for their children.

Collaboration

Some progress has been made as well in working within the legal system, with the courts, and with the juvenile justice system. There is growing recognition that an individual from a violent home who has committed a crime may need additional services if rehabilitation is to be successful. The schools are also becoming collaborative partners in violence reduction. Many public school systems, in part funded by National Institute of Education initiatives, are providing programs for anger management, social skills, and antibullying, all in the service of creating a safer school milieu where children's respect for themselves and each other can thrive.

☐ Needs in the Area

Basically, as is apparent from the previous chapters, needs in the area are considerable. We will delineate a number of recommendations regarding what we see as needs in research, in intervention, in prevention, in funding, and in policy.

Needs in Research

Complexity.   In general this area could benefit from more specific and focused research. There needs to be research on the various factors discussed in all their complexity, using developmental and ecological perspectives. We also need to understand mediators, moderators, and mechanisms of impact, as well as the context in which they function. It is important to continue examining child factors plus family/situational/contextual factors, more than one factor at a time, and using models that reflect this complexity. For example, it seems that sometimes the same factors are mediators, and sometimes moderators, and that they may function differently, even with regard to protective status given the particular context.

Therefore, probably the major need in this area has to do with a shift in emphasis when considering a child exposed to parental violence. This child needs to be considered within a broad context of both the intra- and extrafamilial difficulties the child faces. This is clearest for exposed children seen in a shelter where there are typically a number of risk factors in addition to exposure that constitute a package of adversity (e.g., poverty, homelessness, exposure to community violence, frequent school changes, inconsistent health care, and so on). What this means is that all professionals working with children exposed to wife abuse, including educators, officers of the court and law enforcement agencies, clinicians whether in private practice or community agencies, policy makers, and researchers, need to take a more multidimensional view of the child.

Emphasis on a multidimensional view of the child is reinforced by Simons and Johnson's finding (1998) that a model that gives a prominent role to the antisocial behaviors and orientation of families of grandparent generations was more predictive of subsequent marital conflict and harsh parenting than were models that give a prominent role to observational learning or the legitimization of violence transmitted within specific roles (e.g., spouse or parent). This type of orientation spans traditional disciplines, dimensions, and singular-mechanism explanations. The possible presence of a more global orientation highlights the importance of taking into account all of the mechanisms discussed in preceding chapters that may promote violence. These included poor judgment and new learning capabilities and achievement due to trauma symptoms and distress, the observational or instrumentally conditioned learning of aggressive behaviors to gain control or reduce distress, the development of expectations that others are dangerous and associated poorly fostered social skills, the reinforcement of accepting attitudes toward violence both within families and society, the depression and stress suffered by abused mothers, and difficulties of abusive fathers and their role in creating dysfunctional family systems. Effects of these mechanisms can cascade through different parts of a family, the parenting system, and interactions of family members in the community. Effects also appear to cascade across development for one individual or for generations to produce the kinds of complex ramifications we have seen documented in the foregoing chapters.

We simply must map out systematic strategies in all domains of professional effort that face the challenge of complexity when it comes to understanding the effects of children's exposure and planning intervention and prevention efforts for family violence and wife abuse. This will likely take generations, because the Holocaust literature tells us that severe violence and traumatic exposure reverberate in the lives of victims across second and third generations. But we need to continue to believe we can "start somewhere." There are places to direct our efforts.

Developmentalists (e.g., Cicchetti, 1989) have for a decade recommended taking an Organizational Perspective on child development, wherein many aspects and levels of a child's functioning and environment are considered. This Organizational Perspective needs also to be applied to families wherein many aspects of their environment, functioning, and learning are considered within the context of our communities, society, and world. This means that the paradigm shift moves us away from single- or few-variable explanations, research studies, intervention programs, or educational and policy strategies to multivariate thinking, assessment, intervention, and policy making. We need to honor the principles of multifinality (Cicchetti, 1989), wherein a single antecedent experience, which we have in the past targeted as exposure to wife abuse but now appears more complex, is thought to be associated with many different outcomes, and, of equifinality, wherein one type of outcome is thought to be associated with differing antecedents (i.e., there are different experiences of wife abuse in different contexts and all may increase the likelihood of interpersonal violence in the future lives of those exposed).

Research Methodology.   In order to investigate in all their complexity the myriad of factors discussed above, enhanced research methodologies are needed. Research methods could be improved in the following areas. Definitions of abuse, violence, and exposure need to be delineated and agreed upon in some consensual fashion. Moreover, multiple areas of impact require study for knowledge to advance. Behavioral, emotional, social, and cognitive problems, plus trauma reactions, as well as difficulties with attachment and self-esteem all need further attention and inquiry. Careful and consensual definitions of a standard set of dimensions of exposure that are always reported would represent a huge first step. Then dose-response models with modifying factors could be more precisely examined as well as implications for assessment and intervention.

Measures and Techniques.   At this point in the development in this area, we need a variety of measures and measurement techniques. Researchers would benefit from using some variety in techniques but also providing some consistency across studies through the use of common instruments as well. We need measures that are general to child adjustment and child psychopathology as well as to develop scales and methods that are specific to children exposed to interparental violence. In addition, greater use of multimethod approaches could make significant contributions, including qualitative and quantitative techniques. Each methodology has its advantages and disadvantages, and each can enhance knowledge.

An entire area needing further work is the development of a set of commonly used multiple-domain assessment tools additional to behavior checklists (e.g., for trauma symptoms, developmental status, etc.) to act as anchors across studies much as the CBCL scores for behavioral problems have anchored past research. From the individual differences in children's outcomes noted, it is clear that not all children experience all problems, but that problems may interact and cascade such that those most troublesome for a child need to be identified. A national standardized assessment battery would go a long way toward furthering the cause of needs assessment. More universal or specific needs could then be coordinated with validated intervention components and strategies to provide better services for children.

Results of this type of comprehensive needs assessment could inform primary and secondary prevention efforts in communities and allow them to "take the temperature" of those they serve. If likely needs are known, such as difficulties with reading or problem solving, it may be possible for communities to determine how adequate their services are for responding to those needs. For example, a reception classroom program was established in Toronto, Ontario, to accommodate children living in battered women's shelters. This allowed educational personnel to be trained in the emotional needs of exposed children as well as to immediately assess and identify achievement deficits for the children and to plan appropriate programs for each child. A broader-based needs assessment—including health, mental health, and educational/occupational information for each family—could allow communities to identify factors such as difficulty in accessing health or educational/occupational services that may be supporting the existence of family violence through fostering poverty and a sense of hopelessness and little to lose by adopting an antisocial lifestyle (and perhaps much to gain in terms of financial survival or the self-medication possible through substance abuse).

Samples. It is apparent from the discussions in the chapters above that a moderate range of families has been studied. A clear need is for investigations of a wide variety of families. Currently we are uncertain what parts, if any, of the knowledge we have are generalizable to unstudied types of families (e.g., the very wealthy). We need higher-income samples to see if the results from the very few studies conducted with middle-income families can be replicated. The few studies of middle-income families show that there is an impact of exposure to interparental violence for them also; we need to continue to investigate which factors play a role there also. Definitely there is a need to study the influence of cultural diversity among families and diversity within cultural groups since those differences may interact with violence factors. What is the influence of culture on the occurrence of woman abuse and its ramifications for exposed children? Clearly we need to continue to investigate interparental violence in lesbian and gay families as well.

Data Analysis. Another area of need is for more sophisticated data analytic techniques to answer some of the more complex questions that arise when considering multivariate models. Using multiple regression and structural equation modeling for aggregate data, for example, will be helpful to test models and mechanisms of impact.

For a look at individual children, specialized techniques such as cluster analysis are helpful, because researchers are able to focus on commonalties among and differences between subgroups of children. This allows for more focused and precise treatment planning.

Design.   Ideally, there is also a clear need for more researchers to use longitudinal designs. It would be most heuristic to follow high-risk families prospectively. Because those types of investigations are so difficult to conduct, at the very least families identified through shelters or though domestic violence programs could be followed for at least 12 months. This would allow for better identification of factors related to resilience and vulnerability, as well as take into consideration the transition in the family that takes place as they attempt to establish violence-free lives.

Needs in Intervention

Development of New Approaches.   There are evident needs here to continue to develop interventions that are also developmentally and culturally appropriate, ecological in perspective, and are collaborative. Additional treatment programs/approaches need to be designed based on both clinical experience and conceptual/theoretical rationale and then evaluated.

One place to start regarding new intervention approaches is by gaining more longitudinal information about factors across time that may allow children to be more resilient, or more vulnerable, to effects of exposure. Another approach, which is now in place in some jurisdictions, is to provide more inclusive law and practice in courts and in custody cases so that wife abuse is carefully considered as a factor. A third effort being made in some communities is to provide places for battered mothers and their children to live in safety and receive assistance with both adult and child development to support them in forging violence-free lives. One of the few longitudinal intervention projects to date for battered mothers and their children quickly noted the breadth and complexity of the needs of these families if they were to remain violence-free and development promoting (Jouriles et al., 1998). Programs of this type need to be tried in different sites with appropriate evaluation efforts, such that effective components of these programs can be identified and results replicated.

Also, a high priority relevant for interventions is to expand our knowledge of and response to the needs of the diverse families who require services. Diversity arises from the many ethnic backgrounds of families we must serve, as well as from the sexual orientation of the parents or from the physical or mental handicaps they experience. These diversity factors may provide additional stresses for the parents and children. We know relatively little about special needs of these families. Research informed by knowledgeable community boards and experts is called for, in addition to efforts to locate, constitute, and advertise services in user-friendly ways, including the provision of services in the family's language of choice. These issues provide a great challenge to academic, educational, community, and legal and law enforcement agencies as our society becomes even more representative of different cultures, religions, and traditions. These challenges cannot be ignored if the ultimate goal is to move to a society less dependent on interpersonal violence as a means by which individuals can achieve goals.

Evaluation. One of most basic needs related to understanding interventions and what works for which families is to evaluate agency and shelter programs for children in all their forms. To the best of our knowledge none of the 800 shelter programs for children has been formally evaluated. This is not surprising. Some shelters would like to do systematic clinical outcome program evaluation but have few resources to put toward that effort. Many families come and go so quickly that it is a struggle to even consistently deliver a certain number of systematic child treatment components. The shelters have only a short time (often 30 days or fewer) to work with families, and pragmatic goals of helping battered mothers find safe housing, jobs, and so on take appropriate precedence. Some residential programs do not even have designated children's programs. However, when and wherever possible this type of program evaluation would go a long way in helping us understand what approaches are beneficial for children while they are in shelters.

In addition, we need to evaluate the most common type of intervention, the psychoeducational group approach, more rigorously. At this point it would be beneficial to see what is appropriate for youngsters of different ages and genders and with different issues. Moreover, we need to evaluate individual approaches for children with the more serious difficulties as well to see whether the approaches that work with the same symptoms in other populations work for these children, too. The Jouriles et al. (1998) work is promising in suggesting that some traditional approaches in addition to components honed specifically for violent families can be successful. It is also important to study relational issues and over time evaluate whether long-term interventions focused on attachment and self-esteem can interrupt the intergenerational transmission of interpersonal violence.

In keeping with an ecological approach, there is a need to evaluate approaches for other family members as well. The success of interventions for mothers, regarding their parenting role, discipline, strategies, stress management, trauma, or depression, must be assessed. At some point some collaboration with the offending parent might be in order, and it is critical that we evaluate whether and when that might be possible. This evaluation might include whether it is appropriate to have the offending parent together with the other members in family treatment approaches. Another critical need is to determine how the often-required visitations with a battering parent might be carried out to be the most helpful or least disruptive for the child. Evaluation for different models of visitation for exposed children should be carried out. As previously discussed, it is important also to assess the effectiveness of outreach and support programs. We must provide follow-up to the families and evaluate the outcome and impact of outreach contacts.

Needs in Prevention

The Public Health and Community Psychology models continue to suggest the need for primary and secondary intervention, in addition to tertiary (i.e., direct services to victims). The examples of primary prevention in the schools and community noted earlier are a wonderful start. Existing secondary prevention efforts for high-risk groups (e.g., where neighborhood violence is high) need to be continued and expanded. There are a number of promising approaches, although communities often find it difficult to get sufficient funding. It does not make sense, as the villagers realized with the monster, to continue direct treatment without directing efforts toward prevention.

Needs in Policy

Given the above daunting needs, a final need is that we be realistic and establish a national agenda through greater cooperation among governmental, educational, and private agencies. We cannot address all of these needs at once, but there should be a plan with prioritized goals that respond to all of the needs over time. Policy that instructs the aggressive implementation of restraining orders and expansion and safety of community visitation centers will increase the safety of children and battered mothers. Policy that mandates serious community prevention efforts with safe follow-up for victims who self-identify as a result of these efforts needs to be expanded. One of the most difficult aspects of policy change is not just the creation of law or service guidelines or even the training of professionals to implement the policies. It is the follow-up to ascertain that implementation is taking place in a consistent manner in any jurisdiction. This will require additional resources since it is both difficult, given the stretched energies of the implementers, and logically inappropriate that the implementers are the only verifiers. The continued formation and implementation of policies that reward local, state, and federal agency cooperation and program integrity can go a long way to improving the lives of struggling and violent families and advocate for the safety and developmental needs of exposed children.

Needs in Funding

Unfortunately the above recommendations all cost money to implement. Hopefully governmental and private agencies can continue to recognize the importance of setting aside monies for research (e.g., for multisite longitudinal investigations or clinical trials of intervention programs), direct intervention, primary and secondary prevention, education, and knowledgeable policing and legal system function. Priorities for funding include the development of projects that are collaborative, ecological, and developmental. A truly critical but not necessarily highly expensive method may be to invest at the local level to fund a coordinator for local domestic violence agencies and task forces (Sullivan & Allen, 1999). Unifying the service and program evaluation and verification efforts of all concerned agencies and networks and funding them so that they are not always competing for the same funds could be a powerful use of money. But there is also people power to be tapped. Volunteers will (and do) invest a great deal of time and energy for an important cause when the goals seem clear, coordinated, and reachable, and when progress can be documented. We need to continue and enlarge our commitments of money, time, effort, and spirit.

☐ Conclusion

Work on this volume has consistently been guided by three themes. These are an ecological perspective, a developmental perspective, and a collaborative perspective. The ecological view has been apparent in our emphasis on looking at larger systems than just the child and looking beyond the family. Factors such as culture and society members' attitudes also play a role in impact. The developmental perspective is evident in our stress on taking a developmental view, over time where possible, looking for continuities and discontinuities, and assessing a child's developmental status as well as immediate needs and symptoms.

The collaborative perspective deserves special mention at this point. We must collaborate across areas of work in this field if we are to truly understand the plight of exposed children and respond effectively. Research, prevention, intervention, and policy need the combined power of the disciplines and people who create them and the integration of ideas from child protective services, child development, developmental psychopathology, trauma, clinical child psychology, and juvenile justice, just to name a few. Each one of these areas has much to offer. In addition, there needs to be collaboration across the agencies and settings that inform and serve these youngsters, including schools, shelters, domestic violence programs, child protection, juvenile justice, legal services, and family clinics. There are commendable efforts to provide this type of coordination of effort, message, and purpose taking place. Such collaboration has become imperative as we become wiser about the multiple factors that support interpersonal violence, but it is difficult because many of these agencies are already stretched to provide their mandated services and because they have often survived by gaining grassroots support that came from maintaining a specific focus. In addition, it is just difficult to coordinate a number of people and efforts without the whole network beginning to resemble the "power" structures that have been the anathema of many domestic violence agencies. Our well-intentioned specific efforts of the past have kept us from moving into greater peril, but they have also left us with only partial successes. Many of us had thought we could achieve the goal of violence-free families as we enter the new century. This was not to be. The task is too large and its complexity is only becoming apparent. It has, however, with the proliferation of school shootings among other events, become painfully clear that we need to continue to strive for zero tolerance of interpersonal violence and to coordinate as a society to understand and change the multiple factors that support continued violence with its developmentally devastating effects on children.

☐ References

Cicchetti, D. (1989). How research on child maltreatment has informed the study of child development: Perspectives from developmental psychopathology. In D. Cicchetti & V. Carlson (Eds.), *Child maltreatment: Theory and research on the causes and consequences of child abuse and neglect* (pp. 377–431). New York: Cambridge University Press.

Jouriles, E. N., McDonald, R., Stephens, N., Norwood, W., Spiller, L. C., & Ware. H. S. (1998). Breaking the cycle of violence: Helping families departing from battered women's shelters. In G. W. Holden, R. Geffner, & E. N. Jouriles (Eds.), *Children exposed to marital violence: Theory, research, and applied issues* (pp. 337–370). Washington, DC: American Psychological Association.

Simons, R. L., & Johnson, C. (1998). An examination of competing explanations for the intergenerational transmission of domestic violence. In Y. Danieli (Ed.), *International handbook of multigenerational legacies of trauma* (pp. 553-570). New York: Plenum.

Sullivan, C. M., & Allen, N. E. (1999, February). *Evaluating coordinated system approaches for abused women and their children.* Paper presented at the Asilomar Conference on Children and Intimate Violence, Pacific Grove, CA.

INDEX